Understanding Women

A Guidebook For Guys
Who Are Often Confused

Ben Goode

Rebuttals by Erin Allred

Illustrated by
David Mecham

Published by:
Apricot Press
Box 1611
American Fork, Utah
84003

books@apricotpress.com
www.apricotpress.com

ISBN 1-885027-13-3

Cover Design & Layout by David Mecham
Printed in the United States of America

PREFACE... a couple of starting premises:

Beginning premise #1:

Although I have some strange ideas wafting about in the crevasses of my mind at times, there is nothing in my imagination that could ever compare to the reality of a woman's brain. Things that seem perfectly normal from a guy's perspective frequently set females off fidgeting, hollering, or even more confusing, refusing to say anything at all. Most of the things they do could never be predicted or understood by normal people because they make absolutely no sense whatsoever. Let's face it, women are weird! The problem is, girls can also be sort of fun sometimes in a twisted, masochistic sort of way; they are also breathtakingly attractive, and they do have some practical uses. Many guys like them.

So what are we supposed to do? Frankly, I have no idea, but I feel a moral responsibility to do something. My motto has always been: "even bad information is better than no information at all." And so, I'm writing a very important book. You can see that there is a desperately compelling, even lucrative need to provide this valuable information to paying consumers and, by golly, even if it's misleading, I'm going to provide it.

Beginning Premise #2:

When it comes to important and controversial topics, most peoples' minds are closed, finished; they are made up. Human beings close their minds as a sort of primitive survival mechanism. It improves their efficiency because once a guy makes up his mind about something, he no longer needs to waste time looking for facts, weighing evidence, or worrying about looking like an idiot; he is pretty much free to spend his whole life searching for people and

information which agree with his ideas.
Whenever he finds some, it makes him feel
reassured that he's not an idiot, or even if he
is, he has plenty of company.

Most of us are very very nervous about new
facts. Facts threaten to undermine our
positions and force us to spend time and
effort re-tracing our steps, rethinking our
arguments so we can explain away the facts,
justify why we ignored these facts, and give
us some new ammunition to argue with
people who disagree with our poorly
supported opinions.

So, when writing a book about women, I
figure in order to have a best-seller, I first
need to pretty much avoid facts. So, you
won't need to worry about too many of those
being in here. And then, I figure the next
thing I need to do is come up with a bunch of
stuff to support guys' pre-conceived notions
and biases about women so they don't lose
their self-esteem. If I can do this and sell

through the first printing, I will consider this book a success.

This, however, is easier said than done, especially because I know there are a whole slew of women out there who, when this book becomes a famous best seller on Oprah and Jay Leno, are going to want to read it to find out why all the guys are getting so smug. Since I am an expert writing a book to help guys understand women, if you have any ideas about them, could you please send them to me? but only if they agree with my pre-conceived notions... Oh, and, no facts please.

– Ben Goode

Contents

Understanding Women...

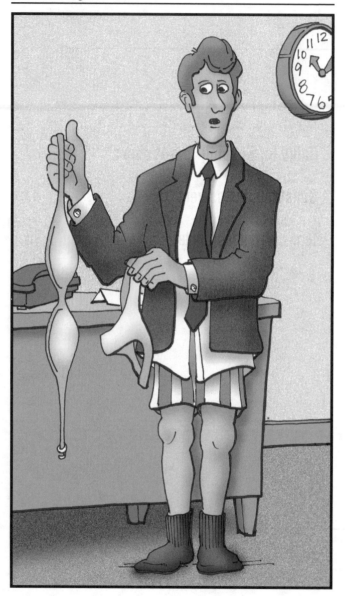

1 GAINING THE PROPER PERSPECTIVE...

"If you're planning on coming back as a chicken, maybe you should limit your consumption of omelettes."
- Hindu Maxim

Girls have been around for a long, long time; some since before computers, football, and even dirt and rocks. That's why it's so frustrating to discover that there are still men out there who haven't figured them out. The way I see it, after all this time I can accept no excuses.

The truth is, the vast majority of people do understand women. More people have them

figured out than not. More than half the people
you run into on the street, once they get over
being mad at you for bumping into them and once
they get the police notified and have your
insurance information, would tell you that women
are not at all hard to understand. In fact, if you say
you don't understand them, they get disgusted
with you. Take my wife, Robyn, for example; she
has no patience whatsoever with people who say
they can't understand women. She knows
perfectly well that for anyone of her gender,
they're simple to understand.

Women sales people are another group in society
who have a terrific grasp of women. They always
know just what to say and exactly what women
want. Grandmas, mothers, lady school teachers,
woman doctors, ladies from all walks of life, fall
into this category. Well over half of the people in
the world seem to have women totally figured out.
So, get with the program guys. I'm getting sick of
these lame excuses. Get yourselves together! Be
a man!

OK, so that was a little harsh; relax and stop
worrying. This book is here for you. After you
read it, never again will you stick your size 11
smelly Doc Martin into your mouth. Never again
will you sleep out in the dog house. Never again
will you wonder why she's avoiding you or why all

her friends giggle and point every time you walk by. Never again will you wonder why we are making these outlandish claims when you know perfectly well that we can't hope to back them up.

How to Discover What You're Doing Wrong

We must start by altering your perspective: Just like the fact that you can't really understand your car's engine problem without looking under the hood, or even sometimes crawling underneath, or just like you can't tell what's been biting your behinder until you find the spider carcass in your underwear, or just like it's hard to know why none of the traffic on the freeway is moving until you get all the way up to the front of the line and find out that the construction guys have died or retired, it's pretty tough to understand women until you gain the right perspective. In order to truly understand women, a guy has to prance around for a mile or two in her pumps, so to speak, to symbolically talk for three or four hours on her cell-phone, or to type for an evening while suffering with her pre-menstrual cramps all the time wearing slinky lingerie. And that's just what we're going to do here. So, get ready to change your perspective, to get down and dirty, to gain enough insights to see things through the eyes of a woman. That's what this book will do for you:

give you a better understanding of women by giving you a man's perspective of a woman's perspective.

Developing the Proper Mind Set

If you are a guy who sincerely wants to thoroughly understand women, start by doing everything you can to change your perspective. Put on a bikini; shave your legs, put on some earrings...oh, I see, many of you already are doing this...OK, get some headaches at night; begin to nag the men in your lives; drive poorly. All of these things will help you gain perspective, and hopefully, along with reading this book, give you a deep understanding of the female mind.

We have chosen a question and answer format for no good reason, mostly because we just did. So leave us alone on that one, but if, after you finish this book, you still have questions about women unanswered, we have no idea what to do; you're on your own.

FASCINATING FACTOIDS ABOUT FEMALES...

• Even though most ladies don't want to admit it, it would take 272,000 cockroaches to equal the weight of only one standard woman.

• Because men generally have bigger eyebrows, nature has compensated by giving women extra closet space.

• If you were to stack all of the women living today into one huge pile, most would not want to be on the bottom.

• The average woman consumes enough chocolate in one month to provide an entire years dietary requirement of saturated fat for a child in the Congo.

• It is virtually impossible to distinguish a female rooster from a male rooster.

• During the nineteenth century, it was considered obscene for a woman to expose her ankles. In the twenty-first century, we struggle to think of anything considered obscene anymore.

THE MOST BASIC OF ALL QUESTIONS

"Men with hairy legs should remove duct tape carefully."
- Ivan, The Tolerable

O.K, it's time to get right down to the nitty gritty. We must examine the most fundamental of all questions relating to women. That question is: "Is this really a woman?"

Life is such a challenge. Nowadays there are guys who wear earrings, long hair, shave their legs, sing soprano, eat tofu, ask directions, have babies, go through menopause, and wear womens' underwear. To further complicate things, there are also women who take steroids, wear men's clothing, shave their heads, wrestle, play football, smoke cigars, pick fights, go to prison, and grow facial hair. So it can be pretty tricky to tell for sure who is who. There are, however, a few tricks of the trade that I've learned which can help you be reasonably certain whether any person in question is actually a man or woman. The following are a few clues:

Some Clues

• If you've lived with her for a while and everything you do annoys her, she's probably a woman.

• If she doesn't understand football, you should at least be suspect.

• Does she like movies like "Steel Magnolias," "My Best Friend's Wedding," "Nottinghill," "Ever After,' or anything staring Julia Roberts? Be careful. She's probably a woman.

• If she is a lousy driver, yet feels no embarrassment when she criticizes your driving, she's most likely a woman.

• Does she swerve to try to run over cats? Then, probably not.

- If she knows nothing about basketball, but cheers for the Lakers, she's probably a woman.

Other Differences Between Guys and Girls

- Girls use tons more toilet paper than guys; guys have no idea what they do with it all.

- Girls travel in groups to the restroom; guys prefer to be alone.

- Girls usually don't make disgusting noises in mixed company.

- Girls think guys should get it; guys don't get it.

- Girls like to talk about things; guys never know what to talk about.

- Most girls don't torture cats.

- Guys shop quickly; girls don't.

- Girls notice filth and clutter; guys live in it.

- Girls interpret non-verbal cues; guys interpret referees' signals.

- Girls generally don't scratch in public.

Understanding Women...

• Girls have sympathy for wretched, bumbling guys, except for ones they just dumped; guys insult wretched, bumbling guys.

• Guys play to win; girls are nice unless they are playing to win.

• Guys drive aggressively; girls drive aggressively, but often giggle while doing it.

• Girls take forever getting ready; guys need help getting their clothes to match.

• Girls seek to understand people; guys whack them.

• You will probably find that girls' voices are generally higher than guys.

• Girls are obsessed with chocolate, but only eat it when no one's watching; guys just pretty much eat whatever they want and burp.

• Every girl thinks she has chubby thighs; guys think all girls who have chubby thighs have chubby thighs...but usually they're cute anyway.

• Guys grow scraggly hair in their noses, ears, on their toes and legs; some girls do too.

• Girls feel compassion toward loser guys...if

they're cute. Guys sometimes feel compassion toward their dogs.

• Girls love to torment guys. Guys are often too dense to know they're being tormented.

10 Things You May Never Live Long Enough to See a Woman Do

1. Go alone to the restroom.

2. Have all the girls over for a night of beer, Nintendo, and football.

3. Send one of her kids to school (or church) with a grape juice mustache, blobs of Jell-0 down the front of his white T-shirt, and a quarter-inch of dirt all over his bare feet.

4. Use a urinal.

5. Pick her nose at a stop light.

6. Adjust herself while playing baseball.

7. Blow one nostril of her nose in public.

8. Belch and ask her friends to rate it on a scale of 1 to 10.

9.   Choose her clothes from the pile of dirty laundry on the floor by smelling the shirts to see which one smells the best.

10.   Follow a guy for 15 miles right on his bumper because she knows that eventually he has to stop when he runs out of gas, and then she can beat him up because he cut her off in traffic.

In What Ways Are Women Superior to Men?

Although they would have you believe otherwise, evidence suggests that women are superior in many ways to men. I know this may also come as a shock to some of you guys, but hey, we promised to play fast and loose with our facts, and by golly, we're going to do it. The following are some proven ways that women are superior to men.

1. They are better looking.

2. They are better smelling.

3. They are generally not as hairy.

4. They seem to possess better intuition.

5. In many ways they are more intelligent.

6. They are usually not influenced by bozos like you.

7. They are generally aware when they offend, harm, or hurt someone's feelings.

8. Indirectly or directly, they control most of the financial assets in the world.

9. They live longer than men.

10. They make most of the consumer choices in the world.

11. They can cook and clean.

12. They often notice when metric tons of formerly useful organic material is decomposing in piles throughout the house.

13. They genuinely don't need men in their lives.

Then, Do Men Possess Any Advantages Over Women?

Yes, definitely, for example:

1. They are generally bigger.

2. They are usually stronger.

3. They are often more violent.

4. They are certainly more impetuous.

5. Some are not all that much less intelligent.

6. They are normal and easily understood by virtually any cretin.

7. They can belch on demand.

8. Their distinctive odor frightens away many predators.

9. They can sometimes tell when they're being insulted.

10. They like to shoot things, break things, and blow things up.

11. They can be perceived as impervious.

12. Some could be perceived as vulnerable.

13. They are often perceived as obnoxious.

14. They can eat large quantities of questionable food.

15. They generally don't cheer for the Lakers.

16. They possess opposable thumbs.

17. They rarely notice and are generally not bothered by rats, mice, roaches and other vermin who live with them.

18. They are vastly superior at playing video games.

So, you see, in 12 or 13 ways, women are superior to men, but men are superior to women in at least18 ways. Advantage: MEN.

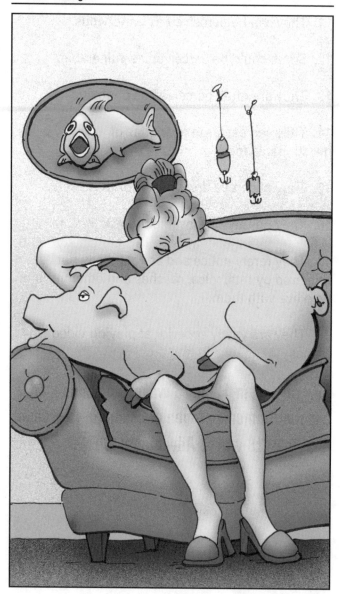

HOW CAN I GET ONE OF THESE WOMEN?

"Never bet big money on the runner who's shoelaces are tied to the fire hydrant."
- Roger Pythagoras

Our research, even though it isn't very scientific, concluded that millions of men would buy a book if they were convinced it could just show them some fool-proof and legal ways to get women. So, now that you know how to tell a girl from a guy, I am going to teach you some fail-safe, scientific ways to attract women.

How to Get Women

To start with, if you want to get women, you must dress nice. Regardless what you may have heard, along with water, fluids, sodium and a few chemicals, clothes are what make the man. I'm a little older than some of the young bucks reading this book, and many of my buddies have no clue about today's clothes. The problem is, people of my generation have an entirely different perspective on advertising than people of today.

Years ago, before we ever even thought of parading all over advertising for a company, we expected to get paid for it. In my day, if someone had come up to me and asked me to wear a shirt with the manufacturer's name plastered all over it, I would have insisted that they pay me reasonable compensation. After all, they were asking me to be a sponsor. That's because when I was younger, designer labels hadn't been invented yet. In those days, about the only way to advertise how cool and expensive your clothes were was to either brag or else to leave the tags on. Today, no self respecting female (Okay, I know that there are quite a number of guys who don't want anything to do with a self respecting female, but work with me here.) No self-respecting female will go out with a guy unless he is wearing clothes advertising the price he paid by flaunting the correct labels.

The problem comes when a guy can't afford to pay way too much for clothes just so he can impress self-respecting women. In this case you have only two choices: #1, is of course, the age old approach of avoiding the self-respecting type of women all together and concentrating on those without any self-respect. If this won't get you what you want, you can try choice #2 and take a lesson from modern politicians. Be a fraud. Hey, no one will know, and if they do find out, focus group polls have already proven conclusively that most people don't care. You can invent your own designer labels and then act as though anyone who doesn't know how expensive these labels are is a loser-dork from some third world country. Using this method, you can feel free to buy all of your stuff at Good Will, K Mart, or wherever. Anyway, go ahead and buy whatever clothes you can afford, then just get yourself some fingernail polish and create your own designer labels.

Being Hot

The next most important thing when trying to get women is to look "Hot." Some guys have problems with the concept of "Hot." This is at least partly because some guys have serious flaws in that they are genuinely not very hot. For example, some guys can't get their hair to do what they want it to; this is particularly tough when they have no hair. Some men have facial features which are unattractive to many women along with everyone else, except for maybe their dogs, and honestly, a guy shouldn't expect that his dog would ever tell him he looks disgusting. Finally, some guys are fat and disgusting and have no clue how to dress or how to act, and they have poor personal hygiene, whiney little voices, and get beat up all the time because everybody hates them. If you are this pathetic, maybe you could use some tips on how to be hot.

How to be Hot

One of the first keys to being hot, is being skinny. To be hot, you must be skinny. Remember the old adage, "You can never be too rich or too thin." While this is pretty much a bunch of hooey, it's still a good thing to remember. The problem comes when you are not skinny and you have no six pack. Then you have only two choices. Either you can get skinny, or you must hang with people who are much fatter than you so that you will seem skinny by comparison. If there are no disgustingly fat people around you, or if you can't always choose your backdrop or companions, you have no alternative but to get skinny. The best way to do this is the way wrestlers do. I don't know about you, but I've always been amazed at how much weight and color wrestlers could lose. I once had a friend who played football weighing 215 pounds, and who looked healthy, tan, and virile. Within a few short weeks after football season, he was on the wrestling team determined to make weight at 63 pounds. In order to make it, he would put on these plastic sweats and run around in any steamy, hot place he could find, spit into a cup, and for three months he would never eat anything except eye droppers of water and an occasional ex-lax.

And he was a nice guy too. He used to come outside on warm days during lunch and watch the basketball players eat their lunches, until tragically one day in the early spring, one of the robins returning from the south mistook him for a worm and ate him. There was nothing we could do, although I have many regrets and an occasional nightmare.

So, there you have it. If you are hot, thin, have a six pack and a nice butt, dress nice, and have lots of money to throw around, these virtues all will help you get women.

Pick Up Lines

Unfortunately, just being "hot" isn't quite enough when it comes to getting women. Some pretty hot guys can't get a date for anything. That's why most guys need proven, successful pick up lines. Girls can be pretty complicated, but if you know the secrets, picking them up is surprisingly easy. I can't imagine any guy having a problem picking up all the women he could ever want with the pick up lines in this book. I'll bet these lines would probably work on the wife of the Pope.

Direct Pick Up Lines That Will Never Ever Fail You.

• See that red porsche parked over there? It's yours if you go out with me tonight.

• I have lots of money; do you want some?

• Some of my friends and I were planning to spend this weekend yachting to the French Riviera. Wanna come along?

• I have an extra diamond tennis bracelet; I don't know what to do with it. I think I'll give it to the next girl who goes out with me.

• I have a whole bunch of hot, new sports cars. Want one?

• I have $15 million that's burning a hole in my pocket. I'm just going to cut loose, go crazy, and spend it today. Wanna come along and help?

• I'm looking for a friendly, honest, faithful girl who doesn't mind having thousands of dollars lavished on her with no strings attached. Know anyone like that?

Sympathy Lines

As you can see, some of these lines assume that you possess some special charms, and sometimes it's important to be a billionaire jet-setter. Since some of my readers are short on money and looks, we must work to come up with some alternatives. Fortunately, women have other soft spots too. One of life's great secrets is that most women are suckers for wretched, pathetic, miserable guys. They think they can fix us!

Historically, this has often worked to guys' advantages, because most guys are naturally genuinely miserable and disgusting. They could never hook up with any women if they had to do it legitimately. If you're unusually ugly, dirt poor, a total dweebe, or something even worse, don't despair. There's hope; however, in order for you to get women, you might need to have no shame for a while. Without looks and money, in order to attract women, you have no alternative but to advertise your wretchedness and ineptitude. The women in your life will misinterpret your bumbling pathetic incompetence as "vulnerability"

and they will love it! Trust me! So, take heart.
The sympathy route might offer you some hope.
Now, all you need to know is what to say. If you're
pathetic, here are a few lines that might work for
you.

• My wife was murdered this morning. I need
someone to talk to. Got a few minutes?

• I just came home from the hospital. Tests
confirmed that I'm dying of terminal brain
flatulence. Could you hang around and keep me
company for my last few wretched hours on earth?

• My last girl friend ran off with a corrupt lingerie
salesman, cleaned out my bank accounts, and ran
over my best friend, my dog Sparky. Now I have
no one to talk to. Will you be my friend?

In spite of all this help, I know that there are still
some out there who are having a tough time
following what I'm saying. You just don't get it.
Let me be very direct here. Stop using those lame
pick up lines that you and your buddies thought up
yourselves. They just make you look like a dork.
In fact, quit acting natural and being yourself all
together. Girls hate that. Whatever you do, don't
use any of the following pickup lines, even if you
thought them up yourself.

Pick Up Lines That Probably Won't Work

- Bet you don't want to go out with me!

- Cool! Your thighs are bigger than mine!

- Hey, let's go out. Why don't you buy?

- I was planning to go run over some cats tonight. Wanna come along?

- I just got out of the big house on parole. I don't have any money. I was hoping to find someone to take me out and buy me something.

- If we got married, do you think out kids would look more like me or you?

Things A Guy Should Never Do

We know that some guys need special help. Even with tried and proven pick up lines, you still have to act partially human. Here are a few more tips.

These things won't impress women:

- Combing your scruffy beard up past your ears to partially cover your bald head.

- Having her help clean your toilet and calling it a date.

• Introducing her to the lice on your head and calling them by their names.

• Sharing your innermost thoughts with her.

• Blowing booger bubbles.

• Bragging about all the cats you run over in your 4x4.

• Chewing your toenails.

• Chewing her toenails.

• Blowing your nose on her cat, Muffy.

• Using your ear wax as chapstick or as make up to cover a zit.

• Holding her down and giving her whisker burns.

• Having her pull on your finger.

• Pulling on her finger.

• Letting your pet pot-bellied pig, Gus, sit on her lap while you watch a fishing video.

• Wearing the head and antlers of the elk you

shot on top of your head when you go out to a nice restaurant.

• Telling her what you are honestly thinking.

• Giving her a back massage using any of the following: a jackhammer, a wrecking ball, a duck, a 4x4, or a rhino.

• Making your date sit in the litter box.

• Blowing garlic cloves out of your nose and into her purse.

• After spending the day shoveling manure, going to pick up your date without showering first.

• Whacking her on the old arm muscle hard enough to raise a knot.

• Introducing her to your friends.

• Introducing her to your relatives.

• Describing your hemorrhoid bypass surgery in graphic detail.

• Making her eat your cooking.

• Having her over to do your laundry and wash your dishes and calling it a date.

• Hitting her with a pie in the face as a joke just as she opens the door to go with you all dressed in her best gown for a formal dance.

• Taking a corner too fast, opening the door, and rolling her out of your car onto the highway just for fun.

• Using her sleeve to clean out your ears.

• Letting her help clean the fish you caught.

• Biting off a piece of your beef jerky, spitting it out of your mouth, and sharing the piece with her...unless she's about to starve to death.

• Putting an inch of mousse on your bald head.

• Burying her in the sand at the beach and leaving only her feet sticking out.

• Making her dinner from the things you catch scurrying across your floor.

• Looking at your retainer under the microscope.

• Letting her spend time with your friends and roommates while she's waiting for you to get ready to go.

FASCINATING FACTOIDS ABOUT FEMALES...

• The average woman has more intelligence than 4.5 springer spaniels, 3.9 elephants, 2.7 dolphins, 14 men, and 1,250 night crawlers.

• Women consume 84% of the world's iceberg lettuce, 72% of the world's chick peas, and 92% of the worlds lotion crop.

• In the Arctic, Inuit women grind their teeth down chewing animal hides to make them soft for their men to wear. In Peoria, men grind their teeth down trying to understand why their women won't balance the checkbook.

• According to animal trainers, it is virtually impossible to teach a female duck to sing alto.

• The amount of toilet paper an American woman uses in one weeks time, if laid end to end, would make a disgusting, soiled, bacteria infested eyesore that would be very long.

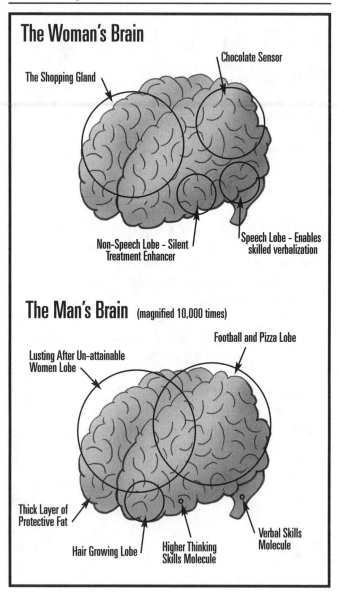

4

SECRETS

"Orange juice always tastes better
before you brush your teeth."
- Ponce de Leonard

Feminine Mystique: Girl Secrets

Girls have secrets, big secrets. Some of them are
deep and dark, I think. After years of being
married to and observing women, I have
unraveled some of this mystique. The party's
over. Write these down guys. If you are capable
of comprehending them, the following are some of
the main secrets which, up until now, have given
the women their mystique:

31

Secrets All Girls Know Which Guys Don't

• After the oil light comes on, you can sometimes drive 4 more days before the car quits completely.

• If you act ornery enough, people will give you what you want and then leave you alone.

• If 8 of you all turn on your hair dryers at once, you can make the lights go out in the entire house.

• After the engine has seized up and the car shuts down, the cooling fan in front still runs for a while. You can use it to make your nails dry faster.

• When all the money is gone out of your checking account, you can still write checks for a few days, even longer if you have a nice guy who keeps filling it back up.

• If you are busy using your rear-view mirror to apply lipstick or mascara, the mirror can no longer be used to avoid running pick-up trucks off the road.

• If you ever run out of toilet paper, pictures of old boyfriends work just as well and you get a little extra satisfaction as a bonus.

• If you forgot to service your transmission for a

decade or so and it melts down, the CD player will work for a very long time even if the car won't get you anywhere.

• If you are in a hurry, men will eat almost anything if you mix it up, cook it, and call it casserole...but the kids won't.

• The policemen at speed traps will generally just wave at you as you fly by at double the speed limit because they're waiting for an opportunity to catch a guy with a broken tail light.

• Having a baby hurts worse than hitting your thumb with a hammer.

• A Chevy Suburban will climb up and over a Subaru if you're not watching what you're doing.

• For some reason, nobody except your mom ever knows how long it's been since you dusted on top of the fridge.

• The amount of enjoyment you get from your bathroom experience is in direct proportion to the volume of toilet paper you use.

• Paper machet wrapped around a balloon can replace the pipe under the sink, but not for very long.

• You never have to write anything down in your checkbook ledger if you don't want to, or if you choose, you can pick any number you want out of the air and write that in. It won't matter; some guy will make it all right.

• No matter how big a mess you're in, if you cry, you will always get some sympathy, and often tears will fix everything.

A Few Guy Secrets: Things Guys Intuitively Know That Most Girls Cannot Comprehend

• You can cover up spaghetti sauce stains on your shirt with duct tape.

• You can catch more fish with dynamite than you can with a pole.

• If you put the pans in the dishwasher still stuffed with food, you don't have to mess around filling little containers (which will just turn green anyway) and putting them into the fridge.

• If you hit a golf ball at a ceiling fan, every once in a while you can get the fan to automatically return your ball to you without breaking a window.

• If you're staying at a guy friend's apartment

and during the night you get cold, although they're not as good as a real blanket, pizza boxes will hold in quite a bit of heat.

• The cat will go away and stay away for weeks at a time if someone puts loaded mouse traps in its little bed or shoots it in the tender parts with a pellet gun. (Remember, cats are not endangered.)

• If your car is really dirty, You should arrange to take your wife or girl friend's car to be fixed. When you come back, she will have cleaned your car, probably out of gratitude.

• The best way to keep your finger from pulling a trigger and shooting other rotten drivers on the road is to keep it tucked away safely in your nose.

• If you're planning a romantic dinner and you must have everything just right, hire professionals and have it catered.

How To Understand What Women Really Mean

Many hapless guys struggle to understand what women mean when they speak...or don't speak. The problem is that too many guys are, unfortunately, just too dense to figure things out on their own. Don't despair. What you need is someone to tell you everything so you don't have to do any of your own thinking. Don't be embarrassed. Lots of guys need to be told what to do. They can't drive without someone helping them. They can't get dressed without someone helping them, and of course, without help, they are always saying something stupid. I know I have certainly learned to appreciate my wife's ability to finish my sentences for me. So you see, guys need lots of help. This chapter comes in the form of a direct translation. Whenever your woman uses one of these lines, you need never again wonder what she means.

For example, the last time a woman asked you: "Do you think I look fat?" You, being a dumb guy, may have erroneously thought she meant: Do you think I look fat?" Boy, would this ever lead to some doozies of mistakes, especially since what she was really saying was: "I want a compliment, and I want it now!" She wasn't even asking a question! Imagine some dumb guy interpreting her question this way and answering in typical guy sarcasm with something like, "Not compared to Shamu."

After reading this book, you would know that she was really giving you a very direct, and emphatic command to give her a compliment, and you could respond with something like: "Whooee baby! You sure rev my motor!" And all would be wonderful.

Interpreting what she says

If you're a real idiot, you will want to commit these bits of womanese to memory, assuming you have one. If you don't, carry flash cards or something:

• Whenever she says: "I don't care where we go to eat." What she's really trying to say to you is: "I know exactly where I want to go; let's play a fun guessing game and see if you can read my mind."

• When she asks: "Do you think your shirt matches your socks?" What she really is saying is: "Change your clothes. You look like a dork."

• When she says: Do you know what today is?" What she really means is: You forgot my: birthday, anniversary, Valentines day, the anniversary of my cat, Fluffy's, automobile homicide, etc..., and if you screw up, I will make you pay for months. (If you are going to misinterpret a question, whatever you do, don't screw up this one. This question is often intended as a test to gauge the depth of your devotion to her.)

• When she says: "What does this song remind you of?" What she is really saying is: "I need you to lie to me, and I need it now! And sound convincing."

Understanding Women...

• When she says: "Please don't call me any more." What she is really saying is: "Call me multiple times every night."

• When she says: "I don't want to see you any more." What she is really trying to say is: "I want to see you every night."

• When she says: "Leave me alone or I'll get a police restraining order." What she is trying to say is: "I love you."

• When she refuses to talk to you and lies about being home and two 280 pound thugs appear on your doorstep with pipes, chains, knives, and brass knuckles and warn you to stay away. What she is really trying to say is: "Love hurts."

• When referring to some other attractive woman, she asks: "Do you think SHE looks good? What she's really saying is: "Do something quick to build my self-esteem."

• When she asks: "What are you having?" What she's actually asking is: "I really, really, really want the $50.00-a-plate lobster, but I will be embarrassed if you don't order it first."

• When she says: "It not a big deal to me." What she really means is: "I care a great deal, but I don't want to tell you because I'm going to determine the future of our relationship based upon how well you can read my mind and then how caring and sensitive you are when you respond to what you think I want."

See! now you can have her fooled into thinking you're a caring, loving, sensitive touchy-feely kind of guy.

Author's note: Discussing gender can be controversial, even painful. Since I started writing this book, women in my house have become really weird. They observe everything I do very carefully. In order to be fair to both sides, keep my food from being poisoned, and so the girls in my house will give me a little electric heater to plug in while I sleep outside with Sparky, I have invited my 21-year-old daughter, Erin, to provide some balance in my book by writing a few rebuttals. Here they are. Pretty good, right on the money – don't you think?

A Rebuttal

Give me a break. Men know exactly what women mean. They just pretend they don't so they can remain lazy bumbling idiots. Nobody, not even a guy, is so dense that he can't pick up on the <u>obvious</u> cues that most women give. This "stupid" act is just another way for guys to try to manipulate women to avoid expending any energy and so they get what they want. Most men are just trying to avoid having to put forth the money, effort, or time to do what women want or to do it right.

In their quest to manipulate women by acting stupid, guys have formed a right and left-wing conspiracy of ill repute. It looks to me like groups of men get together every Monday night on the pretext that they are watching Monday Night Football. But we all know better. By pooling their collective brain-power, they are barely able to generate enough intelligence to discuss such things as hair loss, Ultimate Fighting Challenge, their most recent flatulence, the female anatomy, wrestling moves, or car problems, and of course, this elaborate plan to make women think that guys are too stupid to do anything for themselves.

For example, before a women ever criticizes the way a guy dresses, the guy knows perfectly well that he doesn't match. He knows he just didn't think far enough ahead to have clean, matching clothes ready, and he's too darned lazy to do anything about it. He would rather have his women pick out an outfit for him so that he doesn't have to remove himself from his favorite chair. He knows that if he acts stupid enough, she will go back to his room, get his cloths ready and lay them out on his bed in the shape of a little man. All he has to do is leap from the couch during a commercial break, throw on his clothes and be back at the end of the timeout without ever dropping the remote.

Now that the truth is out, I think that women must do something about this problem. Try letting your man go out in public wearing mismatched clothes and be willing to drive around for a few days until he decides on a restaurant. Soon, either he'll get the hint and start behaving like a real man, or you'll kill him.

23 Things You Can Do While Waiting For Your Woman To Finish Shopping

1.   Go into the hardware department, fire up all of the chain saws and see how many you can keep going all at the same time.

2.   Put packages of gum on layaway.

3.   Find other bored guys and get into a hot game of shopping cart demolition derby.

4.   Hide inside the clothes racks and make animal noises.

5.   Plant a garden. Radishes, especially, will come up quickly.

6.   Read an entire set of encyclopedias.

7.   Find the intercom and announce wacky sales.

8.   Get some other guys together, and using cool stuff from housewares, make a pots and pans band and march up and down the aisles of the store taking requests and entertaining people.

9.   Do donuts in the parking lot.

10.   Go into the restroom and yell at the top of your lungs: "Hey! we're out of toilet paper in here!"

11.   Hang out in lingerie and try stuff on.

12.   Re-think all of your goals in life.

13.   Pretend you're an artist and paint stuff on the store windows like: "Going out of business" and "Everything in the store is FREE!" or "Everything 100% off." You can use her lipstick for paint.

14.   Count how many squares of tile are on the ceiling.

15. See how long it takes to try on every fragrance of perfume in the store.

16. Set off the fire alarms and blame it on someone else.

17. Figure out which video surveillance cameras are on and put on an impromptu independent film performance in front of them for security to enjoy.

18. Do something dangerous or obnoxious to get thrown out of the store and then conjure up creative ways to sneak back in.

19. Polish up your pick-up lines by trying your new stuff out on all the women who walk into the store.

20. Write cool, innovative graffiti on the mens' room stalls.

21. Play dead outside in the bushes and see how long it takes the police to arrive.

22. Offer candy to all the little kids who come in.

23. Bring dark glasses and a cane, sit at the door and see how much money you can make selling pencils.

Another rebuttal by my daughter, Erin:

Oh yea?! Well here are 23 things you can do while waiting for your man to get off the computer!

1. Get on a friend's computer and go into your man's chatroom under the name, "Hot Stuff", and see what he says to you.

2. Sell all his underwear on E-Bay.

3. Take his new BMW for a spin. It should be pretty clean since he just made you spend 2 hours wiping it down with a diaper.

4. Call that really cute handy man to fix your sink.

5. Ask him if you can buy that new bedroom set you've been wanting. Then you can just answer "yes" for yourself because when he's in the zone you wind up answering all your own questions anyway.

6. Moon him and see if he notices.

7. Rip on him. Tell him everything that is wrong with him and your relationship. You don't have to worry about doing any long term damage. You can get it all off your chest and he won't hear a

word you said, because as soon as you started talking about relationships, he tuned you out.

8. Call a friend. Oh, wait; he's on the internet; never mind.

9. Eat all the chocolate you want.

10. Go through his cloths and throw out that old bright yellow, "Don't Worry Be Happy" t-shirt and anything else that annoys you.

11. Set the house on fire and see if he notices.

AN UNSCIENTIFIC, BUT HIGHLY ENTERTAINING STUDY IN GENDER CONTRAST

"If you're a failure with women, don't despair.
So is Woody."

- An obscure line from a '60's beach movie

Sometimes the clearest way to gain understanding is with a good visual. In this chapter I have tried to provide a little contrast. Here you will see the vast differences in the ways men and women complete the same tasks.

An Example Of What Might Happen If Men Were Allowed To Decorate Houses

If a guy were allowed to decorate his house, this is how it would probably look: As you walk in the door and look to your left, you would instantly see your first clue that a guy was the decorator. This would be the pizza stain on the wall right below the moose head. By contrast, we all know that if there was a pizza stain just below the moose head on a woman's wall, she would do something artsy and cute with it, like turn it into a lady bug or sunflower or clever moose saying.

Next, you walk into the bathroom. Clues that a guy decorated this house might be the obvious fact that the people who had showered there this morning had used newspapers for towels and that they had hung them on the moose antlers on the wall and in piles on the floor by the TV. You might also notice that the color of the moose head and towels had been cleverly coordinated to match the trendy colors of the mildew and other residues building up around the toilet, and that these fungis (pronounced fun-guys) were bearing offspring and planting gardens, obviously planning to stay for the long haul.

From the bathroom, you might move into the kitchen, where, if a guy decorated, you would notice the striking absence of any kind of cute decorations...except for the cool moose head over the sink and the abstract toast-crust, fungus, jam and month's supply of soiled dishes in and near the sink. Having such drab colors in a kitchen would be totally unnatural for a woman.

If, from there, you were to go anywhere else in the house, you would notice the walls. Except for an occasional hole where someone accidentally punched a golf club through, and the occasional moose head, that would pretty much be it. Yes, I believe the world would be a different place if men were allowed to decorate the houses.

If Men Helped Other Men Drive Cars

Freeway driving is an important dimension of life around which speculation is particularly fun. If, instead of helpful woman navigators and wives or girlfriends for driving coaches, guys were allowed to make helpful suggestions when other guys drove cars, highway safety would be radically different. In reality, if helping were left up to guys, a driver would pretty much have to go it alone because his coach/helper would either be scoping out women in other cars or sleeping. This would pose some definite risks because we all know that regardless how much driving experience a guy has, women know that he could never survive without help. The fact that guys do survive occasionally, whenever the woman is not around just proves guys don't really drive when women are not around. Women know the truth which is that guys lie. They only SAY they went somewhere, when in reality, they sat trembling and sobbing behind the wheel too terrified to start the car. Then, when the women reappear, they put on their faces of false bravado and wait for their instructions.

Also, as you can imagine, sometimes it's dangerous to both avoid serious accidents and still have enough concentration to retaliate against the incompetent drivers on the road all at the same time. If we follow all this through to its logical conclusion, we are certain that having guys coach guys on their driving would result in many more accidents than we experience under current conditions with woman helper/drivers.

If Men Ran The White House

Going back many generations, from the Hillary administration to the Nancy administration, and even as far back as the Cleopatra administration, there have been some reasonably compliant first men in the Whitehouse. There was, however, one important period when the president was a bachelor, and we can assume that he had at least some marginal input into the country's affairs. I think it was either Millard Fillmore, Martin Luther King, or Ben Franklin who lived all alone in the White House for a term or two. I'm pretty sure that during this all-male administration, they started the Civil War or the holocaust or something.

If Men Did Laundry

No doubt, if men were to do laundry, the world would save a lot of money in detergents and fabric softeners. There would be no need for such equipment as washing machines, dryers, irons and ironing boards, because the only thing guys would be capable of getting ready for women to wear would be low-maintenance items like swim suits and lingerie. Of course, guys' clothes would need to be low maintenance too and consist of pretty much just a loin cloth and a tattoo. But they would always look nice.

If Dads Did Their Daughter's Hair

I think we can all pretty much just imagine this one.

If Men Were To Start Making Some Of The Important Corporate Decisions

Imagine, if men were to start making corporate decisions. For at least a while, bosses, CEOs and presidents would be completely lost. Blank stares would come across their faces; they would be falling asleep without their coffee, as they grappled to plow totally new ground being forced to make their own suggestions about how to improve working conditions and corporate bottom lines. Not knowing what else to do, they would probably head off 'en mass to go golfing while they sorted things out in their minds. With all these other orphaned executives trying to do the same thing and get on the #1 tee at about the same time, golf courses would be like freeways: no fun at all. Pretty soon fairway rage would start breaking out all over the place; there would be fighting, killing, and violence, and pretty soon we would all plunge back into the dark ages.

If Guys Started Having Children

If men were to have the children, they would go into the hospital and with their first labor pain, if I know guys, they would probably pull out their guns or chain saws and take it out on their wives and the doctors and staffs. Not a pretty sight.

Finally... If Guys Planned Weddings

First, women view weddings much the same as guys view the superbowl: as the biggest competitive event going. And so, just like the athletes in the super bowl, they spend a lifetime preparing for this event.

A guy, on the other hand, has a reaction to a wedding like: "No way am I getting messed up in that!" and for a good reason.

The only reason guys even allow such things as weddings and receptions is because the whole idea of a wedding and reception is usually sprung upon them at the last minute, so they don't have time to adequately prepare a response. They have absolutely no idea what's happening to them.

Women have lists of guests which they and their moms have been compiling since before either of them were born. These lists include everyone they know and a very large group of people they don't even like. (These undesireables are on there for valuable "in-your-face" points) That's one reason why it's so important that everything on the wedding day is absolutely perfect and if not perfect, at least expensive. If anything fails to work out perfectly, a normal woman will only be able to avoid suicide if she has the peaceful

assurance that tons of money was spent on it
by guys.

GAME DAY

Women begin mental preparation the night before.
They begin to close their eyes and visualize a
perfect fantasy wedding coming off, which, of
course, it never does. They have every detail
worked out in their minds like a scene from a Julia
Roberts movie. Then, when nothing goes right,
beginning with the weather, they begin taking
cheap shots at the men for ruining the event.

The guys' reaction, on the other hand, is: "What is
going on here? Who's paying for this carnage?"

Being a woman, a bride's top priority is to cut the
honeymoon short so she can get back and open
presents and see if any money came in the mail.
All during the honeymoon, the suspense is so
thick the groom can cut it with a knife.

Brides are driven by instinct stronger than a
salmon's determination to swim up waterfalls to
know symbolically what the old wedding "score" is
compared to other women she is competing
against.

Unless he gets a new ball or racket of some kind, the guy, on the other hand, will generally fall asleep while his bride opens gifts.

WEDDING COLORS

To all the women involved, after the gifts, nothing is more important than the colors. Everything, right down to the sushi must be wrapped in ribbons matching the bride's colors and coordinated with the theme.

Guys, on the other hand, honestly can't even tell what matches.

Guys view the whole process of the wedding and reception as a deterrent to marriage. Psychologists have studied guys' apparent inability to make a commitment. The truth is, they have no problem committing to be married; they are just terrified by the prospect of witnessing, let-alone paying for, a wedding reception.

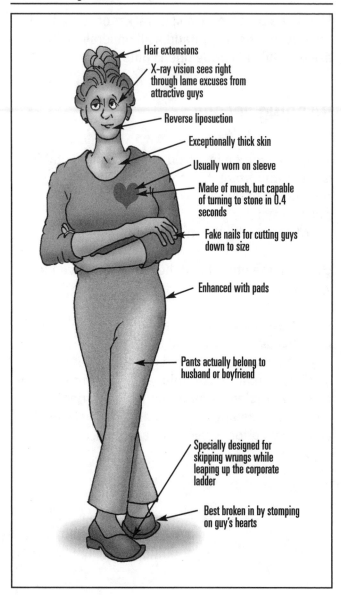

Hair extensions

X-ray vision sees right through lame excuses from attractive guys

Reverse liposuction

Exceptionally thick skin

Usually worn on sleeve

Made of mush, but capable of turning to stone in 0.4 seconds

Fake nails for cutting guys down to size

Enhanced with pads

Pants actually belong to husband or boyfriend

Specially designed for skipping wrungs while leaping up the corporate ladder

Best broken in by stomping on guy's hearts

6 RULES FOR KEEPING YOUR WOMAN

> "The home fires always seem to burn brightest
> before the fire truck arrives."
>
> – Nero

Now that you've got her, how do you keep her?
This is a question that has troubled poor and
middle class guys for centuries. The following are
just a few very simple secrets which, if carried out
meticulously over a period of years, should
convince your average, garden-variety girl to stay
with almost any guy.

Understanding Women...

1.   Give her all the money she can ever spend.

2.   Never tell her "No."

3.   Don't get a belly.

4.   Become an expert in communication and talk everything through.   Share with her your most intimate secrets and thoughts...never mind...bad idea.

5.   Make sure her bank account never runs out of money.

6.   Don't lose your hair.

7.   Become an interesting, even fascinating person, and be constantly intrigued by things that interest her.

8.   Give up golf, basketball, football, and any other interests you have and get into shopping.

9.   Keep bringing her lots and lots of money.

10.   Become a good listener.

11.   Let her hold the remote occasionally.

12.   Clean up after yourself.

13. Never ask her to pull your finger.

14. Always fill her bank account with plenty of money.

15. Wake up and take care of the kids in the middle of the night.

16. Become fascinated by romance novels, a clean house, and other people's business.

17. Get a cat.

18. Whenever her bank account balance gets low, fill it back up again.

19. Wash your face.

20. Use deodorant.

21. Buy some clean clothes.

22. Shower her with loads and loads of money.

23. Stop sneaking off to see other wild women.

24. Fix her car.

25. Fix her toilet.

26. Fix her cat.*

27.   Fill up her checking account daily.

28.   Play tennis or volleyball.

29.   Thank her and be genuinely appreciative whenever she gives you input about your driving.

30.   Be good looking, fit, and romantic pretty much all the time.

31.   Be certain that she never runs out of money.

32.   Accept all of her criticism with gratitude.

33.   Never leave whiskers in the sink.

34.   Never leave a smell in the bathroom.

35.   See that she always has an adequate supply of money.

36.   Never be afraid to ask directions.

37.   Always let her decide when it's OK to be amorous.

38.   Never let her think for a moment that you might be running out of money to give her.

This is just a joke.

Making Points with Women

Keeping her around is one thing; having her tolerate you, is something else all-together. Now days it's not enough to give a woman everything she wants. While money may get her to stay around for a while, if you want her to act like she likes you or to be nice to you in front of other people, you must do much more. In guy marriage counselling we call this getting "extra points."

Dealing or living with women can be just like a big football game. If you miss your extra points, no matter how many touch downs and safetys you score, you will still be a pathetic loser. Before you know it, you will be symbolically lying face down in that giant mud puddle in the middle of the field of relationships, while the meanest person on the other team is twisting your foot around and rubbing your nose in the dirt, all the while trying to manipulate the referees so the other side gets all the calls which will give her the house, the car, the 401-K and the boat, and leave you with the kids. So you see how important it is to make those extra points.

How To Make Points With Women

The easiest way is to give her a little extra money. We understand that most guys work super hard to make it look like they're making as much as their wives. And since a guy's paycheck usually goes toward the house payment, car payments, child support, groceries, medical bills, utilities, and golf, it's tough to squeak out enough extra money to impress her, since she gets to spend her entire $3,000.00 check on clothes and luncheons with the girls. But hey, that extra $5.00 here and there says to her, "splitting up with this Bozo would cost me lots of money." Knowing this might just save your marriage. Extra point!

Next, one of the easiest ways I know to have a woman melt into putty in your hands is to wash the dishes ...without being asked. Now, I know this sounds radical to some of you, but work with me here. You don't have to do it every night. Just keep your eyes open for an opportunity to do those dishes when she comes home toting a bucket of Kentucky Fried Chicken or Chicken McNuggets. Then, as soon as everyone is finished eating, with great pomp and dramatics, announce that tonight is your dish night. She'll never know the difference. And even the dorkiest guy should be able to figure out how to get a couple of plastic sporks clean. Just watch. This will get you tons of extra points.

The final way to score no-fail extra points is to let her hold the remote. Now, you don't want to just do this randomly and with no ground rules, or you could end up watching some lame chick flick like "Martha Stewart Shops With Platonic Guy Friends, or "My Best Friend's Opening Wedding Gifts." Just let her hold it for brief 5 or 10 second intervals when there's a good beer commercial on or while your thumb is resting. This will get you extra points. Oh, and always try to look pathetic.

How To Humor Your Women

Women love bonding. They also have a great sense of humor and love to laugh. This laughter and bonding can greatly solidify a relationship...at least on Television Sit-Coms and in the minds of clueless guys. Here are some great ways to humor your woman:

• Spend your evening building cool stuff out of your dirty laundry.

• Have 25 of your guy-friends over to watch football, call her "the old ball-and-chain," and every 2 minutes yell, "Hey woman, bring me some grub!"

• Be sure and tease her about her chubby thighs

in front of all your guy friends even if she doesn't have chubby thighs.

• Call her on the phone every so often and just breathe loudly.

• Send yourself roses and write your old girl friend's name and, "Thanks for a wild weekend" on the card.

• Accumulate all of your dirty dishes, dirty clothes, and rotting Chinese take-out in the middle of the living room floor, refuse to allow her to clean it up. Call it "Art."

• Spray her with whipping cream, PAM, or WD-40.

FASCINATING FACTOIDS ABOUT FEMALES...

• Most people won't be able to distinguish a female earthworm from a male just by looking at it's shape... or it's hair.

• The average woman spends a total of 11 days in her lifetime removing unwanted facial hair.

• Female electrical outlets normally don't have mammary glands.

• Women who regularly nag men are much more likely to be run over by a truck, abandoned while unconscious, or hit by lightning than those who just have nagging lower back pain or headaches.

• The female sea turtle has very little in common with the female weasel.

# 7

QUESTIONS & ANSWERS

Question:

How do I tell if a girl likes me?

Answer:

This has long been a problem for guys. We men seem to have a hard time reading non-verbal and verbal clues, interpreting their body language, and comprehending when they're ambivalent, clear, vague, or right to the point.

Asking a girl out for a date demands every molecule of a guy's courage. This typical true-life example might illustrate: A guy dials the phone and lays a couple of slick lines on her which he tried earlier on his guy buddies, and which got a definite laugh from them. He then brags a little bit, and eventually hits her up about going to the movie the following night. This is where things get confusing. The girl gives him an evasive response like: "I have another commitment that evening." The guy then thinks, "I'll bet she really likes me; she just has another commitment that evening." And so he asks, "Well then, what about the next night?" to which she responds, "Sorry, I'm busy then too."

Your typical guy will need to think about this for a while because things didn't go at all the way he planned, so at this point, he says "thanks," and hangs up.

In his ponderings for the next few months, he considers the possibility that maybe she really doesn't like him. But the typical guy, believing that he is irresistible and that all women secretly lust after him, dismisses such thoughts as irrational and assumes that since she told him she was busy, she is, and waits a decade or so for another opportunity to ask her out.

Sometime later, he again dials the phone and asks her for a date. Sounding distant and disinterested, she responds: "Sorry, I'm busy that evening."

He naturally interprets her disinterest as feminine mystique. "She's just acting coy," He concludes and tries again.

"How about the following evening?" He asks, to which she responds,

"Sorry, I think I'm going to be busy flossing my teeth."

"And the next evening?" He asks.

"Busy then too." She snaps, and by being persistent, he finds out that this busy girl is calendered through the next millennium.

Now, after this, he is absolutely certain that she is totally hot for him, lusts uncontrollably for him, and he's hooked by the challenge of sorting out these intriguing signals she's giving off. He runs back to his buddies and describes how crazy she must be over him to act so coy. For the next few days he is unable to sleep or eat because all he can do is think about her and how it's going to be.

A few days later, he calls her up just to talk, all the time hoping to confirm his suspicion that she is dreaming about him. Her family says she's not home, but he thinks he can hear her voice in the background telling them she doesn't want to talk to him.

Now he's hopelessly in love. After he hangs up, he can think of little else but her, and he can't wait until the next time they're together.

The very next night, he calls her, hoping to come over and just hang out together, but to his surprise, she's not home again. Only this time he can hear her voice whispering in the background. Frustrated and confused, he hangs up the phone. Out of control with feelings of confusion, pain and tender affection, he dials her number again. This time her mother answers, and after a few minutes of muffled whispers, the shy lass grudgingly takes the phone and firmly, but kindly, explains to him that while she would like to be friends with nearly everybody, she would rather date an ax-murdering alien musk ox than him, and would he please stop calling her. In her mind she is being honest, since she truly would rather date an ax-murdering alien musk ox, or at least a serial killer or a wallaby, than him. (Later he finds out that she is dating a serial killer and hanging out with wallabies.)

He is now TOTALLY confused..."Why are women so hard to figure out," He wonders. "Why won't she just come right out and say what she feels? Has she somehow stopped loving me?"

Guys. Read the following very carefully:

How To Know If A Woman Truly Loves You

Clue #1 - She doesn't.

Clue #2 - Not even one little bit. Deal with it.

Clue #3 - And, especially if you really, really like her, you can be absolutely certain that she doesn't like you. That's a dead give away.

Clue #4 - If you find her very attractive, more than likely, she doesn't like you.

Clue #5 - If you don't travel frequently to the French Riviera, and bop around the beaches of the world, if you don't own garages full of exotic cars and vacation beach houses in numerous locations, if you haven't showered her with diamonds, more than likely she just doesn't have any feelings for you. You should try to find someone else.

Clue #6 - If she is married to you, more than likely she has very little interest in hanging out with you either.

Question:

How do you make love last forever?

Answer:

Even though you now know the secret to keeping a woman with you forever, life's still not that great if she hates your guts. The joy and happiness of knowing that your woman loves you, hey, now that would be something. Here's how the pros do it:

First, you need to marry a woman who loves you and loves everything about you and will always love you and everything about you no matter what. In fact, it would help to marry one who is so infatuated with you that she is oblivious to your stupidity, lack of sensitivity and consideration for her, cowardice, ignorance, poverty, whiny voice, body odor, tooth decay, beer belly, smelly feet, gingivitis, tone-deafness, lack of decisiveness, decisiveness, male-pattern baldness, tooth decay, and the fact that you're doing time for assault.

Once you've accomplished this, the rest is easy. The challenge comes when you screw this one up and marry someone who notices your flaws, or who grows to genuinely dislike you. Avoid women like this whenever you can.

Question:

How can I reduce a woman to tears?

Answer:

Since the beginning of time, or at least the beginning of prime time, making girls cry has been an entertaining and useful life skill most boys work hard to develop. Any guy who ever had a sister or annoying neighbor girl knows how satisfying and gratifying it can be to tease a girl to the point that you get her blubbering or hollering to high heaven, and to know that you did this all by yourself, that it's your accomplishment and yours alone. This can really build a guy's self-esteem and give one an enormous sense of satisfaction and control.

One thing that makes teasing women so refreshing is if you spend a lot of time around guys, you know that the tear button for guys can be mighty hard to find, if it exists at all. You can work for days trying everything imaginable, and unless those tears are chemically induced, it can be nigh unto impossible to get them going. This is partly because guys are genuinely insensitive and shallow and are pretty much devoid of the kinds of feelings that most people would consider civilized, or even human. Although girls and women are determined to believe otherwise, normal guys are pretty much devoid of any kind of tender feelings. They are genuinely shallow and insensitive and most of the time pretty rude.

Women, on the other hand, have complex and tender feelings, completely beyond mortal comprehension. Because of this, they also have cry buttons sticking out all over the place, some of them even with little symbolic "push me" signs hanging off the end. Often, guys bump these cry-buttons, which are sticking out all over, completely by accident. And, if you can imagine, simply being thoughtless, rude, funny, or normal can bring tears in buckets-full. If he's not trying too hard, a guy can bring on a woman's tears by casually dropping a common every day insult like calling a girl "thunder thighs" or "fats-ooo" or by asking an innocuous question like "is that a zit or a third eye?" or by loudly proclaiming some terribly personal or embarrassing tidbit about her, like that she kisses like a mackerel, in front of a crowd of people.

I know what some of you guys out there are thinking. You're saying to yourselves, "You're kidding, right? Making girls cry can't be this easy. We do this to other guys a thousand times every day and expect nothing more in response than a simple obscene gesture or loud belch. Do you mean that to make girls cry, all I have to do is talk to them like I do other guys? If I had thought it would be that easy, I would already be doing it all the time."

Yep, that's about it. And if you are thinking this, you're a real wiener-head, pencil-neck lard butt. But then, you probably knew this already. The point is even YOU can make girls cry. It's true! Go to work. Experiment a little. See how much fun it can be.

Pretend Tears, A Second Frontier

So far, I have been talking exclusively about genuine tears, about things which truly humiliate, offend, or hurt girls. There are, however, times when girls turn on pretend tears for show, to make a point, or in order to manipulate guys. (Phony tears never work with women, because they always know when one of their species is faking it.) So, if you ever want the satisfaction of bringing on these fake tears, all you have to do is put a girl or woman into a position where she thinks she needs sympathy.

Take for example, a typical, every-day work situation. You, a hard-core guy, have been pilfering the company supply closet for decades for your personal use and bragging to a female co-worker about how easy it is. As a practical joke, you give this girl, who is perfectly innocent, a fake memo listing the penalties for getting caught pilfering, salt the area around her desk with extra stolen company pencils, a few staplers, some drug paraphernalia, and illegal assault weapons. Then, one of your buddies from another department stops by posing as a company big shot and pretending to bust her for theft of the pencils and threatening to fire her. If you can pull something like this off with a straight face, just sit back and enjoy the fireworks. Watch as the old artificial manipulation tears flow. It will be great!

Question:

Why do women look so good when men look so ugly?

Answer:

Apparently, much more effort went into the design of women than men. Not only do they look better, they live longer, endure child bearing, cook meals, scrub floors, do the laundry, wash dishes, intuitively know all the correct answers to every question, clean the house, and put up with guys. This could never have come about purely by accident.

Question:

How can I avoid housework?

Answer:

This is a problem many of today's men struggle with. It seems like every day, because of lack of skill in avoiding it, more and more men are getting stuck doing more and more household chores. If we're not careful, pretty soon we'll be doing as much work as the women. It didn't used to be like that in the old days. I can remember when women did pretty much all the work. They moved the TeePee, dug roots, chewed on the old buffalo

hides, milked cows, and generally treated guys like
the royalty they truly are. Unfortunately, they
aren't making too many girls like that any more.
We may even live to see the day that guys are
forced to change diapers and iron their own shirts.

Lucky for you, you have found this book. Here are
a few simple tips:

First, the old tried and true method of pretending
to be working all the time might work for you.
Many women buy this line; some even go beyond
the "buy" stage and actually appreciate all you do
for them. A problem, then arises if you don't want
to be working all the time, or when you need to
come home to eat something or to get your golf
clubs, or to change clothes. What do you do?

One thing that works for some guys is to complain
loudly all the time they're home about how tired
and overworked they are. Since many women
have an overactive sympathy gland, they will
usually feel sorry enough for them that they won't
ask them to do anything. This may, however,
foster a little smoldering resentment which can be
bad, especially if the woman is working longer
hours at a more distasteful job than the guy is, or
if he needs her to do something for him. In a
cases like this, you might have to become even
more aggressive and fake an injury. I have a friend
who had a real MD put a fake cast on his leg and

then had some of his friends vouch for the fact that his leg was really broken...and it worked for a while, too; she was just killing herself with tenderness waiting on him hand and foot until too many guys got talking and their stories didn't match very well. She started smelling a rat, then, because with the cast, he couldn't move very fast. She was able to catch him and duct-tape him to a wrecking ball. So if you're going to use a technique like this, I recommend that you only let a couple of buddies in on your secret and that you rehearse a little and make sure your stories all match.

A Second Alternative

About the only other thing you can do is exercise your macho guy muscles and delegate the chores to one of your kids.

Question:

Why do girls giggle so much?

Answer:

Scientists suspect that giggling is a response left over from an earlier time when it was necessary for survival, much like the fight or flight mechanism, the gag reflex, and the urge to kill telemarketers and inconsiderate drivers. More than likely, long ago, when a group of prehistoric girls were out digging roots and grubs, and a group of prehistoric guys from an enemy tribe came along intent on whacking them over the heads and dragging them off to their caves, they would begin to giggle. When the guys would hear this giggling, they would become so confused that they would run off in all directions and kill the first large animal they could find out of frustration. This also explains the extinction of a number of large species of animals at about this time.

Question:

Why do women hate me?

Answer:

A woman needs someone she can talk to, someone who is her intellectual equal, someone to bond with, a soul mate with whom she can share her innermost thoughts.

Unfortunately, being a guy, you are also a moron. Assuming you were capable of rational thought, nobody cares about your thoughts. I mean, who wants to share intimacies about pizza, jock-itch, the super bowl and office jokes? This is a problem.

Question:

Why do women get so excited about silly little things?

Answer:

It is true that women appear to get all worked up and excited about such ridiculous things as a bouquet of flowers which some clod gave her that she could just as easily have picked herself, hand-made sunflower-looking toilet paper holders, a large pine cone made into a pig-looking object, and a new outfit. There are a number of possible reasons why this is so.

One theory advanced by Brent, and Calvin is that women don't really get all that excited. They just want you to think they are excited so you can't say they never get excited because they don't get very excited when you win your ball game.

Another theory advanced by Boris is that because so many of them are married to guys, they have very low expectations. Their lives are so pathetic that it just doesn't take much to get them excited.

Question:

Why do women hate me?

Answer:

A woman wants to feel secure. She wants to feel stability, trust, comfort.

Unfortunately, being a typical guy, you are something of a flake. Since you lack the competence to successfully run nylons, let alone your life, and because of your distorted, over blown self-image and over-inflated ego, if all women were to stop hating you, you would just become a sexist, egotistical, lying hypocritical bigot, who's head turns every time an attractive woman enters the room. Who wants to pay 9 private detectives to follow some loser like you around to try and keep you faithful? You're not worth it.

Besides that, financially, you're the Titanic. You owe everybody. You can't hold a job. With her luck, she would decide to go with you, sacrifice 10 years of her life supporting you while you try to finish school, and after all that, you would stumble across some 19-year-old floozy in History 121 and vanish to the Bahamas, never to be heard from again. This is a problem.

Question:

Why are some women always ornery?

Answer:

You're on your own on this one. I have no idea.

Question:

Why do women hate me?

Answer:

Women like to have a good time. You've undoubtedly heard the old adage, "Girls just wanna have fun?" Oh, you haven't? Well, that explains a lot. Anyway, being a guy, you are no fun. Going out with you has been compared to reading the tax code. Your idea of a great time is watching bass-fishing videos, repacking bearings, or playing Tetris. This can be a problem.

Question:

Why do you see so many hot-looking women with ugly guys?

Answer:

Although it may seem like it, this is not a case where ALL ugly looking guys get hot women. Just some do. The fact is, there are simply not enough attractive women to go around to all the ugly guys. In order for every ugly or squirrely-looking guy to get a hot babe, some would have to share, and this is highly unlikely. If YOU want to be one of the ugly-looking guys who gets a gorgeous babe, you may have to do something a little different than the others do. For example, if you're really disgusting, filthy, smelly, etc..., as outlined in previous chapters, try for pity. Hot babes love to feel sorry for pathetic guys. They think they can fix them.

Question:

Why do women hate me?

Answer:

A woman dreams of being close to a real man, one who has taught, bulging muscles, a guy with a teasing, manly scent.

If you are reading this book, more than likely you are a slob. You have no muscle tone at all. You lack a six-pack, but enjoy a keg. You couldn't fight your way out of a wet paper bag. Every time you play touch football with the guys like they do on beer commercials, you wind up spraining an ankle or pulling a stomach muscle, and she then has to listen to you complain about it for months afterward.

You have the personal hygiene of a walrus. Your

feet smell so bad they actually keep flies away. Your laundry is crawling with roaches, silverfish and bacteria. This can be a problem.

Question:

What do women like about men?

Answer:

Question:

Why do women hate me?

Answer:

Women want someone they can be proud to be seen with, someone they like to show off to their friends, someone who is cultured and articulate, who knows just the right thing to say and do in every situation.

You, unfortunately, are a jerk. You offend everyone. You think you're hot snot on a silver platter, but everyone knows you as only a cold booger on the paper plate of life. The whole world has heard all of your lame jokes many times. If you weren't too dense to know it, you would stick your foot into your mouth BEFORE you start talking, just to save yourself the trouble of doing it later.

Get a clue. Nobody thinks you're funny, really! Give it up. This can be a problem.

Question:

Why do women live longer than men?

Answer:

Adversity makes people stronger, and women have much more adversity than men do. For example, most women battle for their entire lives putting up with the stupid things guys do.

The average woman builds a strong heart and cardiovascular system by desperately groping to overcome rational thought and reason, struggling against fierce mental opposition trying to come up with a way to assuage her conscience after she has broken every commitment she ever made to herself and completely over indulged, literally wallowing in chocolate, ice cream or some other forbidden delicacy she previously swore to forsake. This struggling takes great courage and stamina, much more than a man could ever develop.

She has a much stronger overall constitution than

her husband from being forced, day after day, to watch daytime talk shows and soap operas where the most wretched, miserable, and conniving people on the planet wallow in pathetic misery. This toughens her up so that when she is having a busy day, and some trivial thing causes her to have to change her plans, she is able to recognize the contrast, count her wonderful blessings, and then go out and easily cope without coming apart hardly at all.

Whereas, guys, generally don't have time for daytime TV because they're working to pay alimony and child support to their two former spouses and their 4 former children all living with different mothers and their dead-beat boyfriends, and so they don't have the opportunity to have their constitutions properly strengthened. Then, later on, hypertension, high blood pressure, and heart disease find easy pickins with the guys. And so they die early.

A third rebuttal by Erin:

So, women live longer than men, Duh; the human race could not survive if the women died first. With the women gone, men would soon follow, dying horrible deaths from causes like hard fouls during pick-up basketball games, or being buried and suffocating under their dirty laundry, from broken ribs from patting themselves on the backs, or from terminal stupidity due to brain atrophy from the complete absence of stimulating conversation. This would be the end of civilization as we know it.

Now, as horrifying as this may sound, there are even more reasons why humankind would die off quickly if women died first: First, your average guy would be dead within a couple of weeks of the death of his woman; that's how long it would take him to starve. The men would all be sitting at the dinner table waiting. And they would just keep sitting and sitting, and sitting, and waiting and waiting and waiting... until it would finally dawn on them that there was no woman bringing food.

After this realization, one of two things would happen. Some of the more frail guys would simply lay down and die on the spot, but a few more hardy souls would get up from the table with a determined look on their face and head right over to the nearest Burger King. Unfortunately, these men would be just delaying the inevitable. It would only be a matter of time before their poor little hearts couldn't pump those blobs of fat and cholesterol from a thousand Whoppers through their pathetic guy veins any longer, and their hearts would roll over and put their little cardiac feet up into the air and croak.

There is one additional killer that would certainly destroy womanless men: their own children. Without Mom, little Debbie would be forced to kill her dad, because she would become a social leper from her Dad fixing her hair for that special date using cool stuff from his fishing tackle box and duct tape. Since this would force him to shave her head, and even though she would look like his favorite basketball player, the absolute social ostracism would cause her to take matters into her own hands. She would kill him.

Obviously we have a kind and loving God who knew that this would happen, so he made the men die first.

TERMS, DEFINITIONS, INDEX... OR SOMETHING

<u>Aardvark</u>: Usually the first word in any dictionary or phone book.

<u>Abuse</u>: What a guy gets from his buddies whenever he gets so wound up in a woman that he spends all his time with her instead of the old gang.

<u>Alone</u>: Something a guy needs regularly from his banker after he finds himself in a relationship with a woman.

<u>Babe</u>: Very large mythical blue ox largely responsible for the deforestation of North America.

<u>Belch</u>: One of 4 things a woman never does.

<u>Benedictette Arnold</u>: Traitor to one's gender. Woman who chooses to use her energy and ability to stay at home and raise a family instead of competing with guys in every conceivable way.

<u>Boy</u>: Male of any age who finds himself in a situation where there is no woman to watch over him, supervise him, and tell him what to do. He can usually be found frolicking in blissful joy playing with either a ball or a mechanical object.

<u>Bride</u>: Woman whose mother has lost all sense of reason and whose father is catatonic and impoverished.

<u>Chick</u>: Something exceptionally cool or trendy as in "Lookie there at that chick tractor!"

<u>Chivalry</u>: The art of taking credit for every lucky and fortunate thing that happens in the world in order to

accumulate a large store of positive points (See extra points) for the times when one comes home two-days late from fishing.

Chocolate: Brown, sweet stuff highly prized by women, which is generally consumed in large quantities when they think no one will know. Was used as money by primitive women.

Friends (See Chums) : 1. Someone who will cover for you, lie for you, loan you clothes, tell you you look good no matter what, but who will steal hot guys from you without any guilt if she gets the chance. 2. The guy who secretly wants you but who accidentally got off on the wrong foot making you think he was only interested in a platonic relationship. 3. Former lovers who outwardly act as though it's over, but who secretly fantasize and scheme to get back together.

Girl: Small woman or unathletic guy.

Gold digger: Female over the age of 4 wanting to establish a serious relationship.

Grandmother: Older woman who still bakes desserts and feeds men without making them do the dishes.

Hot: Temperature of the seat a guy is generally always sitting on because he forgot something or screwed things up.

Ice Cream: Consumed in large quantities by women who can't get chocolate.

Man: Sean Connery

Menopause: Brief, often split-second, pause between the time a girl dumps one guy and begins hustling another one.

Sex: (See "Parents")

Parents: (See "Public Educator")

Public Educator: (See "TV")

TV: Source of intentionally ambiguous, titillating, inaccurate, misleading, and often harmfully stereotyping, but certainly entertaining information about gender roles and behavior. (See "Friends")

Toilet Paper: Substance made from old growth forests used in mysterious ways and gargantuan quantities by girls and women.

N.O.W.: Organization of angry, unattractive, miserable, humor-disadvantaged women who have taken a vow of misery for the purpose of training and encouraging other, less miserable women to participate in vices, and addictions formerly reserved exclusively for men with poor morals and bad judgement.

Pervert: See "guys."

The Pope: After we got to thinking, we figured that maybe he's single.

Woman: Person who uses all creativity, talent, and energy to subtly stick it to rival women and for toll painting.

Zelda: A woman we once knew.

Additional Apricot Press Books

'The Truth About Life' Humor Books

A Rather Lovely

Inheritance

New American Library
Published by New American Library, a division of
Penguin Group (USA) Inc., 375 Hudson Street,
New York, New York 10014, USA
Penguin Group (Canada), 90 Eglinton Avenue East, Suite 700, Toronto,
Ontario M4P 2Y3, Canada (a division of Pearson Penguin Canada Inc.)
Penguin Books Ltd., 80 Strand, London WC2R 0RL, England
Penguin Ireland, 25 St. Stephen's Green, Dublin 2,
Ireland (a division of Penguin Books Ltd.)
Penguin Group (Australia), 250 Camberwell Road, Camberwell, Victoria 3124,
Australia (a division of Pearson Australia Group Pty. Ltd.)
Penguin Books India Pvt. Ltd., 11 Community Centre, Panchsheel Park,
New Delhi - 110 017, India
Penguin Group (NZ), cnr Airborne and Rosedale Roads, Albany,
Auckland 1310, New Zealand (a division of Pearson New Zealand Ltd.)
Penguin Books (South Africa) (Pty.) Ltd., 24 Sturdee Avenue,
Rosebank, Johannesburg 2196, South Africa

Penguin Books Ltd., Registered Offices:
80 Strand, London WC2R 0RL, England

First published by New American Library,
a division of Penguin Group (USA) Inc.

First Printing, January 2007
1   3   5   7   9   10   8   6   4   2

LIBRARY OF CONGRESS CATALOGING-IN-PUBLICATION DATA:

Belmond, C. A.
A rather lovely inheritance / C. A. Belmond.
p. cm.
ISBN 978-0-451-22052-3
1. Americans—Europe—Fiction. 2. Inheritance and succession—Fiction. I. Title.
PS3602.E46R37 2007
813'.6—dc22   2006016657

Set in Bembo
Designed by Ginger Legato
Printed in the United States of America

For Ray

Part One

Chapter One

THE CASTLE IS DARK, AND THE WIND BLOWING AGAINST ITS STONY ramparts seems to evoke evil echoes of all the intrigue, murder, incest, piracy, scheming and passions of the past. There is a dank dungeon in the bottom of this castle where unspeakable torture and misery were the fate of anyone who got on the bad side of kings. Below us, the sea is crashing against the rocks, tempting anyone desperate enough to hurl herself into its cool, caressing oblivion. And in fact, there is a woman poised high on the rampart, decked in elegant crimson brocade and gold-encrusted jewels that catch the envious gleam of the sun. Her long golden hair is streaming in waves that whip around her shoulders as she gazes down at the sea with such a dramatic, defiant look that perhaps she truly is contemplating choosing death over whatever foul destiny the men in her life have decreed for her . . .

"Fuckit!" the actress cried out, her brow furrowed into a furious scowl. "There's sand and crap blowing in my eyes, I'm drenched in sweat under all this stinky upholstery I'm wearing, and now there's no more sun so I'm freaking freezing in this wind. Will you get the lousy shot before I go goddamned blind and die of pneumonia up here?"

"Cut," the director, Bruce, said disconsolately. "Bitch from hell," he added to no one in particular. And then somebody's mobile phone rang. Bruce turned and glared at his crew.

"Whose phone is that?" he demanded. "Tell whoever it is to kiss my ass!"

We had all chucked our phones into a pile in the soundman's van and turned them all off, as we always do. Or so I thought.

The soundman's assistant pawed through the phones, selected the offending one, and answered it. "It's Penny Nichols' phone!" he announced. Everyone turned around and stared at me as he added, "It's your mother calling."

"Better not tell her to kiss Bruce's ass, then," said my boss, Erik, our set designer.

"She's says it's important, and terribly urgent, but not life-threatening," the assistant called out. The whole cast and crew waited.

"Ask her if I can call her back in ten," I said, mortified. The guy spoke into the phone, then gave me a thumbs-up.

It's just like my mother to chat with strangers like that. And it probably didn't faze her in the least to be informed that our little rag-tag production company was in the middle of a shoot. I am a free-lance historical researcher and set-design consultant for Pentathlon Productions, the cable TV company that has cornered the market on historical sagas and sudsy "bio-pics," usually filmed in New York State even though our movies supposedly take place in the most glamorous capitals of the world. Cleopatra, Helen of Troy, and Queen Elizabeth all sailed up the Hudson River to view their kingdoms, and what they didn't find on the banks of New York was provided in B-roll stock film footage. We never, ever get sent somewhere beautiful on location—except this time, because the new production assistant is a society girl whose overseas connections actually got Pentathlon its first co-production deal with additional European financing to make

Josephine, Queen of the Romantics—otherwise known by its old working title, "Napoleon's Wife."

For once we were really shooting in Europe, in an authentic castle on the gorgeous Riviera coastline near Cannes, where Napoleon landed on the beach to make his comeback. There's only one problem, from my humble historical perspective. I couldn't find any evidence that Josephine actually came to this castle and hung out on the walkway, scanning the horizon for signs of her emperor-husband's boat. But nobody cares because it looks so great.

Josephine Bonaparte was being played by Louisa Santo, a pop singer who goes by the stage name of Larima. A beautiful girl from Spanish Harlem, she did a stint at modelling before the music industry got hold of her and spun her into one of its golden canaries. Her music is tinny but mainstream, the kind you hear in department-store fitting rooms and hair salons, with repetitive tunes and fake-defiant lyrics about bad boyfriends. However, she surprised everyone by being able to act well enough for television, which she instinctively knew requires a sphinx-like stillness of the face; and she looks dignified and regal in a gown, instead of bridesmaidenly. In short, the camera loves her. Unfortunately for Larima, she signed on to do this production for a modest fee, just before her first big record hit, so she's stuck with us and has made it very clear that she wishes we would all sink into the sea.

From my perch on a rampart below, I could see how bloodshot the director's eyes were. Bruce is a bit of a Napoleon himself: balding, stocky, tyrannical, with a short-man complex. He truly loves his work and has no further ambition to be anything but a regularly employed movie-of-the-month hack, as he cheerfully calls himself.

"At least we don't have horns honking," the assistant director told him consolingly.

"Horns? Of course we don't hear horns. We can't hear the dialogue, either. The minute she opens her mouth the wind snatches every word she says," Bruce snapped.

Sound has been a terrible problem every step of the way on this shoot. No matter where we're scheduled to film, there always seem to be hopeless traffic snarls barking at us. Even way up in rented villas or in obscure village churches we could hear the roar of trucks, the shouting of workmen, the shriek of sirens. Already today, high up on the ramparts of this castle by the sea where car traffic is not allowed, we had to halt filming when a wealthy-beyond-reason retired basketball star and his pals went zooming by on speedboats and power skis, whooping and shouting and spraying each other with expensive champagne that they shook up and uncorked. Machinery is the bane of our existence as we struggle to re-create romantic history.

But at least this time we're really here on the glorious Riviera, we keep telling each other. We have authentic ruins for backdrop, genuine castles to shoot in, better antiques to borrow. At least we're not parked in the same old vans, eating out of the same old plastic foam boxes, shooting under the same old tree—whether it's the story of Catherine the Great, Nefertiti, or Madame du Barry—on the banks of the Hudson River in New York.

For the company's real specialty is to take any woman of history, no matter what century, rank, or nationality, and run her life story through the formula of plucky-heroine-with-many-lovers, jewels, dresses, furniture, and untold power. The blueprint is simple. The Heroine of History is born either high or low, but in any case she's flung into an early, disastrous marriage, love affair, or rape with the master of the house, who's enough to put any girl off sex for life; and she's often cast out into the street. Nonetheless, being plucky, she steers her own destiny with remarkable ease, collecting various lovers, especially the One True Love whom she usually loses in the end. She compensates for her heartache by achieving business or political World Domination, becoming as scheming and ruthless as everybody around her. Still, you admire her, because she has nice hair and good wardrobe. Were you in her place, you'd do the same. The Heroine of History is just like you and me, only with money, palaces and servants.

I don't really mind the sudsing up of history, except for the one big lie: that the past was no different from the present. In our movies, the Heroine of History acts just like a modern, twenty-first-century gal, flaunting ancient taboos without ever fearing being stoned to death or burned at the stake. Our scripts contain the modern lingo of therapy, such as "our relationship isn't going anywhere" and "you know how bad she is at parenting" and "you really are distancing yourself from your family." At the same time, some favorite quasi-anachronistic words are liberally sprinkled about for atmosphere, especially "myriad" and "forsooth" and "betoken." The characters say "hear me now" and "mark this" a lot.

Of course, we at Pentathlon Productions know that aside from providing the quaint details of costume, sets and furniture, it's our duty to ignore the facts of history whenever they get in the way of modern fantasia. Which is practically all the time. Bruce just keeps admonishing us to *Share the fantasy*.

Bruce had now talked Larima into sharing the fantasy by taking one more shot at the dialogue. We all fell silent, holding our breath, and this time, miraculously, the wind died down, the speedboats didn't swing by us, and Larima delivered a genuine sob with the dialogue that worked beautifully.

"That's it," Bruce said cheerfully. "Lunch." But somehow it felt like midnight, since we'd been shooting since dawn because of the tight restrictions for the use of the castle.

Erik, the man who keeps hiring me for these jobs and insisting that I accompany him on the set even though nobody's really sure what I do, turned to me at this point and said teasingly, "Penny Nichols! You'd better go call your mama now."

There is just so much dignity you can have with a name like mine. Nobody calls me Penelope, because sooner or later they realize how hilarious it is to call me Penny Nichols. I went off shamefacedly and climbed into the sound van, ducking around the crew, who were already dragging cables and microphones to pack in it. I found my phone and sat on some cool stone steps where I'd have privacy. I wondered whether my parents had returned to Connecticut from their winter migration in Florida. I decided to try them in Connecticut first. At the time I had no idea what I was getting into, because, if you knew my parents, you'd understand why I wasn't the type of girl to expect any kind of "start in life" as my English relatives call it. And this is how my mother put it to me on that "fateful" day:

"Hallo Penny, is that you, dear?" she asked. "You sound so far away. I am *so* sorry to disturb you at work, but I'm afraid I must ask you an awfully big favor," she said briskly. She's lived in America since she was eighteen, but she's never lost her English accent, nor that vague aplomb with which she delivers the banal and the most devastating of news alike.

"Because the doctor said your father and I are both too sick to travel," she continued. "Can you hear me, darling?" she added as the line began to crackle with static.

"Yes. Did you say sick? Both of you? With what?" I shouted so she could hear me.

"Do calm down, darling. It's just a wretched flu. We both had a temperature of one hundred two the day before yesterday, but it's down now and I honestly believe that we're over the worst of it. Normally I wouldn't dream of bothering you about it—you *will* over-react sometimes," she said in a familiar reproving tone, which indicates that my reaction is too emotional for the daughter of an Englishwoman.

I sighed. It is practically impossible to have a conversation with my mother without rapidly plunging into Alice-in-Wonderland territory. At some point in your life (right about when you turn thirty, as I did last year) you realize that your parents have begun the slow slide toward senility and you mustn't encourage them to lapse any sooner than necessary.

"You said you needed a favor, right?" I called out helpfully, just as the line cleared.

"Yes, it's got to do with the inheritance, you see, and they all said I simply *had* to reach you tonight about the will," she said.

"Are you and Dad writing a will?" I asked.

"Not *our* will. Don't be silly. It's not *us* who are dead!" she said, insulted and slightly exasperated. We will never grow old, is what she means.

"Well, then, who died?" I fairly shouted.

"Your Great-Aunt Penelope," my mother said.

"Oh," I said with a pang of regret. I'd met her only once, but she'd been kind to me.

My mother said, "You were named for Aunt Penelope, you know. She liked that."

I still can't get used to my name. There's no good reason for my crazy parents to have named me Penny Nichols. All right, the last name comes from my father's family. His dad was an American GI who got stationed in Paris and married a pretty French girl, my Grandmother Aimeé. I never met either of them; my paternal grandfather died rather young of a heart attack, leaving my dad, Georges, a teenager with a wistful and abiding affection for all things American. He managed to pick up a degree in American literature while working as a chef and taking care of his mother. She died when he was twenty, so he came to New York, where he cooked in fine restaurants. There he met my mother, Nancy Laidley. She'd left what she called her "stodgy relations" in England for art school and a career as a free-lance children's-book illustrator. They fell smack-dab in love as soon as they "clapped eyes on each other."

But really, there's no excuse for my first name, not even my mother's airy explanation that they wanted to get some of her own family into my name. My English grandmother was called Beryl, and my mother defensively claims that she *knew* I would not be happy with that.

Mom didn't give me her own name because she said it would be tiresome to have another Nancy around. She didn't have any sisters, just a stuffy older brother named Peter. So that left Great-Aunt Penelope, my grandmother's sister who never married, and they all thought it would be cute to call me Penny. Little Penny Nichols, that's me.

Actually the name may strike you as familiar, if you were the kind of kid who liked to read children's detective stories. Because not only did my parents give me this ridiculous name, they also took it into their heads to invent Penny Nichols, Girl Detective—a picture-book character supposedly based on me.

She was a spunky little sleuth who went around snooping for her friends and neighbors, solving scientific puzzles and natural phenomena as if they were murder mysteries and crimes and kidnappings, by using deduction and logic, certainly, but also memory and intuition and instinct. She carried a magnifying glass, and she had copper-colored hair like mine, which she wore in pigtails.

My mother drew the pictures, and my father, with his literature degree burning a hole in his pocket, wrote the stories. What started out as their little "extra pocket-money" project to supplement their incomes became a modestly successful series of books about the adventures of Penny Nichols, Girl Detective.

Sure. What did they care if they doomed me for life? My fictional counterpart didn't have to face real people in school like I did. It was a huge embarrassment to me because by the time they wrote those books I was already on the brink of becoming a teenager. Yet there I was, Penny Nichols, kiddie detective, heroine of picture books. Ugh.

Of course, the royalties, Mom always reminded me, paid my tuition and would "come to" me in that far-off future when she and Dad were "gone." But time did not stand still circa my parents' era with its milder, 1970s cost of living. So, on my twenty-first birthday, after they presented me with a nice diamond-pendant necklace, my father gently explained that as far as a legacy went, there was the modest house in Connecticut where I grew up; the tiny retirement bungalow in Florida where my parents winter around the pool happily drinking gin-and-tonics; the dwindling royalties; and a few unexciting investments to pay for my wedding and "a rainy day" . . . but that was it. I barely listened; I didn't want to think of my parents being "gone," ever.

"You do remember going to meet dear Aunt Penelope that summer, don't you, darling?" my mother was saying encouragingly. "Because, evidently, she remembered you."

"Yes, but I was just a kid then," I said. I was nine years old when my parents took me abroad, to be looked over by my English grandparents at their pretty stone country house in Cornwall, where the sea was freezing cold even in July. It was our only visit overseas; Mother didn't like going back to see them in England, only to be told how silly Americans were and how foolish she was to choose to live among them. So our relatives were more mythological than real to me, like people in a history book.

"We got the sad news about Aunt Penelope from your cousin Jeremy," my mother was saying. "It was a positively stunning conversation. You remember Jeremy, don't you, darling?"

Unexpectedly I felt a sudden warm tide, a distinct physical sense of absurd happiness at the mention of my cousin. I'd met Jeremy that same summer in Cornwall, when he and his folks showed up for a week at Grandmother Beryl's house by the sea. I was nine and he was thirteen; old enough to admire and embarrass each other. Which we did. I remember that the day he arrived, his folks made him wear his good blue suit instead of jeans like everybody else. I could see that there was some strain between his parents and mine and that he, too, had the coolness of a boy who knew he was richer than me.

Still, he wasn't above climbing trees, and devising codes and hiding places for messages, when we were pretending to be Secret Agents, sneaking around reporting on the movements of the adults. I was a little afraid of his father, who was quick to blame Jeremy if one of us took a spill or broke something. Uncle Peter was my mother's brother, and he never quite forgave her for leaving England permanently. But, as I recall, he seemed to disapprove of everyone, especially his own son; as if, despite Jeremy's impeccable manners he was a delinquent-in-the-making unless quickly pounced upon by his dad for the slightest breach of good behavior. Even at uneventful moments there was tension between Jeremy and his father, so Jeremy learned to use good manners as a secret weapon. Uncle Peter died ten years ago.

"Jeremy is a lawyer now," my mother informed me. "A very good one. His firm specializes in international law, I think," she added in that vague tone of hers, "but anyway he says one of us should fly to London right away, to be there for the reading of the will. Your father and I can't possibly do it because of this beastly flu, and you're already in Europe. By the way, there was no funeral or burial ceremony to attend. She wanted it that way."

"Mother," I said sternly, "are you serious? Fly to London? I'm working here, remember?" Honestly, for someone who was part of a groundbreaking wave of women who entered the workplace when it was a feminist thing to do, my mother still refuses to believe that I have an actual career. She wants to keep thinking of me as a girl, not a full-grown woman, because that might make her become the very thing she dreads, a woman of *un certain âge*.

There was a click and, to my relief, my father entered the conversation as if he knew exactly what was going on. "Hello, my Pennee," he said in that affectionate French pronunciation he always uses when he says my ridiculous name. "I was making the coffee and your mother sneaked off to call you. Have you heard? Your great-aunt has left your mother and you some-zing in her will, so we want to give you power of attorney to handle it for her."

"Why, yes, that's what I've been *saying* all along!" my mother exclaimed, and she truly believed she'd been just that clear and precise. "It was Jeremy's idea; I wanted to give him that power-of-attorney thing, but there are complicated reasons that he thought it should be you. He'll explain it all. I can't imagine what Aunt Penelope's left me, but it's going to be all yours someday anyway, so you might as well handle it from the start."

"Sorry for the short notice, Pen-nee, but these things happen quickly, and we would have taken care of it ourselves, until we came down with *la grippe*," my father said. I heard him sniffle a little, and it occurred to me that they actually had been a bit ill; it wasn't just one of their hermit excuses to avoid traveling to London to face down the in-laws.

"All right," I said. "When do I need to be there?"

"We already booked you on a flight to London from Nice at seven p.m. your time," my father said. "Jeremy reserved you a hotel room in London for an overnight, because the reading of the will is at nine o'clock sharp the next morning. Is that okay?"

"Wow. Well, I guess I can get everything done by then . . ." I said, working out my schedule and wondering how, exactly, I would pull this off. We'd finished shooting the tricky interior scenes of *Josephine, Queen of the Romantics* and moved on to the exterior location shots, where they don't need me as much. Tomorrow would be the last day of the shoot anyway. Once my boss, Erik, threw a perfunctory fit, I figured he'd be intrigued enough about the will to give me permission to leave early. It meant that he'd have to squeeze in a meeting with me on his lunch break today about our next project, *Lucrezia, A Woman of Intrigue*. So I'll owe him a favor.

"It's all paid for. Let's see, oh dear, where did I put all that information—ah, here it is . . ." my mother murmured. I could hear her shuffling papers. And then, in spite of her daffy air, she reeled off all the flight numbers, addresses and directions with perfect aplomb. That's the thing about her. The vague, scatterbrained act is just a way of not having to be pinned down into what she calls the "achingly boring" parlance of life. Underneath it all is the shrewd business-woman who counts up all the receipts and handles all the accounting and investing.

"Now, when they read the will, don't act disappointed if it isn't much," she warned, as if still teaching me how to behave among the English. "Aunt Penelope was a rather reckless flapper in her day, and she didn't have any children of her own to put money aside for, so she probably didn't save much. Perhaps a small investment and some nice costume jewelry. She never worked a day in her life, you know— except for that little singing and dancing she tried—so I'm sure she lived off her savings and whatever her parents gave her. Why, Penelope was ninety years old, and she wasn't thrifty like my mother." I heard my father mutter something about the phone call becoming expensive. My mother spoke quickly now.

"When you see Jeremy, do be sure to ask after his mother—you know, your Aunt Sheila."

"Okay," I said. "I'd better get going on this." Now that I'd adjusted to the idea of returning to the hotel to tell everybody that I must take time off for my personal affairs, this, oddly enough, cheered me immensely. I've never really had an important, grown-up, financial reason for time off, since as a freelance consultant I'm usually too busy trying to drum up more work so I can make sure that I'm not "off" for the rest of my life.

"Sweet dreams," my father said tenderly.

"Break a leg," my mother added in her own tart version of affection. She thinks that if you work in film you use the same lingo as in theatre. And with that, the pair of them rang off.

Chapter Two

THE SUN WAS SHINING BRIGHTLY AS I CLAMBERED DOWN THE STEPS of the castle. Several of the production vans had already left, but I flagged down the sound truck and hitched a ride back to the hotel. It took all my concentration just to stay in my seat and not get bounced out of it each time the driver shifted gears, with a bone-jolting lurch of the clutch, as he struggled up hills or careened around a corner on the narrow back-roads. His radio was blaring sports scores and loud commercials in French the whole way, so conversation was not only unnecessary but impossible. That was fine with me. I needed to mull things over.

Every time I get off the phone with my folks, my own life seems a tad more unreal to me. Perhaps it's because my parents are so sure of everything they do, so utterly convinced of the authenticity of their existence. I don't see how I can ever match that. In photos they grin confidently, always arm-in-arm. In their youth they were tall, slim and trim, Mom with the same copper-colored hair I have, and Dad with his delicate light skin and brown hair, and the brown eyes that I inherited. Nowadays my parents are a little bit heavier, but not much, and more gray-haired, with crinkly lines around the eyes and mouth, but with that radiant look of people who've done what they wanted with their lives.

As for girls like me, we just toddle off into modest careers that we choose because we like the work, not because we want to make money. So I went to art school, and after graduation I freelanced as a historical researcher for authors and academics, but that wasn't enough to live on. Mercifully my friend Erik, who'd become a theatre production designer, hired me to help him authenticate the sets, props, backgrounds and costumes of the historical time periods in the plays, and then movies, that he worked on.

This may sound faintly glamorous, but in reality it simply requires me to research, paint and generally help create fake versions of the decor, doodads and bibelots of dead rich people. I spend most of my days in silent solitude, working from my tiny apartment in New York City, where the sun makes a brief morning appearance, then vanishes; where the kitchen has just enough room for a mouse to cook in, and actually is now beset with strange rustlings in the walls at night which indicate that mice have returned after a mysterious interlude when even they had gone off in search of a better life.

I myself rarely abandon the Manhattan rat race when I go out to do my research, shuffling around dusty old libraries full of books and photographs, and museum archives and used-furniture shops, scurrying through the dark underground hallways, vaults and lairs where most historical artifacts are kept. No matter the time period, I'm looking to find out what they wore, how they did their hair, and what chairs they sat in.

When I've completed my research I present it to Erik, at the occasional lunch-or-cup-of-coffee meeting that keeps my social skills relatively intact.

My friends ask me how I can bear to work alone, with nobody to talk to for days on end. But somewhere along the way the modern world lost its charm for me, and fortunately my job provides me with a legitimate way to spend whole weeks, even months, dreaming of living in someone else's more elegant past, where I would ponder life's verities whilst wearing exquisite ball gowns to fabulous parties and drinking champagne on a balcony with a man who loves me.

I don't really think of it as the past, but more as a sort of secret future. With remarkably thickheaded perseverance I harbor a steadfast hope that I might one day defy the odds and the gods, and use the past as a key to open the door of a more intelligent parallel universe. The only trouble with this sort of thinking is that whole years of your life can go by unnoticed. I'd always assumed that my personal life would automatically blossom alongside my professional development, never dreaming that one could feel slightly mummified by one's own career.

There was a loud roar from the engine of our sound van as the driver heroically steered us onto the main seaside road in Cannes. The Boulevard de la Croisette was mercifully flat and, though full of traffic, less hair-raising. Having been jostled out of my reverie, I resolved to focus on living in the present instead of brooding about the past. Our schedule had been inhumanly tight, with no breaks for sightseeing, devised by a line producer with the personality of a student crossing-guard. But now I squinted in the sunlight and shaded my eyes for a better look.

On one side of the boulevard were the grand, glamorous old-fashioned hotels with their beautiful French windows, built by kings and tycoons for their vacations and mistresses in centuries long gone. On the other side were the beach, the sea, and the famed "Croisette" walkway itself. Despite the town's present-day hurdy-gurdy atmosphere, there was still something elegant here, left over from another era. You could even see it in the way the dapper French traffic cops waved you on, vigorous and proud, intent on keeping the flow of life moving at a snappy pace, and the yachts chugging by in the deep blue sea.

We'd arrived here a few days after the famed Cannes Film Festival had ended. But I noticed that even though the actresses and movie moguls had flown away, largely replaced by elderly French ladies out walking their dogs, still, the stylish Croisette was sprinkled with glamorous young women languidly sunbathing in cushioned lounge chairs with old-fashioned blue-and-white-striped umbrellas, or strolling along the promenade in their gilded high-heeled sandals, skimpy chiffon dresses and sparkling jewelry.

Clutching my bulging, battered leather portfolio of scripts and notes, craning my neck to peer out the dusty window, I reflected that surely, if there was any place on earth where elegance could still be found, it was here on the Côte d'Azur—where those beautiful French doors are still flung open by begowned women and their lovers, gazing out at the sensuous Mediterranean on a warm summer's night.

Naturally, being an incurably hopeful romantic fool, I had imagined that I, too, would be staying at one of these glamorous *belle epoque* hotels with balconies and balustrades and potted-palm dining rooms, but instead, our "affordable" hotel, located way down a side street off the main boulevard, is one in a boring chain that prides itself on identical rooms so that no matter where in the world you stay, if you wake in the middle of the night you can always stagger in the same direction for the toilet. We might just as well be in Akron, in our dimly lit rooms of uninspired gray-and-brown, which feel—and smell—like the inside of a refrigerator.

When our sputtering van pulled up to the front door of the hotel and the sound guys began to noisily unload their equipment, I jumped out and went inside, passing through the lobby, where the newest wave of conventioneers, selling everything from dental supplies to beauty-parlor accessories to computer software, were all lined up with their suitcases waiting to check in. There must have been at least fifty of them arriving this afternoon.

I spotted Erik on his way into the conference room that had become our film crew's private cafeteria. I had my portfolio under my arm to show him some of my initial sketches, notes and samples for *Lucrezia, A Woman of Intrigue*. Pentathlon Productions is producing two bio-pics back-to-back. Since we don't usually shoot at authentic locations, Bruce depends on Erik's beautiful sets to conjure up mood and time period; and because Erik relies on my research, I'm known as the History Lady, whom directors tolerate having around mostly because I keep Erik calm. Erik is supremely motivated and well-connected, able to get a lot of good people and materials for less money than someone else might, which makes directors clamor for him.

He was surveying the chow line and crowded tables when I asked him if we could squeeze in a meeting over lunch about the Lucrezia Borgia set, so I could leave the shoot ahead of schedule and go to London for the reading of Great-Aunt Penelope's will.

Erik furrowed his bushy blond eyebrows as he stood there listening to me. He looks like a big shaggy wolfhound, six feet two and large-bellied, with a full head of floppy white-blond hair and a scruffy beard that's inexplicably darker brown, shot with only a few silver strands.

"What!" he shouted. He waved to the prop-master, who'd just arrived. "Timmy, come *here*. You've got to hear this with your own ears." Timothy, Erik's longtime companion, is thin, trim, wiry and dark-haired. Now he trotted over to us, looking intrigued.

"An heiress!" Erik told him in a stage whisper. "Our little Penny Nichols has turned out to be a bona fide heiress."

Sheri, the line producer, sidled over to eavesdrop, which she considers part of her job. I could tell that she heard what we just said, because she wore a studied look of feigned nonchalance. If she had her way, I wouldn't be on the set at all. I'd overheard her complaining to Bruce about having "extraneous people" around.

"Aren't you having lunch?" she asked us now, looking for an excuse to listen in.

Erik sighed and said to Tim and me, "The cold-buffet line is shorter. Let's grab some sandwiches from the trough, tuck them under our arms, and run like gazelles to my room."

Bruce, the director, saw us rushing for the elevators and became instantly paranoid.

"What are you three up to?" he demanded warily. "Why aren't you in the conference room, eating with the rest of us?"

"Penny has to leave early today. She must go to claim her inheritance," Erik announced pleasantly, as if it were the most obvious thing in the world. "But don't worry. She was up working all last night, making sure we could carry on without her this afternoon. We are having tomorrow's meeting today, on our precious lunch hour, which you so rudely interrupted."

Bruce stared at me, impressed. "Are you serious?" he asked. I nodded. "Fine. Fucking fine; leave early," Bruce said, lapsing back into perfunctory and mostly feigned hopelessness. But he won't miss me on the set. Even now I think he isn't quite sure what I do for Erik, except fuss over details that can only delay shooting.

As Bruce walked away, Tim tugged on my sleeve. "A word to the wise," he warned. "Paul's here in Cannes. He's come to make deals and harass us all. But he's been looking for you especially."

I tried to ignore the instant jolt of dread in the pit of my stomach. Paul is the executive producer of this project, a hotshot VP from the cable network brass—and he's also my ex-boyfriend. I want you to know that I had this career *before* I got involved with him. When we met, he was just an ambitious young producer who'd hired Erik's crew for one of those documentaries where they dramatize scenes from history. It was about Julius Caesar, and there were lots of clanging swords and shadowy orgies.

I was on board to do costume research, so Paul was therefore a boss, which is a disastrous way to begin a relationship, because the power balance is already tipped against you. Before him, I never thought of power. It was the first time that I engaged in that game-playing I so despise, and for which I am ill-suited. It was unnatural for me to play "pretend" with a man seriously—to pretend that you don't care, to pretend that you're not jealous, to pretend that you're interested in other men because that makes him respect you more, to pretend that you aren't fed up and bored when, finally, you are.

After much on-again off-again, we truly went our separate ways. Paul zoomed up the corporate ladder . . . and I'm still alive, which, for a freelancer, is an achievement, of sorts.

"There he is now, over in the lounge. Just wave at him and be cool," Erik advised.

Paul was easy to spot, sitting across the lobby at a table in the bar. Blond, athletic, sickeningly healthy-looking, there's something magnetic about him that makes strangers instantly assume he's important. It's in the arrogant tilt of his head, the mesmerizing effect of the handsome face, the expansive gestures, the carefully toned and weight-lifted muscles framed by his self-consciously selected bespoke suit, and the general cocksure attitude, no matter whom he's talking to—heads of corporations, finance men, politicians.

As he looked up from his table and waved at me, my stomach, just out of habit, felt as if I were in an elevator that suddenly plummeted twenty floors down. I waved back with what I hoped was nonchalant gaiety, and he was momentarily distracted by the cocktail waitress, who was already fawning over him, serving him his favorite scotch, no doubt. Then he turned his attention back to a couple of other important-looking hotshot businessmen seated at his table.

Erik patted my shoulder sympathetically. "You see, it's an omen," he announced. "You are being summoned to London just in time to dodge Mr. Bad News. Come, let's scuttle upstairs to my suite and have our meeting so you can run off before Paul knows you're gone."

We dashed across the lobby and into the elevator. Although Erik had "upgraded" to a junior suite instead of the allotted crackerbox the company gave each of us, the dull decor was the same.

"Dig in, kiddies," Erik said, popping open his plastic-encased sandwich, then peering at it dubiously. "Lord, who on earth hired this caterer? Everything's faux French."

Timothy plunked himself down beside me on the sofa, set his coffee cup on the table, and said, "Well, Penny Nichols, you're among only your friends now, so do tell. Are you about to hit the jackpot?"

"I sincerely doubt it," I said calmly, poking with a fork at my rather anemic salad Nicoise. "I never got the feeling that my elderly English relatives had piles of money to burn," I explained. "Besides, there are other relatives I've never met who'll be there. I'm terrified."

"It'll be fun! You must memorize everything they say and come back and tell Papa," Erik instructed. "Why, you should have seen my Aunt Agnes when she didn't get her mother's fur coat. My dear, she tore the sleeve off it rather than let her sister-in-law have it." He tossed the remains of his sandwich to the side and said briskly, "All right, Penny dear. Tell us what you've found out about those wild and wonderful Borgias."

We gossiped about Lucrezia, exchanging what we'd heard, as if she were a living, contemporary movie star. I opened my portfolio and spread out all the sketches I'd made, and the notes on jewels and furniture and clothes and hair.

"Of course, these are just preliminary," I said.

"Gor-*jay*-ous!" Timothy exclaimed at the sample swatches of velvet and gold braid I brought them. These are my happiest moments, when all my solitary work is presented to people who genuinely appreciate the details I've assembled. Tim, who builds all the props, will pass my notes on to the costumer and the wigmaker as well. He and Erik will scour a few Italian and Spanish flea markets before they return home. Then they'll set to work in their shop, a warehouse in Brooklyn, with a fleet of carpenters sawing, glueing and hammering the set pieces. Fake authenticity is what we call it.

On the Napoleon set, my real job was art forgery. I made copies of portraits and paintings that Napoleon and Josephine commissioned. Erik says this is good insurance for the future; I can always turn to crime for a living if we stop making these movies.

"Nice work, Penny!" Erik said admiringly, studying a replica I'd sketched from a photograph of a fifteenth-century portrait engraving of Lucrezia Borgia.

"I'll try to get a look at an actual portrait or engraving. It's hard to visualize her accurately when you're working from photocopies and reproductions," I told them. "I can't always be sure which portraits are really her. And some are considered copies of lost originals."

"We're nearly finished with *Josephine*, so don't bother coming back to the set when you're done in London," Erik said. "Take some time off, then just focus on the Borgia stuff."

"What will you wear for the reading of the will?" Tim asked encouragingly.

"My black silk suit. But I haven't even packed my bags yet," I admitted.

They both tsk-tsked, shaking their heads, and Erik warned, "Don't count on Sheri to get you to Nice in time for your flight. Go, baby, go."

Part Two

Chapter Three

EVERY NOW AND THEN LIFE GOES OUT OF ITS WAY TO REMIND ME why I have fallen out of love with the real world and stubbornly try to exist on my Parallel Planet. Mass transportation is an excellent example. The plane was full tonight, with seats crammed closer than humanly tolerable, and the moment we were airborne, the guy in front of me tipped his seat-back into my lap. I tried not to think about those blood clots you can get from travelling in such tight spots, the ones that later kill you. The lady in the window-seat next to me had hogged up the overhead compartment with tons of "carry-on" parcels that she tossed up there, crushing my raincoat in the process. At her feet she plunked down a blue canvas bag with airholes and outer pockets that held blankets and bottles. When she unzipped the bag, a monkey popped his head out, looking patient and resigned. Then he saw me. I mistook his bared teeth for a smile, so I was unprepared when he hissed and spat on my arm. His mistress smiled at me with fake benignity.

"Look! He likes you," she assured me. I wondered why this animal wasn't in steerage, drugged into a stupor, or making himself useful by stomping on suitcases to test their strength. Later, when the Monkey Lady was dozing, I asked the bright, brittle blonde flight attendant, who just shook her head, saying, "That's a legitimate 'service animal.' For people who need physical or emotional support."

By then everyone else was nodding off, too. Except the monkey. Unlike the adage, he saw but he did not do. Under the circumstances, I thought it unwise to take out the snack I'd grabbed from the fruit bowl in the hotel and shoved into my raincoat. It was probably smashed, and although this flight didn't serve a meal, who in her right mind would pull out a banana in front of Curious George? I decided to focus on London, and Great-Aunt Penelope's will.

I busied myself with my little pen and pad of paper, diagramming the family tree. I'd have to meet some of these people in London. This is what I got:

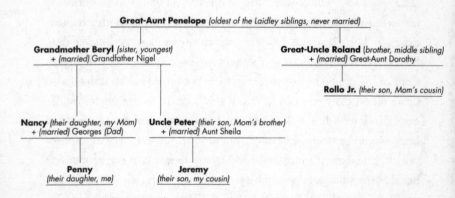

I sat back, trying to recall what little I knew about the actual personalities of my English elders from that brief visit to Cornwall so many years ago. Mom's father, Grandfather Nigel, was still alive back then, and I remember him as a kindly old man who usually disappeared right after breakfast to potter around in the garden. Grandmother Beryl, who normally wore tweeds and a wool alpine hat with a feather in it, donned an old-fashioned wool bathing suit on this occasion and insisted that we all go down to the sea for a *plonge*. As a child I didn't see the point of my grandmother's cheerful hardiness; she seemed so proud of proving how durable she was by doing uncomfortable, difficult things.

But Grandmother's sister, Aunt Penelope—she insisted we call her "Aunt" and not "Great-Aunt" because she said the "great" made her feel like a moose head on the wall—well, she was what the ladies of her day called "a live wire," who simply crackled with energy. She lived in London but spent that summer with Grandmother Beryl. They were both what I considered old ladies, but Aunt Penelope was always slightly subversive. I remember being instantly grateful when she whispered conspiratorially that I didn't have to *plonger* into the ice-cold water any deeper than my knees—my lips were already turning purple. She scandalized the adults with whispered gossip from London, about everything from famous English lords, ladies and politicians who were obscure to me, to the fates of her own past beaus. She was frank and theatrical while telling stories, and Grandmother Beryl ate it all up but then disapproved in a provincial way.

I contemplated the "other side" of the family tree, who were relatives I'd never met. Great-Uncle Roland, the brother of Grandmother Beryl and Great-Aunt Penelope, had died about twenty years ago. His wife was Dorothy, "that dreadful American divorcée," a blue blood from Philadelphia who seemed to regularly offend her sisters-in-law with her careless, offhanded insults. Dorothy had reportedly spoiled their son, Rollo Jr., especially after his father died, so Junior never did what my mother called "a day of honest work." Instead, he gambled away most of any money he got hold of, took drugs in a big scary way, got in trouble and hit up his aunts for cash, then vanished for long periods of time until he went broke again.

The ladies must have been a little afraid of Rollo's sudden, unannounced appearances when he was desperate for money, so his name itself was always shrouded in some dark and vaguely threatening cloud.

When Grandmother Beryl died a few years ago, she'd already sold her house in Cornwall, leaving the money to Mom and Great-Aunt Penelope, who took it upon herself to rescue Rollo Jr., because he owed money, she said, "all over the world."

As I sat there in the airplane mulling this over, I had the weird feeling that somebody else was peering at my family tree. I looked up straight into the gaze of the monkey, ensconced in his slumbering lady's lap, silently watching my every scribble.

"Relatives of mine," I told him. "And how's your tree?"

When we landed at Heathrow, everyone made a mad dash for the taxicabs, but there was already a long line of waiting passengers from other flights. Wearily I joined the queue.

Then I spotted a uniformed driver anxiously walking up and down the line holding up a sign that said, "Penny Nichols." I wondered if I had hallucinated it. I waved to him, and a smile of relief crossed his face. He tipped his hat and said, "This way, miss," and led me away from the envious line as he handed me a note from Jeremy:

> *Sorry I couldn't meet you. All is arranged. Wish I could take you out to dinner but can't. Please feel free to order room service or dine at the hotel on our nickel, Penny Nichols. Will meet you tomorrow morning. Fondly, Jeremy.*

I fully expected to be booked into one of the dreary chain-hotels I'd just left. I did not expect to be whisked past red carpets, liveried doormen, a concierge who acted truly delighted to see me, a bellhop who got my bags up there before me, a butler waiting to usher me into a suite with a view of the park. I would have panicked, thinking it was surely a mistake, but the butler smiled at me reassuringly as he bowed and closed the door softly behind him.

Chapter Four

THE COLOR OF MONEY IS NOT THE VERDANT GREEN OF DOLLARS AND pastoral real estate, nor the red and black of profit and loss, nor the silver and gold of coins of the realm, nor the purple of decadent royalty. The color of money is soft pink. It's that rosy hue of health and well-being, of baby cheeks—no matter how old the heir apparent is—flush with fresh air from a carefree morning horseback ride, or warm and cozy when just awakening from an untroubled afternoon nap before a crackling fire. It's the pink that's somewhere between the pink lemonade of sunrise and the apricot-pink of the sky at sunset. The peachy-pink of the *Financial Times*, the salmon-pink of good champagne.

My room was a cornucopia of every imaginable shade of warm rose. It hung in majestic draperies above the head of my bed; and the Louis XVI chairs were upholstered in a slightly paler shade. The cushion of the chair near the kidney-shaped vanity table was a deeper hue, a bold raspberry that matched the sofa placed in front of the low mahogany dining table in the sitting room. The carpet was patterned with twining flowers in various shades of rose, and even the Italian marble in the bathroom was warm with a pink glow, especially when the soft lighting was turned on and refracted in the needle-etched mirrors. Crystal and silver vases overflowed with pale pink and even a few rogue fuchsia roses, and the entire suite was redolent with their fragrance. It was so quiet after the butler left that the only sound in the room was the slightly shifting champagne bottle as the ice melted in the bucket.

It was ten thirty when my suitcase and I entered the suite. It had been a long day. I was too tired to sweep downstairs into the hotel bar all decked out in a gold lamé evening gown and an ermine-trimmed wrap and high-heeled slippers with a feather on them—even if I owned such clothes, which I did not. But I was hungry. The hotel had a late-supper menu, so I ordered dinner in my room, and uncorked the champagne.

I ran a bath and unpacked my pretty floor-length silk nightgown and matching robe, still wrapped in tissue paper, and my little travel slippers. I'd packed this ensemble at the last minute in New York, in a sudden, stubborn burst of dreamy romanticism, just in case life gave me an opportunity to wear it instead of the long flannel T-shirt I normally wear in frigid hotel rooms.

It was just the right temperature in this suite. No chilly draft, not even after I rose like Venus out of the marble tub that I'd filled with a rosewater bubble bath. Sipping the champagne, I wrapped myself in the hotel's soft cream-colored terry bathrobe, to dry off comfortably.

I was toweling my hair dry when the butler wheeled in my dinner on a gold-and-white trolley, and expertly laid the dining table with silver, crystal, china, and linen that was soft enough to put in your lap without its shedding the telltale lint of streamlined laundering. The tender steak was cooked just the way I'd requested—only barely pink—with asparagus, and sweet red potatoes the size of golf balls, and real French bread. Then I nibbled on a few cookies and sipped a cup of tea that made me feel warm, relaxed, and free of time zones.

While dawdling over the tea, I filled out my order for tomorrow's breakfast of coffee, boiled egg and toast, marmalade and jam, and the day's newspaper to be delivered with it. Then I changed into my silk nightgown and climbed into the enormous bed, which was firm but layered with soft cotton bedding, and I laid my head on the generous down pillow.

Drowsily I thanked my cousin Jeremy for arranging for me to have a good night's rest. The boy I'd known was now an important, grown-up London businessman. I wondered how he felt about suddenly being in charge of the family affairs. His father, my Uncle Peter, who was Mom's brother, had died when Jeremy was just twenty-five; and his mother, Aunt Sheila, who is *veddy* veddy English and whose family was wealthier than everybody on my side totalled up, still lives in London. I recalled the annual Christmas cards that she and my mother exchange, enclosing brief but polite letters and the occasional embarrassing snapshot of me and Jeremy.

Those snapshots ended a few years ago with Jeremy's wedding photo—and my lack of one—but then he was divorced within a year, with no real explanation. In the photo his wife was looking off-camera, so all I could see was a good profile and blonde hair, not much more.

Was he, too, one of the walking wounded when it came to love? The grown-up cousin Jeremy in the photos looked like a smooth-faced, elegant English businessman, yet in the eyes I could still see the slightly rebellious boy from the beach at Cornwall that summer.

He'd been stiff and starchy at first, as we sat primly with the adults over tea and cakes served in the kind of china that Americans use only when somebody dies or gets married. It was all I could do to balance my plate and teacup, for I felt my cousin's watchful eyes and, worse, his mother's. But one afternoon, when we raced each other through my grandmother's walled-in garden with its path leading to the sea, I was able to joke with him and get him to drop his cool, snotty attitude.

He even confided in me that he certainly was not going to be just another Englishman in a suit in another "bloody boring" job, like his banker father. He was going to travel on safari, he said, kicking pebbles in the path; or explore ancient ruins, or start a rock band. I was flattered that he was confiding in me, even though he called me "child." But this important conversation was interrupted by a very buzzy bee that relentlessly chased me halfway down the path until Jeremy commanded me to stop shrieking and "Freeze!" Something made me trust him, so I halted. As the bee circled me to come in for the kill, Jeremy valiantly gave his beach towel one sharp, quick *snap!* and the bee fell down dead at my feet. I was highly impressed.

Our mothers were already ensconced with chairs and umbrellas, waiting for us. The sand where we laid out our blanket was warm, and Jeremy dared me to race him into the water. The waves were crashing and filling the air with a wonderful bracing salty flavor. But the ocean was breathtakingly cold. After the first toe in I hesitated, and that was when Grandmother Beryl splashed past me and dove in, hale and hearty, shouting back for me to join her. Jeremy rolled his eyes at my hesitancy and plunged on ahead. Standing on the shoreline, Great-Aunt Penelope assured me that I didn't have to, but finally I flung myself in, gasping, my hypersensitive skin turning bright red. I swam a bit, but the water never felt any warmer, as it did back home on our side of the Atlantic.

Afterwards I ran out of the chilly sea and dashed, blue-lipped, teeth chattering, back to the blanket on the sand, peering wistfully at a fairly cloudy sky that made the wind feel colder. Jeremy's mother, Aunt Sheila, saw me emerge, and she told Jeremy to run and get more towels and dry me off before I caught pneumonia. He was always an obedient kid on the surface, with blameless manners, yet subversive the moment the adults' backs were turned.

In this case he promptly ran off to get the towels, but when he saw that the grown-ups had lost interest and were deep into their boring gossip, he flung the towel around me in a fairly vigorous rubdown, and when I protested, he told me that I was being a weak, "whinge-ing" Secret Agent who'd just parachuted into an Arctic river and must avoid hypothermia.

Then as we sat there I taught him how to play poker, although he declared that I was totally unable to keep a "poker face." He taught me Morse code. This took awhile, but once I caught on, it came in rather handy when we returned to the house and sat down to dinner. Uncle Peter had put on some droning, fusty old music from his "era," and Jeremy found it so excruciatingly unbearable that he began to tap out a message to me on the table leg.

Crummy music, he tapped. Startled, I stared at him, but he just gave me our Secret Agent look. He was teasing me for my frequent use of the word "crummy."

B-l-o-o-d-y b-o-r-i-n-g, I agreed, tapping back with his favorite phrase. Individually we were both pretty well-behaved kids, but we seemed to bring out the mischief in each other.

"What's that noise?" my mother said, looking up from across the table. I glanced away innocently. Jeremy cleared his throat. Uncle Peter shot him a suspicious look. I held my breath. We ate more, and the adults resumed their conversation.

Jeremy waited until the music swelled louder, then tapped again. *I hate peas.*

I couldn't believe his audacity. I lowered my head so that the sight of his smirk wouldn't make me snort with laughter. Before I could tap out a reply, however, Jeremy's mother cocked her head.

"I heard something, too," she said. Grandmother Beryl looked around, perplexed.

But Aunt Penelope had been glancing knowingly from Jeremy

to me, and now she smiled and said in a noncommittal way, "Oh, it's probably just a pair of little mice again."

Even now, years and years later, as I snuggled into my enormous bed in my hotel room, listening drowsily to the muffled sound of London's traffic in the street below me, I found that childhood memory as vivid as if it had happened yesterday. Time is like that. Whole years whiz by into oblivion, yet certain moments seem eternal. I drifted into the first deep and decent sleep I'd had in months, and I did not move a muscle until breakfast—and Jeremy—arrived together the next morning.

Chapter Five

BLUE-SUITED AND CARRYING AN ATTACHÉ CASE, LOOKING VERY SERI-ous and important, Jeremy entered the sitting room ahead of the butler. I received them both regally, seated on the sofa that was pulled up to the dining table. Actually I'd scurried there in order to hide behind the table so that they couldn't see too much of me in my silk nightgown and robe.

Jeremy strode right up to me, and, as if he were my husband coming home from a business trip, he bent to kiss my cheek, with more warmth than you'd kiss an old aunt, yet nothing to suggest more than cousinly affection. I got a quick whiff of some clean male scent, something suggesting bergamot, lemon, salty sea air, and money.

"Hallo, Penny," he said brightly as the butler arranged the plates unobtrusively, then went out and shut the door behind him. I gestured for Jeremy to take the nice plushy chair opposite me at the table, for he could not resist glancing down at my food, and I recognized a look of hunger and fatigue on his face, beneath that smooth facade.

"You're Penny Nichols, all right," he said, taking time to look at me directly as he sat down, "all grown up, but I'd know you anywhere." This made me feel like my hair was in pigtails, which it never was, so I quickly assumed a grand, sophisticated manner.

"Have some coffee and *please*, help me finish this marvelous break-fast," I said. "They gave me two eggs and a whole basket of breads. If you behave you can have one of each."

And after a little dance of no-thanks-oh-all-right he tucked into the food with the gusto of a boy.

"Thanks. I was in Brussels last night," he said. "Just got in this morning. Wanted to finish up some business so I could clear the way for ours."

While we were eating, I stole a few glances at him. God, he was really so mercilessly good-looking. He was a grown-up now, all right, quite serious and manly, so different from the gangly kid he'd been the last time I was this close to him. His dark, wavy brown hair was expensively cut to look offhandedly hip. His pale skin was smooth as the cream in my pitcher, and his high forehead was without a trace of a furrow, indicating that distinctly untroubled calm possessed only by boys raised with money and the certainty that they will never starve. There were a few wry crinkles around his mouth and eyes. Those blue eyes, framed by dark lashes, were cool and distant as the sea when he glanced at you, but if you caught his attention with something smart or amusing, a flame of deep comprehension, humor, and intel-ligence warmed his gaze, making it astonishingly kind and friendly, even gentle.

This must go over well with his law clients, I thought. Just the kind of man you'd turn to when you needed an advocate in a sticky-wicket situation. For despite his warmth, you had the sense of a panther lurk-ing behind the gaze, a creature who could strike swiftly and lethally if the situation called for it. His midnight blue suit was beautifully tailored, cut narrowly enough to be urban-stylish, not fat-cat middle-aged. He wore a white shirt with thin blue stripes; a wine-colored silk tie, not too wide; good shoes that weren't too shiny-new or old-farty; and expensive socks—aha, here is where a man illustrates any dash of rebellion, in socks patterned with a wild red thread running through otherwise sober dark blues and blacks.

"Mum thinks it's unforgivable that I wasn't at the airport to greet you," he said, pouring coffee for me before he poured his own. "She wants you for tea this afternoon, if you can bear it."

Damn, I thought to myself. First, I was supposed to ask after Aunt Sheila before he mentioned her. And second, I felt momentary panic at being submitted to Aunt Sheila's scrutiny, which undoubtedly would make me feel as if I needed a haircut, badly. But I caught him watching me with a knowing smile, so I said as casually as I could, "Of course. And how is Aunt Sheila?"

"Mother is impossible, as always," he replied enigmatically, stirring cream into his coffee.

"I remember your parents having elegant cocktails before supper that summer, with Herb Alpert playing on the stereo." I kept my face straight, but he winced.

"Yeah, that was Dad's music. Mom was Beatles and Stones, like your folks."

"Was she a mod or a rocker?" I asked, lapsing into our old teasing mode.

"A dilettante," he said, a shade more darkly than I expected.

"I think she once told me she kissed Paul McCartney," I offered. Jeremy glanced up at me sharply, then looked slightly embarrassed about his mother.

"She *will* keep telling people that," he murmured, and took a bite of his croissant.

"Why shouldn't she?" I said. "It's a moment in history."

There was something so familiar about his ironic tone and good manners that it made me think, *Actually, I do remember this fellow.* And after all these years, his mother was still a thorn in his side somehow. I'd forgotten that. I never knew what it was, exactly, that bothered him about his parents. As a kid I'd automatically chalked it up to how impossible adults were. Nobody needed to explain why, back then.

"How are Aunt Nancy and Uncle Georges?" he asked, eager to change the subject from his mother, which, after all, he'd introduced. "Does your father still make those incredible roasted meals? Lamb and pheasant and all those marvelous potatoes, and those brown sauces?"

"Did he cook for you? How can you possibly remember that?" I asked curiously.

"How could anyone forget?" he replied. "I sulked for a week after we left, when we went back to our cook's dull boiled food. You and your parents were like characters in a storybook. I always secretly believed that you really *were* Penny Nichols, Girl Detective."

His tone had just a slight mocking edge to it, but I looked up from my plate in time to catch him glancing at my neckline and my silk negligee ensemble in a way that men simply can't seem to stop themselves from doing when they first meet a woman. He hastily shifted his gaze to the sugar bowl and busied himself with his coffee. I tried through sheer force of will not to blush, by glancing at the day's headlines in the newspaper lying beside my plate. This is how I have learned to control my blushing somewhat, but not entirely, by putting my thoughts somewhere neutral and safe—like on wars, murders, political scandals. Anything that I don't have to personally be embarrassed by. Yet I suddenly felt doubtful that I could pull off this casual grown-up act. But I would certainly go down trying.

"And are you that same kid who rescued me from a very aggressive bee in Cornwall by zapping him dead with one shot from a beach towel?" I asked him.

A light blush rose under his pale skin and then faded quickly. Well, well, I noted. He's a blusher, too. He said, "Ah! Yes, well, I had to do something. You very nearly got us both stung to death." Then he gulped his coffee and cleared his throat briskly.

"I must go over to the office and collect some paperwork for the reading," he said. "But I didn't want you to have to face down the 'vultures' without knowing a few things. There are two wills: one English, the other French, because Great-Aunt Penelope owned property in both countries. The English will is quite simple and straightforward. The French one is newer, because it replaced an earlier French will from the 1950s which originally divided the French assets between her brother—that's Great-Uncle Roland—and her sister, Grandmother Beryl, who were both alive then. But since she outlived them, Great-Aunt Penelope remade the French will to include 'the youngsters'—that's you, me, and Rollo Jr., you see. She made me the executor of the will just before she died. Her solicitor in France had retired, and she didn't like his partners. So she left everything to the care of my firm."

"How did she die?" I asked gently. He looked genuinely regretful.

"In her bed, quietly," he answered. "At night, in her sleep, the doctor thought. Heart gave way, but he said it wouldn't have been painful . . ." He stopped. "She tried to telephone me that day. I was in Japan. Couldn't get back to her in time. I rather liked her," he said reflectively. "One of the few older people with an open mind, who'd lived an eventful enough life to actually like the younger generation. Of course, I didn't know her long. Just when she summoned me to lunch in her London flat, to tell me about the will. She never talked about herself, just asked about me and my life. So I didn't know that she was ailing."

"She was alone when she died, then?" I asked. He nodded. I thought of an old Roman proverb: Live your own life, for you will die your own death. I reminded myself of my new resolution to live in the present.

"Who are the vultures?" I ventured, having already guessed.

"Rollo Jr. and his mum, of course." He looked at me quizzically.

"I never met them," I said.

"No? Well, Dorothy's rich beyond reason but won't give tuppence to Rollo Jr., so he always touched our side of the family." There it was again, that dark cloud around Rollo. "And it's not as if Rollo's dad didn't leave him money," Jeremy added, sounding perplexed. "Plenty, but it's doled out in a monthly allowance. Goes through his fingers like sand."

"Junior must be in his early sixties, right?" I asked curiously. Jeremy nodded.

I thought it over. "Aren't all people vultures when it comes to inheritances?" I said. "Picking at the remains of another person's life?"

He smiled at me. "You couldn't be a vulture if you tried," he said. It didn't sound like an insult, but I felt somehow that it was. After all, he hadn't seen me in years. How did he know that I couldn't be a predator if I put my mind to it?

Jeremy's mobile phone rang, and he quickly scooped it out of a pocket and spoke quietly but urgently, mostly saying, "Right. Okay. Right." When he put it away he looked distracted, then caught my glance and nodded to me apologetically.

"Sorry, but I've got to get over to the office. Here's the address for the reading of the will. It's Aunt Penelope's apartment. Belgravia. It's best that we meet there instead of arriving together. I'll leave the car for you downstairs so you can't possibly get lost, and I'll grab a cab."

The mention of the car prompted a question that had been nagging at me. "Jeremy," I asked hesitantly, "I hate to ask, but—who's paying for all of this? The hotel and the car . . ."

He looked straight at me. "Why, you, of course," he said with a grin. I made a face at him to indicate that while I may appear somewhat gullible in unfamiliar circumstances, I am not a total idiot.

He reached out and ruffled my hair. "The office, child," he said.

"Your father insisted on paying for your flight over here, but the rest is on my account. Your parents are clients, after all. Best not to take too long washing up and getting out. We start at nine."

I appreciated his offhanded generosity, yet his admonitory tone about punctuality jogged my memory of how there were moments when his superior coolness used to annoy me. Something about all those in-your-face good manners had the effect of making me want to shock him by acting like an ill-mannered American delinquent—which, damn it, I'm not—just to make him drop that polite mask. I remembered that when I was nine I gave this a great deal of thought, and suspected that he actually wanted me to play the role of *provocateur,* to bring out his alter-ego, the person who wished so desperately to be bad. Instead of taking the bait, I learned to banter back and forth with him, like a game of table tennis.

"Believe it or not," I said in my own light, superior teasing tone, "I am perfectly capable of attending to deadlines. I do, after all, work in movies, and time is money. Frankly, I think it awfully rude of you not to inquire about my line of work. I'm rather fascinating."

He looked surprised, then shook his head in mock disapproval. "Only Americans immediately ask you about your line of work," he informed me as he headed for the door. "We Europeans think about it, of course, but we bide our time before broaching the subject. However, since you mentioned it, do you know any sexy actresses you can introduce me to?"

"Larima," I said automatically. "Just finishing up a picture she's starring in." He raised his eyebrows, suitably impressed.

"Really?" He cocked his head as if considering a serious offer. "I don't believe I'm her type," he said thoughtfully. "No yacht for her birthday parties." He grinned. "Well, I'm off. See you at nine. Don't be tardy," he couldn't resist warning. He shut the door softly behind him.

I glanced at the clock, which was an ornate gold affair on the marble mantelpiece, with a round mother-of-pearl dial surrounded by some sculpted, vaguely Grecian figures. He was right. There wasn't much time. I'd slept very well in my elegant bed. I headed for the shower. The water pressure was good, and it beat some sense into my head. Or perhaps it was just that once Jeremy was gone I was able to resume thinking clearly again. In any case, it occurred to me that I'd failed to ask him a crucial question: What did Great-Aunt Penelope bequeath to us?

Furthermore, I thought, rubbing myself fiercely with the plush cream-colored towel, Jeremy hadn't volunteered the information. Maybe there was some legal rule about not spilling the beans before the reading of the will. Or maybe, with that European finesse, he'd been waiting for me to broach the subject, and then he'd have told me. Perhaps I'd already failed my first exam, to test how smart and grown-up I was. Then I told myself that Jeremy and his parents always made you feel inferior; the trick was not to get all tongue-tied and klutzy.

Luckily I'd packed my killer silk suit, black and expensive and, for once, perfectly fitted to me, making me look slim and actually even ruthless. I keep it for emergencies. And an ivory silk scoop-neck blouse under it, very nice, and those high, sharp black pumps. New pair of good stockings in a package I now busted open for this occasion. And a good Italian leather handbag I'd picked up at a special price that made it affordable. A marvellous old makeup lady I once worked with years ago taught me how to do my face, so I made it up slowly and restrainedly with eyeliner, white highlight, and just the lightest touch of blush to make me look healthy enough for a fight. My hair is behaving itself today, I thought. This is good. Absolutely no perfume, and minimal jewelry—just diamond stud earrings and the decent-sized diamond pendant my parents gave me when I graduated.

The sort of delicate combo that looks as if you are being understated on purpose, not because you're broke.

There. I stared in the mirror. Everything looked fine, except my eyes, which looked frightened and much too sincere. "Take it easy," I told my reflection. "No need to get all hopped up over costume jewelry and a few nice bonds."

The eyes that looked back at me betrayed that all I really wished to do was just not look like a fool in front of our relatives. They'd probably never see me again and I did not want to live on in family lore as a dope. Poor Penny, for instance. Wasn't she pathetic? She didn't know how to behave. No, no, no. I vowed to keep my dignity, no matter what happened.

Part Three

Chapter Six

WE GOT STUCK IN TRAFFIC, SO I BEGAN TO SWEAT. THEN, KNOWing that I was sweating made me panic a little, sitting there in the back of that discreet, dark, luxurious automobile from Jeremy's law office. But the elderly driver wove his way expertly through busy, workaday London, leaving all the soot and noise behind as we went partway around a lush green park and into a quiet residential neighborhood full of discreet mews and tree-lined squares ringed by immaculate sidewalks and elegant old town houses. We pulled up to a Victorian house with white pillars, and double doors with frosted glass panes.

"Here we are, miss," the chauffeur said encouragingly, as if talking to a shy cat that wouldn't come out of its box right away. He was a small, wiry old man, with a calm, reassuring manner. I nodded, embarrassed that he'd seen through my attempt at poise.

I checked my wristwatch. Seven minutes to nine. Not late, but not a moment to spare. Thanks-very-much, Jeremy, for making me worry about time, I thought. I reminded myself that I was representing my mother here and I simply was not going to mess this up. So, when the driver scurried around to open the door for me, I valiantly plunked my high-heeled foot firmly on the pavement, and, although I wobbled a bit at first, I marched myself up the pretty, clean white steps of Great-Aunt Penelope's town house.

An eager-beaver type of guy in his mid-twenties opened the front door as if awaiting my arrival. He was bright and alert, with obediently short hair, a well-cut suit that somehow made him seem even younger, and a perfectly educated accent. You would never mistake him for a doorman. He stepped aside to let me into the vestibule, where there was a door for the first-floor apartment, and to the right a staircase for the other two flats.

"Miss Nichols? I'm Rupert. I work with Jeremy." His voice was low, as if we were in church. "Go right up to the library, second floor, please." The staircase had a gleaming polished banister and wine-colored carpeting held with gold braces. The carpet didn't keep the stairs from creaking a little as I stepped on them. I stopped at the small second-floor landing.

The door to Great-Aunt Penelope's apartment was ajar, in a way that no living person would leave it unless she were just moving in or out. The inside hallway had a tulip-shaped lamp on a small table, which stood beside a sliding panelled door that was partially open. I hesitated, then slid the door farther open. It moved noiselessly in its tracks.

The library was a charming room, full of light from two sets of bay windows, each with its own window-seat. The furnishings were mostly turn-of-the-century pieces—the twentieth century, that is, Great-Aunt Penelope's heyday. There were deep blue curtains at the windows, tied back with giant gold tassels. The opposite wall had built-in bookcases filled with gold, black, and dark green elegantly bound books protected by glass doors. All the furniture was small but pretty—a walnut roll-top desk and chair in a corner; a "swoon" sofa for delicate ladies prone to sudden fainting spells; and, by the tiny fireplace, two wing chairs with a low, round Queen Anne table.

But then, totally out of symmetry, was a cluster of chairs with high, ornately carved wooden backs and seats with maroon damask cushions. They looked as if they'd been dragged out of the dining room and awkwardly grouped in this semicircle at the center of the room. I figured that only lawyers would stomp in and do such a thing. And, indeed, there were three such likely candidates facing me right now—but none of them was Jeremy.

Dressed in dark suits and ties, immaculate white shirts, and enormous, expensive-looking cuff-links, they struck me as the sort of businessmen who always hunt in packs. The three of them were huddled protectively around a narrow cherrywood table with a glass top, where they shuffled some official-looking files and glanced up at me intently as I entered. They were silver-haired men with mistrust permanently etched onto their faces, and hard, marble-blue eyes that revealed no emotion, making them look like porcelain dolls, the kind that in horror movies invariably run amok and start killing the real humans. One of them flashed the quick, charming smile of an elderly crocodile. The other two simply returned to their papers, indicating that I'd failed to impress them. But I saw that they were excruciatingly conscious of my presence, which only confirmed my significance here. I felt a trifle uneasy.

Two more people entered the room—a petite, spidery old lady in an ash-blue coat and hat that matched, and a middle-aged guy in a navy blazer and beige flannel trousers. This simply had to be Mom's cousin, Rollo Jr., and his mother, Great-Aunt Dorothy. I nodded to them, but they pretended that they didn't notice. The lawyers sprang into deferential action, making an elaborate big deal of getting the old lady seated in one of the chairs, then conferring with Rollo in a low, unintelligible murmur. I decided that it was time for me to stop waiting for permission to sit down. So I went to the window-seat at the bay windows that fronted onto the street. I gazed out imploringly. Where the hell was *my* lawyer? He was late, that's what.

Every time I sneaked a peek at the others from under my lowered lashes, they glanced away, which meant they'd been sizing me up, too. I couldn't help thinking that we looked like a fairly ghoulish family oil painting. First, Rollo Jr., who'd loomed so large in the family lore, sounding so vaguely diabolical and threatening that I'd expected him to be tall and shadowy, lean and mean. I was completely unprepared for a paunchy, rather dissolute-looking, somewhat pathetic aging-playboy type with overly wavy graying hair, and bags under the eyes, his stomach hanging over his belt, altogether looking a bit like, well, actually like Elvis in his later "fat" years as seen in those old record-collection commercials. He was decorously attentive to his mum. Great-Aunt Dorothy was a little birdlike lady with silver hair teased into the bubble shape that women of her generation favor. She seemed dainty but not fragile, with one of her tiny bird-claw hands clutching a silver-topped walking stick. I could see how she might indeed have been a formidable sister-in-law to Grandma and Great-Aunt Penelope. And finally there was me, little Penny Nichols, trying to appear all grown-up, but probably looking as if I was waiting to be interviewed for a job I knew I wouldn't get.

Jeremy and his associates entered just seconds later. It felt like an eternity, but technically I suppose they were spot-on time. The atmosphere in the room changed tangibly. There was no mistaking the shift in power, revealing that Jeremy's team was in charge of this meeting. He introduced me to Harold, the senior partner, an older gray-haired guy with confident gray eyes. Then Severine, their French legal expert, an attractive woman in a bold white silk suit and white pumps, with huge brown eyes and shiny dark hair pulled into a perfect twist; she looked to be Jeremy's age and had the confidence that comes first from being a French female and second from having enough expertise to impress her male colleagues. Rupert, the younger guy who'd let me in, was told that he could go back to the office, once it was clear that all the necessary papers were here. He gave me a bashful smile, as if his lesser importance had suddenly been revealed to me. All in all, a good team to look after my mother's interests, I thought.

Jeremy politely introduced me to Great-Aunt Dorothy and Rollo. Now that I was being formally presented, Rollo looked up with a blameless expression and said, "Yes, of course," with a tolerant kind of nod. His mother, forced to acknowledge my presence at last, gave me a wide smile of exaggerated delight, as if she'd just been presented with a new parlor maid.

Subtly but forcefully, Jeremy and his team took over the glass-topped table with their papers, and put three chairs behind it, where they sat. Severine settled in with the calm attitude of one who will participate only if called upon. Grudgingly, the other lawyers withdrew to the remaining chairs in the semicircle. One was empty, which made it mine. Jeremy saw me hesitate, and gave me an infinitesimal but reassuring nod. Then Harold began to read the will aloud, starting with a preamble about where Great-Aunt Penelope resided, the date, et cetera.

The entire roomful of people seemed collectively to be holding their breath. I dutifully listened closely to the legalese and, for my mother's sake, tried to figure out exactly what was going on, and to be a good representative of her interests. Yet I couldn't help it—what fascinated me about Great-Aunt Penelope's will was the same thing that fascinates me about history in my job: that in following one human being's life, you can pick up embedded clues about eternal truths, about what endures and what vanishes, what's important and what isn't.

Harold read on, in a dignified murmur that had an insistent quality like a drumbeat, and his voice took on a momentum, in the tone of a high priest murmuring incantations: "I, Penelope Laidley, being of sound mind and body . . ."

I focused on decoding the formalities as he announced that Great-Aunt Penelope had left this apartment that we were sitting in and all its contents to my mother, and some hefty English bank assets to Rollo. He and his mother appeared satisfied with this. They did not contest the English will, and everything seemed hunky-dory, perfunctorily dispensed with—but there was nothing for Jeremy, which bewildered me . . . at first.

When it got round to the French will, however, all five of their party raised their heads in alertness and sat closer to the edges of their chairs expectantly. It signalled to me that the French assets were perhaps the more valuable, and this was what the fight was all about.

"My villa in France, including the house and all the property, I leave to Jeremy Laidley. The contents of the house, that is, all remaining furniture, I leave to my nephew Roland Laidley, Junior. The garage and its entire contents I leave solely to my great-niece and namesake, Penelope Nichols."

After the briefest of pauses, everybody started talking all at once. The earlier high-priest incantations were replaced with overlapping spell-casting, and voodoo cursing as Dorothy and Rollo's lawyers objected to the French will, and Jeremy and his team retaliated with polite warnings of time limits to contest it and procedure and other calm but fierce words. Then suddenly it all came to a stop. It was over—at least for now. Like a round in a boxing match.

Harold neatly arranged the papers of the will in their leather folder. A butler hired for the occasion arrived with a tray of coffee and china cups, cream pitcher and sugar bowl, which he put on the round table near the fireplace. This seemed to be a signal, for Jeremy and Severine went over to fill and pass the cups around. But Rollo's lawyers, after murmuring to Dorothy, got up as one and stalked out the door. Dorothy rose majestically and contemptuously. Rollo cast a regretful look at the coffee, but helped his mother across the room.

I was still puzzling out why Aunt Penelope had mentioned me in such a whimsical way. Hmm, I thought. For some strange reason she thought of me as a garage person.

Before I had a chance to mull this over much, I was distracted by the tense figure of Great-Aunt Dorothy, passing by me on her way out. I could feel her pent-up fury, even before I looked up and saw it in the rigid way she was carrying herself. Although her face had a blank, stony expression, her breath gave her away, coming out in sharp little gasps. She paused at the lawyers' table, and as if unable to contain herself a moment longer, she poked her walking stick at Harold's leather folder, knocking it off the table and scattering the pages of Great-Aunt Penelope's will all over the floor.

"We'll just see!" she spat out with a look of triumphant glee, as if somehow by messing up the actual pages she had dispensed with their contents as well. I was horrified and embarrassed for her, as if she'd suddenly and publicly lost her mind. "We'll just see!" she repeated to Jeremy, who had instinctively come to my side. Rollo hastily took hold of her arm to steer her out of the room.

Nobody else seemed the least bit surprised—except me. Harold sighed, and they all merely picked up the papers and reassembled them, then went right on about their business.

As they sorted it out, Severine began a rapid conversation *sotto voce* with Jeremy. She called him "Zheremy" in her lilting French accent, acting very correct the whole time, impeccable, efficient, and not inclined to dawdle. They both nodded vigorously, and then, when they were done with the papers, she raised her eyebrows to Harold, indicating that she was impatient to leave.

Harold shook hands with me rather more warmly than before, which gave me the first inkling that perhaps Mother and I had made out rather well. Severine, who'd earlier given me only the briefest and most professional of nods, now turned her laser-gaze on me more intently as she shook my hand, and then out of the corner of her mouth she murmured to Jeremy, in a wry, slightly patronizing tone, *"Ah, la petite cousine américaine! Elle est charmante."*

Jeremy looked a trifle embarrassed. As well he should, I thought indignantly. I wasn't six years old, for Pete's sake. Why should she call me a "little" charming American cousin? But before I could really size her up, she departed with Harold. I listened as their footsteps died away and the heavy door downstairs closed behind them, leaving me alone with Jeremy.

Jeremy let out his breath as if he'd just played a rigorous soccer game. For the first time it dawned on me that he took his role as family protector very seriously and even, perhaps, wanted to impress his American relatives so they would think well of him.

"So now you've met Rollo and Dorothy," he said wickedly. "What do you think?"

"Geez, nobody looked like I expected," I admitted. "She's so tiny, but for a minute there I was sure that she might clonk us both on the head with that stick of hers. And Rollo! After all I'd heard about him, I thought he'd resemble Jack the Ripper." Jeremy rolled his eyes.

"A case unsolved—therefore nobody knows what he looked like," he pointed out.

"You know what I mean. In the movies," I said. "I certainly didn't expect an aging lounge-lizard with mother problems."

"Well, he's a bit more complicated than that," Jeremy warned, but he didn't elaborate. He turned to me with a professionally bright air. "So, Penny Nichols," he said, "how does it feel to be an heiress?"

"Very funny," I said. "All I heard was something about a garage."

He grinned. "That's not all," he announced. "Your mother told me that whatever property she got, I should hand over to you. Once the will has been officially processed. So you won't have any trouble inheriting it when your mother—erm—when she's gone. You can let me know if you want to keep it or sell it. Any idea what a flat like this, in this neighborhood, goes for? It's worth seven hundred fifty thousand pounds. And people would kill just to get hold of one, because you have to be an insider even to know when one is available. Want to have a quick look around before we lock up? We've got a lot to do in very little time."

Of course I should look around. To report back to my astonishing mother. Honestly, I was going to have to get my mind off romantic history, and learn a little about the greed thing.

My head was swimming, however, as I took in the apartment. The library was the biggest room, then a dark, narrow formal dining room, and a tiny pink-and-white kitchen in the back overlooking a sweet walled-in garden with patio; a small cherry-red second bedroom, which Aunt Penelope had used as a sewing room; a little bathroom with claw-foot tub and gold seahorse-shaped soap dishes; and, around in front again, a big, dramatic main bedroom with white-and-gold furniture. On a raised area near a window was a satin-skirted mirrored dressing table and matching satin-tufted chair. Tucked in another corner was a huge canopied bed.

Jeremy opened a big closet, which was full of sensible old-lady clothes. Peering into it made me feel as if I were trespassing on someone's grave. I was glad when he closed it again.

"Jeremy," I said, suddenly horrified as I stared at the big canopied four-poster bed, "she didn't—die—right here—in this bed—did she?"

"No," he said. "She died at the villa in France." I exhaled loudly in relief. Jeremy went on speaking briskly as we went back down the creaky staircase. "Aunt Penelope's had this flat since the 1920s, and the French villa since sometime in the 1930s," he was saying. "Your father says you're an expert at historical furnishings and art. Think you could make an assessment of the value of her possessions? We must be accurate when we declare their value for the taxes."

"Sure," I said. I'd already been admiring the pre-war moldings, trim, light fixtures, beautiful wood floors and doors. The furniture was good, mostly Victorian, but not spectacular, and although I'd dutifully concluded that I didn't see any fancy *objets d'art* to report back to my mother, I knew that the flat itself was a rare find. It was perfectly situated but quiet and private; it had good light from those pretty windows, and was elegant and charming but still cozy enough to feel like home. The window-seats in the library made you want to curl up with one of the nicely bound books, reading and drowsing until the gold carriage-clock on the mantel chimed the dinner hour. "I can't believe she gave this to us," I said softly.

Jeremy had been watching me for my reaction. "Well, don't cry for Rollo. He'll get about as much in bank assets. Nobody expected old Aunt Pen to have hoarded that much. Guess they wanted that money right away, so they didn't peep about the English will."

"Maybe they want the cash to pay for those lawyers to help them contest the French will," I said. "What a pack of coyotes. Are they as expensive as they look?"

"Super-expensive," he said darkly. "It'll be a good fight, but we'll win it, hands down."

"Is the French property worth a lot?" I asked. "What about that villa? Did I hear that right? It's yours, isn't it?" His face lighted up with enthusiasm and appreciation.

"Apparently so! Haven't seen it yet. Heard it's a bit tumbledown and needs repair, but the value is in the land. Severine's handling that end of things. I don't know why Aunt Pen left it to me," he said wonderingly. "By the time she asked me to help her, she didn't go down there much anymore, until that last week when she went back. She was sharp as a tack, but she *would* keep asking about my life instead of her own legal issues. She told me straight out that she thought Rollo Jr. was a fool, but she felt sorry for him, for being so 'stunted.' Said the kids picked on him at school. He's quite fond of antiques, she said, so I'm not surprised that she left him all the French furnishings and whatnot."

I was picturing Jeremy patiently listening to Aunt Penelope rambling on, peppering him with questions about his life, which he'd rather not have discussed.

"Why is Rollo going to contest the French will? It's pretty obvious that Aunt Penelope definitely wanted you to get the villa," I said.

Jeremy shook his head. "I don't know. French inheritance law can sometimes be more complicated, and perhaps Dorothy and Rollo are hoping it's easier to fuddle with."

When he fell silent I asked tentatively, "Any idea what's in the garage?"

"A car, I should think," he said, looking intrigued. He became brisk and businesslike again. "You and I had better get over there and have a look. We can catch a plane"—he glanced at his watch—"Damn, we could go right away, but Mum insists I bring you round for tea. I'll tell her we can only do a quick stop now, just to say hello. So we'll see Mum, fly down to Cap d'Antibes, maybe have dinner in Nice. I know a good place. Okeh?"

Chapter Seven

Aunt Sheila lived in a pretty apartment building in Chelsea, with the speediest elevator I'd ever been in, which shot us up to her floor in total silence.

"Are you sure she won't mind us just popping in on her like this?" I quavered as I followed him down the hallway, absolutely certain that his mother would blame me for this instead of her adorable son.

"Of course it's all right. She was fine on the telephone," he said, leading me to her door. He had a key and we went right in.

Aunt Sheila was seated on a pale green sofa in her drawing room when we arrived; she'd been glancing at a newspaper in an effortless way, as if nothing the world did could surprise or upset her. Her hand was cool, soft and smooth, and she gave it to me for a brief but sincere moment of welcome.

She looked exactly as she had all those years ago, which would seem impossible but was nonetheless true. Same blonde hair cut into the same chic bob with bangs, same slender figure, only perhaps a bit stiffer. She wore a sleek, expensive cream-colored suit cut perfectly for her; and her pretty legs did not require high heels to look good, so she wore buttery-soft-looking delicate leather flats. She had green eyes, a perfect little nose and chin, and a slightly pouty mouth.

Despite her reserve, there was something sexy about her. She wore gold jewelry—a slim wristwatch, small thick hoop earrings, a short necklace that looked like a golden twisted rope, a few subtle rings that twinkled when she held out her hand, and a bangle bracelet with elegant stones.

"So this is Penny," Aunt Sheila said, glancing back at Jeremy in amusement. "She looks just like her mother. Doesn't she, Jeremy?" Jeremy looked a little embarrassed. "Penny, dear," Aunt Sheila said in a quieter tone, "do let me say that I was most sorry to hear about your great-aunt. Penelope was always kind to me."

"Thank you," I said, not quite knowing how to respond.

"I know you're both in a tearing hurry, but can't I have Alice fix you some lunch?"

I glanced at Jeremy as if to say, *Okay, fella, you handle this.*

"Can't do it," Jeremy said. "Penny's been travelling a lot, and I want to finish up this business in Nice today." A maid in a long black dress and white apron appeared at the doorway.

Aunt Sheila nodded to her, then turned to us and sighed. "Take a couple of sandwiches with you, then, Penny," she said reasonably. "Just in case you get hungry on the plane. They're in the dining room." Jeremy stood aside for her to lead the way across the hall.

The dining room was flooded with light that came from a wall of big windows looking out on the Thames, at picture-postcard views of the city. Little boats were gliding along quietly below us, past fairy-tale church spires and venerable old bridges. It made me catch my breath with delight. Jeremy smiled at me as he noted my reaction. Then I saw that the table, laid with white linen, pale yellow napkins, and gold-rimmed plates and glasses, was set with a buffet platter of little sandwiches, salads, and a plate of cookies, all flanked by two vases of yellow roses and violet-colored sweet peas, and a bowl of fruit. I looked at Jeremy reproachfully.

"Oh, all right, a quick nibble," he said.

"Boy, that's big of you," I said, and Aunt Sheila laughed.

We sat down and ate. Jeremy must have told her on the telephone about how things went at the reading of the will, because Aunt Sheila never asked, never mentioned it, and seemed more interested in "catching up" on my little life so far. "Re-e-eally?" she drawled when I told her, for instance, about the wife-of-Napoleon picture we'd been shooting in Cannes.

"I think history is most fascinating when you can actually watch it being made," she said. "I was in Paris in the summer of 1968," she added, almost boasting. "During the general strike. We hitchhiked to Saint-Tropez," she added, casting a daring, almost challenging look at Jeremy.

"Jeremy doesn't like me to talk about my hippie days," she said.

"Mother, really," he said, mildly reprovingly. "You never qualified as a hippie."

"True," she allowed, "but I was reasonably hip. Jeremy looks just like Peter when he puts that face on," she told me.

It was the one and only time she mentioned her husband, and the effect on Jeremy was to make him raise his eyebrows, ever so slightly. When Jeremy's mobile phone shrilled, he seemed glad to excuse himself and slip out to a back room to take the call. That left Aunt Sheila and me alone, but before I could get scared she turned to me conspiratorially and said, "He's a pain in the arse, but he's awfully good-looking, isn't he?"

"He does look good," I admitted.

"His wife was a positive beast to him," she confided in a low voice. "Made him miserable. She was a nervous type, really, the kind that has to be doing something constantly to distract herself. Club-hopping every night. Endless chatter. You want to pet them and make them calm down, that type, but they won't let you. It makes them nervous to be calm. Anyway, she thought my poor lad was dull when he occasionally wanted to sit home at night in his robe and slippers before the fire in the winter. She never realized how hard he works, how tired he gets after all that travel. In the end, she ran off with his best friend."

This was more than my mother had ever told me. In fact, I was sure Mom didn't know this.

"Do keep that under your hat," Aunt Sheila said in a low voice, her glance darting toward the hallway, anticipating Jeremy's return. "He'd kill me if he knew I'd told you. But sometimes you have to tell people. It's not good to suffer in silence." She sighed. "Look out for him, will you?" she asked. "He won't let me. He'll listen to you. He trusts you. I'm glad, because sometimes life can make you mistrust the opposite sex." She said this in the tones of someone who liked the opposite sex.

Then she leaned forward as if she were working herself up to saying something more, and even opened her mouth to do so, but we both heard Jeremy's brisk footsteps coming toward us. Aunt Sheila straightened up and smiled brightly. She rose, glanced at her slim gold-and-diamond watch, said she had an appointment, kissed me lightly and told me to give my parents her "love," which surprised me a little. Jeremy opened the door for her and summoned the lift, and let her go without us because I'd asked hesitatingly if I might use the powder room.

"You show her, will you, Jeremy, and lock up for me?" Aunt Sheila said as she flitted out the door, waving away my thanks for the nice lunch.

"Where's she off to?" I asked when I returned from the spotless pale blue bathroom.

"She goes to visit a veterans' center once a week," Jeremy said dryly. "On Tuesdays. On Wednesdays and Fridays she shops and takes exercise. On Mondays she's got her land mines and women's shelter. Not exactly the hippie lifestyle she'd have you believe, is it?"

"Oh, leave her alone. Your mother," I said, "is younger than you."

"Yes, well, she's been having an affair with one of those blokes who works with her at the veterans' home," he said a trifle tartly. "He's supposed to be a musician. Composes musical bits for television shows for the BBC. They've been an item as long as I can remember. Father knew it, and I knew it, and the whole fucking world knew it."

I was shocked. Not that Aunt Sheila had been having an affair for years and years, or had cheated on stuffy old Uncle Peter, who, quite frankly, was disapproving enough to drive any woman bats; but that Jeremy had so uncharacteristically blurted out the information to me right here, in his mother's apartment, as he was courteously opening the door for me.

"Really?" I asked, rather hushed in awe. I didn't know what to say, and I wouldn't have said it if I did, for fear he'd bite my head off. But once we got in the elevator he resumed his professional air, as if he hadn't just said something astounding and personal.

"You ought to call your mum," he said reflectively. "Tell her how things went, and where we're headed. I feel certain she'd want to know."

We went back to the hotel, and he plunked himself in front of the television set and watched the news, as if we were in any old hotel room instead of the most gorgeous pit stop on earth, while I hastily packed my duds and phoned home.

I didn't want to be responsible for making us miss the plane, so I was very succinct with my mother. I said, "Ma, I can't talk long because I have to catch a plane with Jeremy. You got the London apartment. It's beautiful. Yes, I love it! But I don't know why you're giving it to me. Jeremy says it's worth over seven hundred thousand pounds. And I got the garage in France and whatever's in it. Yeah, the garage. Jeremy got the villa, but Rollo Jr. got all the furniture. I'm gonna go look at the French stuff now. Yup. I'm getting on a plane. With Jeremy.

It was his idea. Yes, we ate. At Aunt Sheila's. Sandwiches and cookies. I'll tell you later. Oh—and she says love to you and Dad." I lowered my voice. "Yes, she said love."

I think that was the point at which my mother said, "Well, that's what a couple hundred thousand pounds will do for you," but I did not respond because although Jeremy appeared to be focusing on the TV screen, I thought he might actually be listening to what I said.

"Did the other relatives get anything?" My father's voice popped on. Mother must have gestured to him to pick up the extension. I explained again about what Rollo Jr. got, and Dad said, "Good. Then everybody is happy, no?"

"No," I said. "Rollo Jr. is going to contest the French will." There was a silence, and then my mother said, "Let me speak to Jeremy, will you, darling?"

I handed him the receiver. He didn't look at all surprised. He said some reassuring things to her, just as if he were talking to a client and an aunt simultaneously, then I heard him say, "Yes, I'm sure she does." Then he hung up.

"Sure who does?" I asked suspiciously.

"You," he said, gesturing to the bellhop who'd appeared, to pick up my bag.

"I do what?" I persisted.

"Need a little looking after," he shot back. "I wonder, can she mean to protect you from unscrupulous men who chase after young heiresses? Because she didn't elaborate."

I was really, truly embarrassed and could not imagine what had possessed my mother to make her say such a thing. "Of course I deserve VIP treatment," I said. "You should have noticed by now."

By this time I didn't care what I said. Things were moving rapidly and I knew it couldn't last. I knew I was being Cinderella for a day, staying in five-star hotels, acting like an heiress, being invited to lunch. Tomorrow things would slink right back to normal, I felt sure. Those relatives of mine would somehow succeed in taking all the money away, no doubt—not because of any lack of skill on Jeremy's part but simply because thieves focus all their energy on a swindle and are never distracted by useless things like love and work and great conversation.

Yes, tomorrow things would go back to normal, and I would be short of funds again, staying in crummy chain-hotels on a low-budget production if I was lucky enough to be gainfully employed, and my glamorous cousin would go back into his world of money, and we wouldn't see each other again for another hundred years. So why not make the most of this little fairy-tale blip in time?

Chapter Eight

A T LEAST THERE WERE NO MONKEYS ON THE CORPORATE JET. THERE
were, however, some guys in suits—English lawyers and their
male clients who were very jocular, particularly after they availed
themselves of the scotch and other stuff in the bar. The jet was outfitted with an array of crystal glasses in every conceivable cocktail shape,
anchored to the padded bar in some mysterious way so that they
wouldn't go flying about like missiles in the event of turbulence. A
strip of colored light above the bar kept changing colors and bursting
into star patterns against the black background, for no other reason
than entertainment value. And it worked; for about the first five minutes, anyway, when the guys made bets on how long it would take for
the galactic light show to run the gamut of colors and return to its
original blue. While clattering ice and munching nuts, the guys shot a
few more covert, curious glances at me, the only woman aboard. They
acted like rowdy schoolboys who felt compelled to behave at least
minimally well but occasionally guffawed at their own presumably
bawdy little jokes.

Jeremy eyed the other men in that silent way a guy with a girl sort
of warns the other fellows to bugger off. We sat on two of the few seats
that were facing forward, like the pilot. They were wide and leathery,

with ample leg room, but, as Jeremy noted wryly, amazingly not that comfortable nonetheless. The other seats, which could hold eight people apiece, were more like two extremely long black sofas, facing their counterparts across the aisle. The plane was long and narrow, like a limousine, with ebony-colored draperies, carpeting, padded walls. It was apparently designed on the assumption that its passengers would be in groups, like an entire marketing department or a football team, who would earn the privilege of flying privately by discussing how best to kick ass. And indeed, that's what the other guys seemed to be doing.

I told Jeremy that it was awfully nice of him to get hold of the plane for this trip, thereby sparing us the crowds, noise, and toilet lines of commercial flights. "It was luck," he insisted modestly. "The jet just happened to be available. It somehow never is."

Then he settled back and soon fell asleep, in that way you do when you're totally wiped out, where your head is flung back and your mouth drops wide open. Having him asleep made it possible for me to study him a little more closely—the left hand without its wedding band, the elegant understated wristwatch with several time zones. He had honest hands, wide and capable. The corners of his mouth were turned down a little; perhaps this had to do with seeing his mother today. I wondered how often he visited her, and where he lived. I recalled what she said about his wife being mean to him. People look so innocent when they sleep, and Jeremy looked, for once, rather vulnerable.

He woke later, with a guilty, apologetic start. "Sorry. Conked right out on you, didn't I?" he asked sheepishly. I grinned. "Fell down on the job," he said in self-mockery, "right after promising your mum I'd look after you." He glanced at the men, who'd gotten a little louder, then at me. "Seriously," he said, as if our conversation was never interrupted by sleep, "how's your love life?" His tone was protective, not leering, like a vigilant big brother asking a kid sister.

"I've had my moments," I said thoughtfully, "and some pretty bad ones at that—you know, the obsessive relationship—but I can't honestly say I've been really, truly, desperately in love." I meant it. Because if what I had with Paul was all there was to love, I'd shoot myself.

"Desperately," he repeated. "Trust me, you wouldn't want to be."

"Does that mean you were?" I asked automatically, idiotically forgetting for the moment what Aunt Sheila had told me. Then I caught my breath, which made it worse, because it was a natural enough question to ask, but by gasping at myself I betrayed that I'd heard something. Mercifully he assumed it was from my mother. He just laughed ruefully.

"Oh, you can tell your mum that I've recovered from the divorce with at least a modicum of self-respect," he said lightly, "some females here and there, but no steady girlfriend as yet. Which frankly is fine with me. I'm not ready to take the plunge again."

"Are you still in love with your ex-wife?" I dared to ask. He looked utterly horrified.

"God, no!" he said, shocked.

"Okay, okay, take it easy," I said in an equally cousinly tone. "What was she like?"

"Beautiful, neurotic. Elusive. Accused me of giving up on us first. Not sure of that. She said I didn't make enough effort to change, which is true. I'm to blame for getting testy in the end," he said, glancing away momentarily. "Lost my sense of humor, which is deadly. She was surprisingly harsh, once she made up her mind that we were through," he admitted. "Best way to break it off, I suppose, but it left a bad taste. I would have preferred kinder memories."

He'd seemed offhanded enough when he started talking, but looked faintly horrified again toward the end, as if he'd revealed more than he intended and somehow couldn't stop once he got started. Hastily he added, "But you're dodging the question yourself, putting it back on me. Have you got a boyfriend? Should I look him over and see if he's fit for an heiress?" He put on a mock stern expression, but there was something genuine in his inquiry. I shook my head.

"We broke up, and this time it's really for good," I said, suddenly mortified that my voice had just waffled on whether it was over or not, without consulting my brain, which sternly said that it was. My face felt hot, and I was sure that it was beet-red. "Nothing dramatic in the finish, either," I said lamely, trying to sound more definite. "It just ran out of steam. I realized he was bored with me and I was tired of him. It was depressing once I figured it out."

God, it was getting worse, the more I said. I'd better quit while I wasn't ahead.

Jeremy comprehended my lingering agony and uncertainty. His voice was soothing. "I can't see anyone being bored with you, of all people," he said affectionately. "Surely not. I'd expect seething passion, even at the end, like hurling books and bric-a-brac at each other."

"We did that, too," I said. "Before we got too weary to fight. I'm not really boring. I just retreat into my shell when I feel cornered. He wanted to get married just weeks after we met, I think because all his friends were having weddings. It seemed so impersonal. I wanted to live together first, and we did, but he was pissed off the whole time, and he still seemed like a stranger somehow. I felt bullied and rushed, and it just freaked me out more."

"That's because some guys know perfectly well that they can't be trusted," he said quickly and surely. "Hence the big hurry. They want to capture you before you figure out that they're useless bastards. But don't you let them."

"Thanks," I said. "I always wanted a big brother. It's very restful."

He bowed his head. "At your service, anytime," he said.

"I'll have to watch over you, too, and make sure that some gold-digger doesn't go after you and your villa and your devastating English charm," I said. We shook hands on the bargain.

The plane was tilting toward Nice now. You could see blue swimming pools attached to the villas that were nestled into the craggy hillsides, and the soft blue Mediterranean Sea was lapping at the pebbly beaches. My production company had finished the Riviera shoot and gone home now, and Erik and Tim were doing the flea-market circuit, to scrounge for props and antiques, starting in Spain. For once I didn't have to hurry off to a meeting or a shoot. Jeremy had rented a car, and he'd given me a map so I could be his navigator out on those winding corniche roads.

I thought of Aunt Penelope, boldly buying her villa in the 1930s, when she was young, in the time of cocktail parties, slinky evening gowns, sweet love songs amid plunging stock markets, sandwiched between two world wars. None of her relatives remembered being at that villa, and it was quite likely that she'd stopped going there a long time ago. Yet she held on to it all this time, when she could have sold it for lots of money. And she went there one last time, and died there. To me that meant memories of love and a lost era that she didn't want to dwell on, but still, in the end, felt more at home with. Already I could feel that the house would be full of impressions, energies, indications of past passions, sorrows and joys.

Jeremy smiled at the look of anticipation on my face. "You don't want to expect too much of this garage," he cautioned gently. "One woman's treasure is another woman's clutter."

"I know that. I was just thinking of all the ghosts in the house," I said enthusiastically.

"Ghosts?" he inquired, looking faintly alarmed. "Do you know this for a fact? Are you one of those people who can sense the presence of evil spirits? If so, please don't tell me."

"No, not that," I assured him. "Come on. Aren't you excited?

You're the proud owner of a villa in the South of France! Admit it.
You must be thrilled." He smiled indulgently.

"Slow down, child," he said. "It ain't ours till the fat lady sings."

"Oh, phooey," I said. "Let's be the first ones off the plane."

"All right. Got your map?" he asked, looking rather excited himself now. "I'm counting on you to help me find the damned place."

Part Four

beautiful red, white, and pink profusion of flowers tumbling over each other in reckless and joyous abandon. I saw trees with blossoms of an intense color somewhere between purple and violet, a shade I'd never seen before on a tree. I'd hardly seen any sights at all when I worked here days ago with my film cohorts. Just airport, taxi, hotel, locations, libraries, via the inland superhighway, which didn't have these views. The scenic natural world had been barely in my peripheral view, through the fogged lens of jet-lagged exhaustion. Now I lay back in the passenger seat, lazy and happy, nearly drugged with the soft sunshine.

Higher up we climbed, to where stone farmhouses with peach-colored roofs were stubbornly built into any scrap of land that could be found clinging to these impossible cliffs, along with the precious olive trees that for centuries had been coaxed into growing on narrow terraced ledges, to make the liquid golden olive oil prized the world over. Monks and perfumers had labored in these fields to perfect the fine art of harvesting the exquisite herbs that grew here in such fragrant abundance—lavender, sage, thyme, and the borage that knights put in their wine cups to give them strength and courage.

As I gazed out my window with the soft, diffuse sunlight kissing my skin, I could feel more centuries of history flashing by me. These old villas hiding behind iron gates, stone walls, and dense hedges of rhododendrons attested to the Victorian era, when sad sweet tubercular writers, musicians and artists wintered here in hopes of regaining their health and strength, while Russian and English royalty gambled and played bridge with railroad tycoons and rich eccentric botanists. Then came the summer crowds in the glamorous Roaring Twenties and the thirties, Aunt Penelope's time, when Coco Chanel made suntanning chic, and expatriates like Fitzgerald and Hemingway toasted the good life with each other; and artists like Cocteau and Matisse rediscovered their wild-child links to the primitive art of cave paintings and sculpture. Despite the layering of centuries here, that prehistoric world was not so very far away. Whenever we shot through a tunnel I saw that these were not the smooth man-made concrete tunnels of New York, but craggy, ancient Gothic cathedrals carved right into the magnificent cliffs.

When at last we burst out of the tunnels onto the *moyenne corniche* road, I gasped at the staggering view of the open blue sky and the sheer drop to the sea below, where the harbors were filled with bobbing fishing boats and yachts. Every time we rounded a turn the view changed and I gasped again, twisting in my seat to compare the angle of where we'd just been with the glimpse of where we were heading, unable to decide which picture-postcard image was the more perfect and beautiful.

I kept exclaiming, "Oh, my God, look at that! Wow, did you see that? Phew, isn't that gorgeous?" until I finally gave in to the sheer delight of not being able to keep up with one spectacular angle after another after another. I just sat back in my seat and laughed out loud, and my laughter made me think of the endless sprays of flowers tumbling over the walls in such excessive profusion that it must be Nature laughing, too, at how many flowers there were to smell, how many fish gliding through the sea, how many stars glowing in the sky, and how many silly people trying with their minds to keep up with it all.

Jeremy smiled indulgently at me, enjoying my reactions with the amused pleasure you get when you watch someone experience something you love for the first time, like a city or a book or a good wine. When I caught him smiling at me I grinned back.

"It's amazing," I said. "I was just here days ago, working, and I never saw any of this. I was like a little caterpillar chewing on my leaf, just too wrapped up in work, work, work."

That gave him the opportunity to ask me more questions about the portfolio I'd been carrying, with all the Lucrezia Borgia artifacts, sketches, swatches, and samples. I started off with my usual quick spiel about my work, designed to get it over with. Normally, when people find out that you work on set designs for movies, they exclaim, "Oh! Isn't that fascinating! Doing what, exactly?" but the whole time that they're nodding and listening, you can see the wheels turning as they try to figure out how much money you make—and when they realize it isn't much, they lose interest.

But Jeremy didn't act like that. He listened attentively when I told him about people I worked with regularly, like Erik and Tim; and other "wild-card" elements on the set, such as child actors or old veterans or new crew members, who at first might drive you crazy, yet later they sometimes surprised you by emerging with valor by the shoot's end. And often it was a little sad when a production wrapped and you knew you might not see some of those people ever again, after the strange intensity you'd shared with them for a couple of high-strung weeks.

When I ran out of steam and Jeremy ran out of questions, I tentatively asked him about his career. And somehow it was easier for both of us to talk about it today, with the gentle green-and-blue sea sparkling below us, and the great blue sky stretching endlessly ahead, with the soft yellow sun that was serenely fading into a coral-colored sunset.

"Father wanted me to go into corporate law, of course," Jeremy explained. "More money and influence and all that, but I found it too sick-making, to be honest. It's just as well, because the company that wanted to hire me fell like an elephant to a massive stock scandal, and every lawyer and accountant who worked there got a bit tainted when it came to being hired elsewhere."

"Did your father adjust when you told him what you wanted to do?" I asked tentatively.

For once he didn't seem to mind talking about his dad. "Oh, he trumpeted a bit," Jeremy said reflectively.

"After all, it's not like you told him you wanted to give up law entirely and become an actor or something," I said. Then I remembered his childhood ambitions and added, "But you wanted to be a musician when you were a kid, didn't you?"

"A rock guitarist," he said. "Which Father never thought of as a musician. We cut a record, actually."

"Let's see, your group was . . ." I said searchingly, "the Dogs of War."

"Good God!" he moaned. "No woman should have a memory like that."

"So what happened to the Dogs?" I asked.

"We had fights, and stole each other's girlfriends, and broke up when it was time to sit exams and graduate." He grinned. "Besides, we got a good look at the music industry and didn't fancy being told what to record by committees of corporate marketing boys. That's not what produced the Beatles. I guess I didn't want it that badly, and you have to, to survive."

"So—did you and your father reconcile before he . . ." I started out being daring and reckless, but I lost my nerve. Fortunately the landscape seemed to be keeping Jeremy philosophical, therefore not at all offended by my tactlessness.

"Does one ever really reconcile with a father?" he asked. "But we came to respect each other. Forget about ever getting his approval. To some extent he treated everybody that way—a habitual disapproving act that kept people off-balance so they didn't get too close. But I was his own flesh and blood, yet he behaved as if I was genetically disposed to becoming a bum!" He shook his head wearily, remembering. "If I wanted something, no matter how harmless, he'd say I couldn't have it, simply because if I wanted it, then surely it must be wrong. I learned to pretend that I didn't give a damn about the things I wanted badly; and vice versa, which can really fuck you up, because you forget not to do that all the time, with everybody else."

"I have to confess, he scared me a little," I said.

"You knew him at his feistiest. He was pretty tough in those days," Jeremy said. "Even when I began to do well in school, it caught him off-guard at first, until he decided it meant that I was finally 'seeing things his way,' as if he'd been proven 'right' and I'd been proven 'wrong.' He was so insufferable about it that I wanted to turn round and become a jewel thief or a drug dealer. Then I thought, no, that would be just what he expected. Finally I said, sod it, I've got to get him out of my head. So I went to study in Paris for as long as it took. Rather a good moment, that, when you first hear your own voice inside your head." I nodded in agreement.

"But your parents are perfect, right? So you've no idea what I'm talking about," he went on, glancing directly at me with a smile. The intensity of his curiosity gave me an unexpected surge of excitement, and I actually had to turn away for a moment so he wouldn't see clear through me and detect this flash of pleasure I'd experienced, just basking in his company.

"I bet your parents were cool with you," he was saying. I recovered my light attitude.

"Not at all," I said. "My father kept warning me that men were unreliable and I should find my own *métier*, but he never gave me a clue about how to start a career, and he never wanted to give me specific advice for fear I'd follow it literally and not be able to think for myself. I mean, once in awhile you want a cut-and-dried opinion, you know? And my mother simply refuses to seriously believe that her daughter isn't a kid anymore."

Then I gave him a sideways squint. "Wait a minute. We haven't finished with you yet. Tell me more about what you do."

He liked two main things about his field, he said—the global reach of international law, and the human factor in inheritance and estates. "The human factor?" I repeated.

"You learn a lot about national preoccupations," he explained. "I mean, people are basically the same, but, for instance, in France, I think paternity is a much bigger issue than in England. It's a big part of their identity—French men worry a lot more about having a son to carry on the family name, and being sure that it really is their son, et cetera. So bloodlines are very important."

"Inheritance law is so much more personal than corporate law," I mused. "Things must get pretty emotional. But at least you don't have to worry about getting embroiled in some skanky stock-market scandal."

He gave me a scolding look. "My dear girl, if you think that inheritance is any cleaner than business, then you haven't been reading your Balzac," he said.

"We did a movie on Balzac and his mom," I shot back. "He liked unusual doodads. Had a special pocket-watch, a kind of nineteenth-century 'organizer.' Drove me nuts, finding those props."

"He also clerked in a law firm when he was a boy, and said that he learned just how low people would stoop to get their mitts on a tiny, grubby little inheritance," Jeremy informed me.

"Are you saying people would kill their relatives to inherit a couple of *sous*?" I asked.

"Or to inherit a few goats, out in the country," he said, nodding. "Oh, perhaps they didn't kill their relatives outright, but just hastened the end along."

"I think our exit is the next one coming up," I said, suddenly remembering my role as navigator with the map.

"Great. Thanks," he said. We followed the signs to get off the highway, skirting past the actual town of Antibes. Once we pulled away from the main roads, and onto narrower streets, we were on our own, because there were no more road signs. We flagged down an elderly man on a bicycle who actually had a loaf of French bread in his basket and a black beret on his head, like a man in a travel poster. He listened obligingly when Jeremy slowed the car and I spoke to him in my patchy French, and then he pointed out the way.

"That can't be real French bread, can it?" I joked after we drove on. "He's just posing like a tourist brochure, right, for our benefit?"

"Right. He works for Disney. He'll probably yank off that beret the minute he turns the corner," Jeremy agreed. Then we both fell silent, sensing that we were just minutes away from Aunt Penelope's villa.

Chapter Ten

WE WERE ON A NARROW DIRT ROAD WITH ONLY OCCASIONAL driveways opening out onto it, but finally we reached a gravel path half choked with tall overgrown shrubbery, and I spotted a little tiled sign with the name that Great-Aunt Penelope had given her villa, *Temps Joyeux*.

" 'Happy Times,' " I translated. "Funny, isn't it? In French it sounds okay, but in English it sounds like a cemetery or a rest home. You'd think Aunt Penelope could come up with something a little more sophisticated than that."

"We Laidleys are not a very imaginative bunch, I'm afraid," Jeremy chuckled as the car went crunching over the gravel drive. Weeds and underbrush were poking out here and there, but it was the big old trees that were really making headway, overhead, like a shady canopy. It felt as if we were driving inside a green tunnel, because the drive twisted and curved several times before it finally opened up into a straight path to a small gravel clearing.

Directly ahead of us was an unused, peeling fountain in the center, filled with autumn leaves. The villa loomed behind it. Jeremy pulled the car to a stop, and the engine noise retreated into an abrupt silence.

Dust rose around us from the sudden stop of the tires. Jeremy waited till it settled, then lowered his window.

"Hear that?" he whispered. "Total silence. Except for the birds. And if you listen closely, I bet you can hear the sea."

We sat there quietly, and you could indeed hear, far off, a sort of whispering, washing sound of the sea lapping up against the rocks. "Oh!" I sighed, inhaling deeply. "What is that wonderful smell? Honeysuckle?"

"Jasmine," he said, pointing to vines growing against one side of the villa, where little white-and-yellowish trumpets gave off the scent, leaning toward the back of the house, indicating where the sunny side was. The front of the house, which faced us, was the shady side, and the sun was sinking lower behind it, but I could still make out the color of the pale peach walls, the Matisse-blue shutters at the windows, the burgundy door. The back of the house faced south and would have the view of the sea.

I couldn't wait another minute. I grabbed my portfolio to take notes, and I sprang from my seat. "Jeremy!" I cried. "Let's go look!"

I felt as if we were kids again, exploring somebody's abandoned house. I would have run around to the back of the house to see the view and peer in the windows, but Jeremy picked up his briefcase, marched up the front steps, and put the key in the lock. That was when it dawned on me that the new owner of the villa was my child-hood pal, who wiped his feet on the mat respectfully before entering. He deserves this, I thought. It was great that he'd be rewarded for his steadfast protection of the family interests.

"Come along, then," he said to me, amused. I followed him inside. "Be careful, there's no electric on," he cautioned as we fumbled in the dark. Then there was a little beam of light.

"You brought a flashlight," I said, looking admiringly at the slim, compact tool.

"A torch," he corrected. "Will you never learn to speak proper English, child?"

We entered, shuffling together, following the beam of his flashlight into a small circular foyer that was flanked by two opposing staircases leading up. A narrow shaft of sunlight shone from the open door of the drawing room, which was straight ahead, under the stairs, so we gravitated there first. Jeremy led the way in, but we'd gone only a few steps when we both paused.

It looked as though a roomful of ghosts were standing there waiting for us. Then I realized that it was all furniture, draped in white sheets to keep the dust off. There must be a chandelier overhead, I observed, because it was covered with a balloon of white, too, like a puffy cloud. Jeremy reached out and threw back a corner of one of the sheets, then another and another, just enough to reveal a credenza here, a sofa there, a table nearby. I identified most of the pieces from my years of scouring antiques shops, and wrote them all down.

"That's a Russian clock, early twentieth century. That chest of drawers is mahogany, Italian, late eighteen hundreds. The sofa's French Empire. That *secretaire* is to die for. Russian or Swedish, maybe. Yessir, Rollo will do all right."

"Nice to have a pro like you around. Makes it all easier," Jeremy commented. He said he'd pass my notes on to Severine's assistant, who would do a final tally on the French possessions.

"Rollo's welcome to this furniture!" he observed. "It's too heavy and depressing. If I had to stare at these things all day, I'd go barmy."

"What would you prefer? Deco?" I teased.

"Deco would be great," he said. I pointed out the octagonal door handles and blue-tiled fireplace.

"Here's something else you'd like," I said, having pulled back the coverings of an adorable black baby grand piano after I'd spied the foot-pedals sticking out. He plinked a few keys, conjuring up the melody of "A Hard Day's Night," but it sounded positively ghostly.

Even in the shadows I could see that it was a lovely villa, but needed repair. Paint was peeling from the walls, and the wood floors were scuffed. We walked back through the circular foyer, where the two staircases, one to the left, one to the right, met again overhead. The second-floor hallway above was more like a balcony, so that you could gaze back down at the foyer where we were standing.

Jeremy looked from the stairs to me and I practically read his mind, but as usual it was me, the dumb American, who said it aloud. "Race you!" I cried. I took the left staircase, he took the right, and I beat him by a fraction.

"You're still light as a feather," he murmured with grudging admiration. "I could never outrun you. Do you still swim as straight and fast as an eel?"

"Jeremy, look," I said, flinging open doors. "One, two, three, four bedrooms!"

"Watch out!" he said sharply, and a second later I stumbled. The floor had something sticking out of it, but it wasn't a nail. A slat of wood had come loose and was raised—that's all it was. Jeremy took me by the hand as if I were a naughty little girl.

"Come with me," he said sternly. "If you fall through the floor now, they'll think I killed you for the inheritance."

We walked through each bedroom briefly. The master bedroom, decorated with fading blue-and-white-striped wallpaper with pale pink cabbage roses twining through it, was on the southeast side of the house, where the morning sun would come pouring in the windows of the French doors, which opened onto a balcony. This, I later realized, was the only room in the house that had been cleaned and dusted and looked as if someone had lived here. Aunt Penelope had died right in that bed, so neatly made with a soft blue counterpane.

I didn't want to mention it to Jeremy, but he seemed to be thinking the same thing, because after a pause he said, "She must have gotten comfort from this place if she came here to die. But I can't help thinking she'd feel like one of the ghosts."

We were quiet for awhile. Finally he pointed. "Balcony here," he said. I peered out. It was one continuous balcony that ran all along the width of the house on the south side.

"Hey. If your guests walk out there from their room, they can sneak along to your side and peer right into your bed," I observed.

"Hmm, that's true," Jeremy noted. Adjacent to the bedroom was a small white bathroom, with bidet, sink and mirror, claw-foot tub, and the kind of old toilet where you pull a chain from a box above. Over the tub was a skylight, so you could gaze at the stars at night from your bath. There were charming old gold-and-white fixtures. Jeremy ran water in the sink, which came out brown at first but cleared, with good pressure. No pipes groaned in protest.

"Plumbing doesn't look too bad. That's a surprise," he observed. I had recovered from my initial emotional reaction to the bedroom, and now I noticed a teakwood object at the foot of the bed. I drew closer to examine it. "What's that?" Jeremy asked. "A bed tray?"

"A writing desk," I said, lifting the lid and showing him the slots for pens and the wells for ink bottles, all carved smoothly out of rosewood and inlaid with mother-of-pearl. "Antiques dealers love these desks," I said. "They were used by housewives and army generals alike for centuries! You could just pick 'em up and take 'em with you in your carriage as you were fleeing revolutions and overthrowing governments. Every step of the way, people wrote letters because, after all, they didn't have telephones, or even telegraphs. This beauty is from the late seventeen hundreds, I think, and it's English. Probably—" I stopped dead as I pulled open a little drawer where writing paper was usually kept. There was no paper in there at all. Two faces stared back at me—mine, and Jeremy's, in two distinct photographs.

"Hang on!" Jeremy exclaimed. "That's us at the beach!" We peered closer. Somebody had snapped close-ups of us that summer, without our ever knowing it. Goose-bumps rose on my arms. Jeremy had the same thought. "Looks like Aunt Pen took snaps of us on the sneak."

"I look like a redheaded scarecrow," I groaned.

"I look like a tall mop with eyes," Jeremy noted. I turned the photos over, searching for a date to confirm. But the inky script on mine said only *Penny without her braces,* and Jeremy's said, *Musical like his dad,* which made Jeremy snort. There were no other photos in the box. Just a card from Jeremy's law firm with the name and address and phone number.

"Jeremy," I said in a low, mysterious tone, "it's as if she knew we'd come here together. Maybe there's something about this place, and her life, that she wants us to find out about." The more I thought about it, the more I warmed to my idea. "Why else would she divvy it up so that you got the house and I got the garage?"

He stared at me. "And Rollo got the furniture, remember? Nothing very mystical about dividing your estate among your blood relatives so that the government doesn't get it! Penny," he said gently, "you want to be careful about romanticizing this. Most people just sell off what they inherit."

"Phooey," I said in embarrassment, for lack of a better retort. "You won't dare sell off this great villa, will you?"

"Not bloody likely," he admitted. "It's lovely. But is the rest of it in good shape? Come along now. Use your detecting skills to finish this tally-up, all right?" Jeremy said teasingly, as he led me away to the next room.

We started making up names for each bedroom. The first was the Rose Room, because of the pink cabbage roses on the wallpaper.

Next came the Bastille Day Room, because it was red and blue. It was followed by the Renaissance Room, a smaller one, which had tile on the ceiling, painted with cherubs and clouds and doves.

"That's rather pretty," Jeremy observed.

"Italian," I said. "They used to do that for people they loved. For brides, or children, even newborn babies. Paint the ceiling, or even the roof of a crib, to make them see something happy when they opened their eyes in the morning."

The last bedroom we called the Japanese Room, with its wallpaper of pagodas and little ladies with paper umbrellas crossing arched bridges. All four rooms were laid out in a row, one after another, flanked by the balcony on the outside, parallel to the hallway on the inside. The three guest rooms had to share a bathroom at the end of the hall, a pale, sea-foam green, with the same kind of old-fashioned toilet and a narrower tub. Some of the floor tiles were loose.

We went back downstairs, and discovered a door at the foot of each staircase. The one on the right was only a closet, with nothing in it but an awful-looking old mop. The door on the left led to a dining room with heavy, dusty red draperies, drawn together; and a long table with eight hideous-looking chairs with high backs made of carved wooden snakelike squiggles.

Beyond the dining room was the kitchen, which had a door leading outside to a small enclosed porch with a bench, and a shelf containing kitchen-garden tools—a basket, watering can, snippers, gloves. The porch had an outdoor stone staircase that went past those climbing jasmine vines and ended at an herb patch.

The kitchen was most in need of repair, having an ancient black stove, a sink with rusty tap, an old-fashioned icebox, and a pantry. A staircase beside the pantry led down to a wine cellar, with rickety steps that felt more like a ladder. Jeremy flashed his light around, and we examined a few dusty bottles of some old port and sherry, but the racks were mostly empty, strung with elaborately thick spiderwebs that made me dread coming across their architects.

"Looks like Aunt Pen and her chums drank up all the wine," Jeremy said approvingly. I was still worrying about finding a monster spider colony, so I was glad to leave the cellar.

We returned to the dining room, and Jeremy pulled back the drapery, which raised a cloud of dust, making us cough, but it was worth it—there were French doors that opened onto a slate patio with big terracotta flowerpots, a cast-iron table and chairs, and, a few steps down, an old tiled swimming pool filled with nothing but leaves.

The pool was rimmed on the far side with dense shrubbery, where the property stopped abruptly. Cautiously we went out and peered beyond the shrubbery, and there we discovered that this villa, like the olive trees we'd seen all along the way, was simply clinging to a patch of earth on a cliff, one dollhouse among many. There were houses above us, houses below us, all perched on terraced "steps" that gazed out at the gorgeous Mediterranean Sea. The fiery orange sun was just slipping softly into the sweet blue sea far below, leaving a rippling golden path across the waves to the horizon, connecting land to sea in the mind's eye.

"Oh, Jeremy!" I breathed. "Isn't it beautiful? Aren't you so happy, to be so lucky?"

"Yes," he said softly. "And yes, and yes."

I closed my eyes and sighed. When I opened them he was smiling at me.

"Aren't you forgetting something?" he asked. "The garage, my girl."

I gave him a sideways squint. "Thought you'd *never* ask," I said. "See how cool I've been about it?" We dashed across the lawn to the garage.

It was a silly-looking shed, an absurd, relatively pint-sized replica of the house, only it wore its roof at a rakish angle, like a hat on a tipsy guest. Jeremy had to lift a wooden arm that barricaded its double doors. The oak doors were surprisingly heavy and didn't hang quite level, but we managed to shove them open. Jeremy led the way in, shining his flashlight ahead, and I followed. But then he stopped short so suddenly that I collided with him, crashing into his back.

"What is it?" I cried.

"A houseguest," he said in a falsely calm voice. "Look."

There was a car in there all right, with its front facing us. But when Jeremy aimed his light across its hood, two red eyes were staring back at us. They weren't like any eyes you'd want to see on a living creature. They looked unearthly, unblinking, like a stranger from Mars. While I stood there watching, however, the serpent uncoiled itself and shyly slithered across the hood, down to the ground, and made haste for a hole in the stone wall through which some light shone, indicating how it had gotten in there in the first place. Expertly, it vanished.

"Snake!" I said unnecessarily, in a pip-squeak of a voice.

"There goes your first possession," Jeremy said, sweeping his light in an arc around the car. One of the headlights was broken, and looked as if it was stuffed with hay. I hoped it wasn't the snake's nest. I found myself tiptoeing, stepping quickly and lightly so that my feet wouldn't be in one place too long for any other snakes to glide over.

"I hope we don't surprise a rabid raccoon or something," I said nervously. But Jeremy was moving closer to the car, shining his light on a silver hood ornament that looked like a snorting giant lizard leaping on its hind legs.

"My God," he breathed. "It is. I can't believe it, but it is."

"Is what?" I asked nervously.

"It's a Dragonetta!" Jeremy said triumphantly, as he circled around it with excitement, examining the steering wheel and the rearview mirrors and the door handles. "From the look of it I'd say it's a 1936.

I'll bet Aunt Pen was the first owner, too, which is incredible luck."
He peered inside. "Rather neglected, though. Whoa, I'll bet that's the
original horsehair upholstery. Looks like mice have been lodging here,
but, thankfully, nobody's home now. But they tore up some of the
leather, and shit all over it."

"Don't touch it," I said, remembering some obscure thing I'd
read.

"I never touch mouse shit," he said gravely.

"No, the horsehair," I said. "I think you can get anthrax from it."

"Nonsense," he said, getting more warmed up about the car by
the minute. "This could be fixed. My God, an original Dragonetta.
What a find. The engines on these cars were big for the time, and the
body was light, framed in wood, made by hand. The power and lightness mean it just flies down the road. Those engines were built to last
forever, back in the days before all the good ones went into airplanes."
He was still halfway through the window, peering in, but now he
backed himself out and looked at me almost sternly.

"Do you know how lucky you are to inherit a car like this?" he
demanded.

"Why? Is it worth a lot of money?" I asked.

"Oh, you'd have to put some serious cash into it to make it worth
a lot," he said dismissively. "It's not the money, my dear child. It's that
you are one of maybe ten people in the entire world who have one."
Then suddenly he grinned. "Have I actually found the one antique
that I know more about than you?"

"That's right!" I conceded. It was something I'd almost forgotten: his boyish love of great cars. As a kid he'd collected magazine
photos of "orphans," or vintage cars with nameplates that were no
longer made, like Packards, REOs, Franklins. He could reel off car
statistics—year first made, year last made, engine size, performance
ratings—the way most kids quote baseball statistics. When he spoke

about his favorite autos, his normal noncommittal reserve gave way to a radiant exuberance that he didn't exhibit for anything else. But, as I recalled, he'd kept this passion a secret from the grown-ups, perhaps anticipating his father's disapproval.

"Jeremy," I said, "did you ever tell Aunt Penelope how much you love antique cars?"

"Hmmm?" he said distractedly, still examining it. "Of course not. Why should I? Who would have guessed she was harboring one of these babies all these years?"

We examined the car closely together. It truly was ever so elegant, with a cobalt-blue body, a wide, luxurious dark interior of fine leather and horsehair seats, a wooden dashboard and huge steering wheel and all those other glamorous things that nobody puts in cars anymore. A good old auto with an air of loyalty. It deserved to be fixed up and loved. I understood how Jeremy felt—as if we'd found a prize racehorse neglected in an old barn; you wanted to give the animal a decent brushing, feeding and proper home.

With great enthusiasm we went through the glove compartment and perused some faded maps on tissue-thin paper that was practically disintegrating right before our eyes.

"These are the Alps!" I said in delight. "Wonder if she was a skier? Hemingway was sliding around Europe in Aunt Penelope's day! He used to go to remote areas with no lifts where you had to walk all the way up the mountain just to ski down it. He said it gave you the kind of legs that made you a good skier. Hey, there are pencil markings on some of the roads. Looks like she trekked all the way through France, Italy, and Switzerland."

I was sitting on the passenger side, when my foot knocked something under the seat. I reached down and, very carefully, dragged out the object and examined it. A wooden toy soldier, made of cylindrical pegs all threaded through with string, connecting the forearms, upper arms, lower legs, thighs, feet, hands, and torso to the head, so that if you pulled up his hat, you could make his arms and legs jump at the elbow and knee joints, and his little round head wobbled back and forth, all making an amusing clacking noise. He had painted black eyes and a moustache, and a red nose and mouth and apple-red cheeks.

"Look, Jeremy!" I said, playing with the strings. "It's a toy soldier."

"Is it valuable?" he asked.

"Not terribly. They're pretty common, but it's old; I'd say it was made on the Continent between the two world wars"—I turned the soldier upside down so I could see the bottoms of his black-booted feet—"Yes, in France."

Jeremy was checking out the trunk of the car, which he called "the boot," where he found a picnic basket, outfitted in wicker and leather with old crystal champagne flutes in it and an ancient rusty winescrew and some old salt and pepper shakers.

"Could this buggy actually be drivable again?" I asked.

"Of course," he said. I liked the idea of tootling around slowly in a car, instead of rushing about to run errands. Jeremy patted the car affectionately as he walked past it. For pete's sake, he didn't even act this excited over the villa.

We continued our tour of the garage, with Jeremy going around announcing whatever else he found—rusty rakes, shovels and other gardening equipment, old folding chairs. I kept taking notes as we had with the house, for the inventory of the estate. But I began to feel a creeping, familiar feeling of foreboding stealing over me, there in the presence of Great-Aunt Penelope's loyal old auto, which had been young and vital when she was. Now the car was rusting away, still waiting for a driver who would never come back. It struck me now, in a more real way, that Aunt Penelope, who had once been so alive, was gone. And if she could die, then so could I, and Jeremy, and everybody I knew and loved.

Erik calls this Historian's Melancholy. It hits you at odd times, but you know it when it strikes. Every so often, when you're sitting in the dead zone of the library where all the old books end up, or an antiques shop when you come across an old pocket-watch engraved from one stranger to another with a dedication that was so personal to the owner but means nothing to anybody else—all at once it dawns on you that these are really just the used, worn-out detritus of some dead person's life. Whose owner was just like you, believing he'd live forever.

And suddenly the dank smell, the darkness and the dust freak you out and you want to run as fast as you can, outdoors into the light, where you can gulp lots of air and reassure yourself that you're not dead yet. Erik says it's healthy—because it's life warning you that death is no good, that you've come too close, and you the living shouldn't be wallowing in the dust of the dead, but should be out conducting your own life in the sunlight. (And drinking and carousing, Timothy would add.)

I didn't run out of the garage, but I fell silent. "Well!" Jeremy exclaimed, dusting off his hands, when he was done. I handed him the pages of my inventory notes, and he said that Severine would review it and her office would type it up officially. With great reverence he closed the garage doors and brought down the wooden arm that held them shut.

"You okay?" he inquired, looking quizzical. "You're awfully quiet."

"Yes," I said, glad to be outside with other living things, like those fragrant blossoms and stalwart trees. I thought of Aunt Penelope, with her deep, throaty laugh and her love of gossip. I said, "Life is awfully short, isn't it? One minute Aunt Penelope's a gay young flapper, and the next thing you know . . ."

Light broke across his face, and he took me by the hand and said,

"I know. But come on, darling. Brace up, Aunt Penelope would say. We've miles to go before we sleep. Let's take one last look out the back before we go."

We crossed the lawn, which was already wet with dew or whatever it is that steals across the grass at night. The sun's golden path on the water had vanished; now the moon left a silver trail in its place. You could imagine silvery fish swimming under that silvery trail, on their way out to the wider sea. We paused, gazing in companionable silence, and the sky grew darker around us, but like children we didn't really notice until suddenly, it seemed, it was night. The flowers began to give off that mysteriously intense night scent. The air had the mingled songs of late birds, cicadas, crickets, and I thought I might even have heard an owl hoot.

And then, while we stood there, lights started to go on, one by one at first, in the other villas around us. There was something sweet and comforting about seeing other homes nestled into the rocks and cliffs, lighting their lamps and twinkling at us like stars. Signs of life, and hope, like votive candles in a dark church. Finally it was dark enough to make us both sigh like kids who know they have to go indoors now. Jeremy shone his circle of light ahead of us.

As we crossed the lawn I mused that Jeremy would move in here someday, with a new wife, surely, and they'd have kids scampering on the lawn who'd have to be called in at night. One of them would be sent out to the garage to greet me, dotty old maiden aunt Penny, who'd come sputtering up in her silly old car to visit. I could see it now, how hard I'd work to be funny and cheerful. The image made me sick.

Jeremy put his hand on my shoulder to guide me, keeping me closer to him in the dark. "You always used to have scratches on your legs and scrapes on your knees," he said. "I'm not going to let you fall down on my watch, or your mother will have my head."

He opened the car door for me on my side and shone his light into the car, then closed the door after I got in. I saw him cross in front of the car with his light guiding him. Then he climbed into his seat, switched off the flashlight, and started the car.

"Well? What do you think?" he said, as he turned the car around to head out.

"It was awfully sweet of her to give us both a place to live. She could have sold it all off and socked it away in a bank and then left it to some charity or some memorial to herself," I said.

Jeremy glanced at me as if he sensed something. "We were her family, and she cared about that," he said. Then he added, quite deliberately, "I promised you a good dinner, and I know just the place. If it's still there. It's in the old town, in Nice. They make an excellent beef *daube*—it's like a stew in red wine, served with ravioli. It's a specialty there, a perfect combination of Italian and French. You and I are going to have a fantastic meal."

Chapter Eleven

I THINK IT WAS COLETTE WHO SAID THAT ALL SORROWS OF THE HEART can be cured with food. Well, perhaps she was right. When the man who does the cooking greets you as if he's genuinely glad that you've come to his restaurant, which on the outside looks like a hole-in-the-wall in a crumbling building off a cobbled street, but on the inside is all warmly decorated with red walls and white tablecloths and flickering candlelight; and you are encouraged to work your way slowly through a meal, course by course, with waiters flitting quietly like angels, their presence delicate and unobtrusive when they appear at your side just as you want more wine, or to change the forks and knives (which come from a locked china cupboard's drawers) as a herald of each new plate of food, which they handle in an unfussy but respectful way as if it were sacred; and when the food is so spectacularly good that it dawns on you slowly that you have died and gone to heaven; and when the wine is cool and soft and works its magic slowly, gently, like the lapping sea—well, you can't be melancholy at all. You can only be glad that you were born in the first place and are lucky enough to be here on this night, at this table, with this nice person sitting across from you who understands how you feel and is enjoying your company as much as the meal because, for once, the world is full of nothing but people of good will.

"Jeremy," I said gratefully, with my usual talent for foolish under-statement, "what a wonderful place. Thanks for bringing me here."

And because it was such a beautiful night, even my clumsy words didn't matter as much as the tone of my voice, which Jeremy heard and understood, and he looked happy that he'd succeeded in making me happy. I asked him how he knew so much about Aunt Penelope's car, and he was a little embarrassed to confess that as soon as he'd started earning enough money, the first thing he did was to go out and buy a Dragonetta auto for himself. Apparently the company still sold a limited new edition of them each year, made to look like the old model.

"I'll take you for a ride in it," he said. "If you promise to let me drive that car of yours."

When we were done, the proprietor, an elegant man with a bald head and alert dark eyes, walked us to the door with a genuine smile. He shook hands with Jeremy, and gently and lightly kissed my hand.

Then we walked to the Promenade des Anglais, another one of those elegant old boulevards where pedestrians can stroll along the beach and gaze at the gorgeous Mediterranean Sea. It was a warm night and everyone was there—couples with babies, elderly people, teenagers, young lovers—as if the earth was cupping us all in the palm of her hand.

"Beautiful here," Jeremy commented. "I heard that the bay around Nice is called the Bay of Angels. How come?" He peered at me. "Come on, I know you know. About all these historical bits. Go on, do one now."

"This isn't a parlor trick, you know," I said huffily. "It's my career. A little respect, please."

"I am in total *awe* of you," he assured me. "Go on. Why is the bay of Nice called the Bay of Angels?"

"Angel sharks," I said. "And they're not as dainty as they sound.

They kill. But the people who lived here down through the ages believed that they were blessed by them because the sharks chased away pirates and invaders—or ate them."

Jeremy grinned. "I don't know how you keep all these things stuffed inside that head of yours."

"How about you, with all your fancy legalese?" I teased him. "All that 'whereas' and 'the aforementioned.' I saw you in action at the reading of the will, remember? Very impressive indeed." We were laughing at each other, and people who passed by us smiled in knowing amusement.

But we had reached Jeremy's parked car, and, just as we climbed in, I had that terrible kind of moment when you go to collect your belongings and suddenly realize that something is missing. It feels like a hole in your stomach. "Oh, Jeremy!" I cried. "I lost my portfolio!"

I didn't say aloud that if I didn't find my portfolio I might as well kill myself, because it contained months of hard work that I could not possibly duplicate, sketches and swatches and notes and phone numbers and—

I didn't have to say it, because he heard the change in my tone of voice.

"Steady on," he said. "I know that you didn't bring it into the restaurant, because I would have told you to leave it in the car. So, it must still be in the car. It probably slipped off the backseat to the floor."

But we searched the rental car from stem to stern and, as I knew, the portfolio was not there. "Calmly, now, think where you last had it," Jeremy said, looking confident that we'd find it. And just as he spoke I remembered.

"In Aunt Penelope's garage," I said instantly. "I put it on the seat of the car."

Jeremy sighed. I knew enough about Englishmen not to be fooled by the mild, light nature of that sigh. From a man with his talent for reserve, it was the equivalent of anyone else screaming, "You're impossible! I'm full of fabulous wine and food and now you want me to drive all the way back on that treacherous road in the dark? And back again? We'll miss our plane, and we'll be totally exhausted and dusty and all the dinner magic will have worn off, so why did I spend all this money? I'd like to wring your neck!"

Of course he didn't say any of this, but I knew he had to be thinking it. What he did say was, "Well, we'll miss our flight back tonight. But perhaps it's just as well. We can stay in an hotel tonight and face London tomorrow."

He busied himself with making the arrangements via his mobile phone, then he lapsed into total silence for most of the way back to the villa. I could feel the black sky and sea echoing his moody, dark silence. But when we got off at Aunt Penelope's exit and he could feel that we'd made progress, he cheered up a little.

"I know a man in Monte Carlo who could tell you how much it would cost to get that car up and running and beautiful again," he said. "He used to have a dealership in Plymouth, but now he's in a sort of semi-retirement down here."

"Just for my own info, if I didn't fix it up, what's it worth?" I asked, pushing my luck.

Jeremy looked scornful. "You'd be an idiot not to fix it up." Then he duly considered my question. "If you didn't, someone like my friend would probably buy it for several thousand pounds. But that's just a fraction of what it could be worth."

As we headed down Aunt Penelope's driveway, a startled frog leapt across our path in the headlights and leapt again to safety. But Jeremy suddenly slammed on the brakes, cut the engine, and turned off his headlights.

"What's the matter?" I cried. "The frog's okay."

"Somebody's there," he said, nodding in the direction of the garage. "There's a light on, see?" In the silence we could hear men calling out to each other, and indeed I saw lights bobbing, as if somebody was carrying a lantern back and forth; and there were other lights not moving but fixed, glaring out at us. But we were in shadows, and since the men were talking above the roar of their own car, they didn't hear us turn into the far end of the long driveway.

Before I could stop him, Jeremy was out of the car and advancing on foot. I got out, too, out of pure cowardice because I didn't want to be left behind. I crept after Jeremy, who was walking off the path so that he'd be stepping on pine needles instead of noisy gravel. We proceeded quietly, then paused just close enough to see what was going on ahead of us.

A big, ugly truck was parked in the driveway at a crazy angle, its rear to the garage, its tail-lights aimed straight at the doors of the garage, which were flung wide open. As we watched, I saw, to my disbelief, that two men were actually pushing Aunt Penelope's car out of the garage. Apparently it was hard to push because two of its tires were flat as pancakes. Still, they had it pretty far along, just outside of the garage, and one of them had flung down a kind of ramp, as if they intended to push the car up into the open back end of the truck. I couldn't believe it. How could car thieves know about this place?

"Shouldn't we call the police?" I whispered. But Jeremy held up his palm to shush me. A third man, who'd been sitting in the front passenger side of the truck, was the one who evidently had been doing the shouting, because he was calling out now to the two men that were pushing the car. He sat with his door open and his legs dangling out the side, and he was smoking. He wore a white suit and a panama hat. As he hollered, a look of recognition crossed Jeremy's face, and then even I recognized the lazy, condescending voice.

"Mind the windshield, for Christ's sake!" he called out in a contemptuous tone. "And somebody had better start steering it now!"

"It's Rollo!" I breathed. Jeremy took my hand and led me back to his car. We slipped inside, and he got on his phone and murmured quietly into it, speaking some combo of English and French. When he got off the phone, he looked grimly satisfied.

"Sit tight," he said. "They can't get out past us. Severine's assistant is going to have the cops down here right away."

"What if they have guns?" I quavered. "They could shoot their way past us."

"Then stop chattering like a magpie," Jeremy said pleasantly. "Or you'll alert them to the fact that we're sitting here." Then he added, "They don't have guns."

"How do you know?" I hissed. "My mother says Rollo had a drug habit. Maybe still does. Those guys could be—"

"Shut up, they don't have guns," Jeremy said maddeningly. He wouldn't say how he knew, and in fact he wouldn't say anything else, he just kept repeating that one phrase, as if saying it over and over would prove it true, which proved to me that he didn't know. Men. This is what they do when they have no empirical evidence, when their prized logic and rationality fail them, when they are going only on instinct but refuse to say so.

I'm guessing that it took about twenty minutes for the police to come swooping down the driveway behind us. Jeremy heard them and turned on his car lights, so they'd see us, but even so, they came awfully close and their cars squealed noisily to a halt. Then with flashlights bobbing, all four of them ran down the drive and caught Rollo red-handed.

The three thieves froze in the lights, but recovered quickly. The two men who were helping Rollo took off like jackrabbits into the darkness. Two cops went after them, but Rollo just calmly sat there sideways in his car seat and smoked his cigarette.

And he smoked through the whole thing. He smoked through all the gesticulations and translations, especially when Severine's assistant, Louis—a charming young man with curly black hair—arrived, all dressed up for a night out. Rollo calmly and arrogantly made Louis do all the translating for him while Rollo insisted, unbelievably, that he had come all this way, and moved the car, because he was trying to get at a big, old-fashioned bobsled at the back of the garage, which, he insisted languidly, belonged to him.

You really can't argue with a crazy man. The gendarmes tried it, Severine's assistant tried it, and even Jeremy scornfully attempted it, but when someone is sticking to a crazy story you simply cannot carry on a rational conversation. You can say, as they all did, "You must be kidding. You hired a rig, and moving men, and dragged this car out, just so you could come and claim a rusty bobsled that may or may not have belonged to you when you were a kid?"

And you can say, as I did in a hurriedly whispered conference with Jeremy, that there was no goddamned bobsled in that garage a few hours ago when we were there taking inventory, but it was to no avail. Serenely and leisurely, Rollo insisted that the bobsled had been there all along. And he pointed at it—an old bobsled, made to carry a whole bunch of people—which had his name clearly lettered on it, in paint old enough to make it passably plausible that he hadn't just painted it on this minute. I guess he could have dragged it out of the house, from a dark corner in the basement, maybe. But not from the garage. As for the rented truck, he shrugged, saying that the rental agency didn't have anything smaller. He'd intended only to take what was his—the beloved bobsled of his youth.

At this point there were about sixty seconds when it was possible to speak to Jeremy without the others hearing, and I whispered urgently to him that my portfolio was still sitting there on the car seat. I hated to bring this up right now, because I wasn't sure if he wanted them to know that we'd been there earlier.

"Don't be silly. We came here to take inventory," Jeremy said. But when he went to retrieve it, this created an uproar just the same, as Jeremy reached in for my portfolio and Rollo noted it and said in an exaggerated voice, "O-*ho*!" and then everybody started gesticulating and translating all over again.

I took the portfolio from Jeremy and locked it in his rental car. In due course the policemen pushed Aunt Penelope's car back into the garage. They had to do it, since Rollo's slippery friends had disappeared into the darkness and nobody could find them. Severine's assistant produced a padlock, and the garage was locked. All this was done amid tremendous arguing in French, which at first I tried to translate to myself but then gave up.

There was a brief, strange lull, during which Severine's assistant was explaining things to the cops, and nobody was paying any attention to Rollo or me. Rollo took advantage of this moment, reached out, and pulled me by the elbow to his side. He had by now risen from his seat and was still blowing smoke into the air, and into my face as he put his mouth near my ear to speak in a low, urgent murmur.

"Listen, my girl. Don't trust that fellow Jeremy. Mother had him checked out by a private detective and believe me, he is *not* who you think he is."

His tone surprised me, because, unbelievable as his words were, they had the odd ring of truth to them, which I could not ignore. I looked straight at Rollo now. His watery eyes with their pouches of fatigue beneath them looked genuinely distressed. "I'm only looking out for you. We Laidleys must take care of each other. He's very charming with women, this fellow. But don't let him charm you out of what's rightfully yours."

Jeremy looked up now, saw Rollo talking urgently to me, and strode over to us. "Is he bothering you?" Jeremy demanded.

At that moment his phone rang. It was Severine, and she was so agitated that even though I couldn't make out the actual words, I could hear her voice chattering rapid-speed without pausing once to let Jeremy speak. But Jeremy didn't look like he wanted to speak. His face suddenly went pale, and his eyes kind of glazed over. He listened for a long time.

Rollo was staring at us so hard that his gaze, like the beam of a headlight, compelled me to look up. He nodded significantly at me, as if he'd just been vindicated. I looked from him to Jeremy and back again. For the first time, I felt somehow afraid of them both, as if suddenly I was totally among strangers.

Everyone else had fallen silent, looking expectantly at Jeremy for some sign of what to do next. Jeremy spoke haltingly, in English mixed with French again, to Severine's assistant, and handed him the phone so that Severine could talk to her guy. He spoke briefly, gave Jeremy back his phone, and moved quickly to inform the police of something. Then, very abruptly, everyone turned to their cars and looked as if the party was over and they were all going home.

"What happened?" I asked Jeremy. He didn't answer me. He just reached into his car for my portfolio and suitcase, and handed them to Louis, Severine's assistant.

"Can you drive Penny to the hotel?" he asked brusquely. Louis nodded.

Jeremy turned to me. "Listen, Penny," he said rapidly, "I've got to talk to Severine. And get back to London on the first crate I can stow away on. But there's no need to drag you into this all-night fiasco. You're already booked on a flight back to London tomorrow. Rupert will pick you up in London, at the airport. We think it's best if you stay at Aunt Penelope's apartment until you hear from my office. Harold will call you and explain everything."

"But—" I sputtered in disbelief.

"It's better this way," he said in a low tone.

"Jeremy!" I said, exasperated.

"Oh, for God's sake, Penny, get in the car and be quiet," he said tersely, in a tone I'd absolutely never heard him use, not once, not even when we were kids. It was an agonized voice, as if he'd just been stabbed in the gut and he was pleading with me not to make things worse. And then he turned and strode off angrily and got into his car.

I felt another hand at my elbow, this one tentative and respectful. It was Severine's assistant, Louis.

"Come," he said, with perfect gentle manners. "Theez way, please."

I followed him into his little Renault. "What on earth is going on?" I demanded as he turned the car out of the driveway and we headed to the road.

"Rollo, he is going to contest the will," Louis said in his polite, respectful voice.

"But Jeremy expected that," I said. I peered at the kid. "What just happened back there?" I persisted. Louis tried to shrug and act dumb at first, but I kept looking him in the eye and repeated my question and I said finally, "Louis. I know you know. Now tell me."

A look crossed his face as if he knew the jig was up. While we waited at a traffic signal at the edge of town, he turned to me with a very delicate, sympathetic expression.

"Zey are saying zat Jeremy is not a blood relative," he said simply.

"That's insane!" I exclaimed. Louis paused, as if waiting to see if I was going to splutter some more. When I didn't, he proceeded with, "Zey say Jeremy's father was another man, not Mr. Laidley."

"That's the dumbest thing I ever heard," I said. "Rollo must be desperate. But even if it were true, what's that got to do with the price of potato chips?"

"Pardon?" Louis asked, puzzled.

"I mean, what's being a blood relative got to do with the inheritance?"

"Ah!" Louis said as he steered the car on the corniche road. "Well, French law, you see, it eez very, very complicated. When people fight over estates, ze blood relatives could, perhaps, have an advantage. Maybe a court will find that he cannot have so big a piece of the pie, *comprenez-vous?*"

"Shit, yeah, I get it," I said, astounded. I gazed wildly out the window. Here we were again, zipping along at the edge of a prehistoric cliff in the dark. Unwillingly, I recalled Rollo's insinuating tone, and his words about Jeremy took on new meaning.

"We are here," Louis said, as he pulled up to a pleasant little hotel. He jumped out and saw me to the front desk to verify that they had my room.

"Don't worry," he assured me as he left me at the elevator. "Tomorrow it will all be explained to you." The day's events were catching up to me, and I was too exhausted to argue. Once I got into my room and saw the pretty bed with fluffy pillows, I gave in and fell asleep almost immediately.

Chapter Twelve

B UT THE RETURN TRIP TO LONDON TURNED INTO AN ALL-DAY AFFAIR. The plane had to make an unscheduled stop in Paris because of mechanical "difficulties." We were herded off the plane and had to hang around the terminal until they could find us another flight. Even after we boarded the new plane, it sat on the runway, queuing up behind others waiting for takeoff.

That gave me plenty of time to think. Could it really be that Uncle Peter was not Jeremy's father? I remembered every single word Jeremy said about Uncle Peter being a difficult dad; and about "we Laidleys" being a cautious, stodgy bunch; and how Aunt Penelope cared about leaving her possessions to family members. I knew what it meant to Jeremy to be the protector of this family. And how he'd said that paternity was a bigger issue in France than England, but he said it in confident tones, as if he had nothing to worry about.

When we finally landed in London, I spotted Jeremy's assistant, Rupert. He looked relieved and happy to bundle me off into his car.

"We heard about your flight being delayed," he said, pleasantly but authoritatively. "Jeremy left instructions that I take you back to your aunt's flat. Harold will call you—" He glanced at his watch, then said,

"Well, he's out dining with a client away from the office now. He'll have to ring you tomorrow morning."

By then I was fed up with the whole pack of lawyers that had been pushing me around, Jeremy included. "Where the hell is Jeremy?" I demanded. "What's going on?"

Rupert said softly, "He didn't come into the office today, but I'm sure he'll call you as soon as he can."

Something in his tone made me feel like I was being managed, and I didn't like it. I rummaged in my bag and found my address book. My mother, in her infinite wisdom, had given me the address and phone number of Aunt Sheila "just in case" I needed help while abroad. My mother is the only one I know who has always been prepared for national emergencies, terrorist attacks, plague, nuclear war—you name it and she's got a contingency plan for it. So I called Aunt Sheila on my mobile phone. She answered on the second ring.

"Aunt Sheila? It's your niece, Penny. I was with Jeremy yesterday when he got some shocking news. I'm heading toward your apartment, and I'm coming up right now because I can't go into further detail on the telephone. So please tell your doorman I'm on my way in."

I was using my bossiest, most confident voice, which I am able to summon only on occasions when I feel bossy and confident, which are very rare. But I was tired of being bullied, lied to, and generally out-snooted. I wasn't feeling automatically inferior anymore, and it must have been audible, because Aunt Sheila said in the most compliant and respectful voice I'd ever heard her use, "Of course, darling. Come right over. I'll ring them downstairs to let you in."

"Fine," I said briskly, and hung up, then turned to Rupert, who gaped at me. I leaned forward and gave the driver Aunt Sheila's address.

"There's been a slight change of plans," I said to Rupert, pleasantly but crisply. Rupert looked alarmed.

"But Jeremy wants—" he began. I gave him a dead-on, dead-eyed look.

"I'll give you my mobile phone number," I said. "If Jeremy wants to talk to me—which he isn't doing right now—he can reach me day or night. So can anybody else who wants to explain this whole clambake to me." I handed Rupert the number just as we pulled up in front of Jeremy's mother's apartment building.

"But—where shall I say I dropped you tonight?" he stammered.

"Have you got a key to Aunt Penelope's place?" I asked. He quickly handed me a couple of beauties—a heavy gold one with an ornate curlicue at the end, which was for the main door, and another similar but lighter one for Aunt Penelope's inside door.

"You *will* stay on there, won't you?" Rupert asked pleadingly. "Jeremy says you can remain there as long as you like while you're making your assessment of the belongings. And there will be papers to file for the English will tomorrow, which will need your signature."

"Of course," I said. "I'll be there, as of later tonight. Thanks for the lift, Rupert," I added, gently but firmly. "Tell Jeremy it's rude to dash off like that, and if he wants to know more about what I'm up to, he can bloody well ask me himself. At any rate, tell him I expect to hear back from him, personally, *tout de suite.*"

Part Five

Chapter Thirteen

IT WAS DARK OUTSIDE BY THE TIME I REACHED AUNT SHEILA'S APART-
ment. She came quickly to the door when I knocked. She was
wearing a gold and red silk caftan, and flat little black and gold velvet
slippers. Her blonde hair was pulled back at either side with black
enamel hair combs, and she was smoking a cigarette. Her whole look
seemed sort of Moroccan and made me think of rich heiresses in the
mid-1960s jetting to North Africa to throw wild parties in crumbling
palaces with marble pools, where their friends reclined on pillows and
passed the hookah. But then, it is a hazard of my trade to instantly
catalog and attribute time periods.

The curtains in her drawing room were pulled back this time,
revealing a big window with a night-time view of the Thames. One
could make out the venerable buildings from the lights around them,
and the boats strung with lights like jeweled necklaces, silently gliding past.

"Penny, darling," Aunt Sheila drawled, not quite looking at me
directly. "Always lovely to see you, dear, and you sounded *so* upset that
I simply *had* to climb out of bed."

She was overdoing that nonchalant yet aggrieved tone, but she'd
accomplished a lot with her brief speech, designed to make me feel

like a rude buffalo for intruding on my elderly auntie. I was supposed to start stumbling through apologies and feeling foolish for insisting that we had something so important to talk about that it couldn't wait till morning. And normally that's exactly what I'd have done. But tonight I wasn't so susceptible to games of manners.

"Jeremy got some pretty astounding news last night," I said, not yet sinking into the chair she gestured for me to take. "And he got it from Rollo. So he dumped me off in France, and nobody will tell me what's going on."

She looked momentarily taken aback. "Would you like a drink, dear?" she asked.

"No," I said rudely and deliberately. "What I'd like is a straight answer from somebody around here. Is it true that Uncle Peter was not Jeremy's father?"

She seemed unsurprised by the question as she poured herself a little glass of gin, into which she dropped a tiny peel of lemon. She sipped it delicately, having placed her cigarette onto an ivory-colored elephant figurine which, it turned out, was an ashtray and a cigarette holder combined. You laid the cigarette across the back of the elephant, whose ears held it firmly in place. At the elephant's feet was a little trough where the ashes collected.

"Yes," she said quietly, tucking one leg under her as she sat sideways on the sofa across from my chair. "It *is* true." This time I did sit down, and I gazed at her wonderingly.

"But Peter adopted Jeremy, perfectly legally," she added. "I thought we'd arranged to keep those records private. I don't know how Dorothy's dreadful people got their hands on them."

"Then—who's his real father?" I blurted out. The whole situation was a strange dream that I was struggling to wake from. If I felt this way, I could imagine how Jeremy felt.

Aunt Sheila retrieved her cigarette from the elephant before answering me in a tone that was level and unoffended. Her gaze was deliberate and direct now, but her chin was raised just a trifle defiantly.

"His name was Anthony Principe," she said calmly. "American, actually. His parents were Italian-American. I met him in the late sixties, when he came to London on his own."

"What was he doing in London? School?" I asked, prodding her to continue.

She shook her head. "He was a guitarist and singer in a rock band. His group came for the music scene. They cut a few records. They were pretty good."

"A guitarist?" I repeated. "Ohhh!" You might say it struck a chord. I was thinking of Jeremy's garage band, and his passion for rock and roll, which always drove his father—Uncle Peter, that is—crazy. The feeling that this was all a dream was evaporating now, like a fog, and I began to believe, for the first time, that it could possibly be true.

Aunt Sheila was watching me warily, like a cat. "Yes," she said softly. "Guitarist. Just like Jeremy. I thought about that a lot, when he was making all that noise rehearsing with his friends. I thought how familiar the whole scene was. I suppose Jeremy could have inherited that from Tony. Music is a hereditary thing, isn't it?" This was entirely too casual for me.

"Maybe it explains all those fights he had with Uncle Peter," I said crossly. "We just thought Uncle Peter hated rock and roll. There was a little more to it, wasn't there?"

"Oh, no," she said. "Peter was always a Burt Bacharach man. It had nothing to do with Tony, because he didn't know Tony personally, didn't know about his music."

God, she was maddening. And it struck me that in this conversation, and the one we'd previously had over lunch, and in fact, probably always, she referred to her husband as "Peter" and never as "Jeremy's father." I hadn't noticed that before.

"So—what happened to Jeremy's real father, then?" I asked.

"Tony got drafted into the Vietnam War, you see . . . the year that Jeremy was born . . ." She had started so confidently, but then her voice trailed off as if she couldn't trust herself to say another word. I felt a stab of sympathy, watching her struggle not to let her voice reveal what was already evident in her eyes.

"Did he die?" I asked, after a moment of dread.

"First he was—wounded," she said. Her voice was small. She looked away from me now, so all I could stare at was her profile, elegant as Helen of Troy. She gazed at the end of her cigarette, then continued, "Sent to a veterans' hospital, which was beastly for him. When he was released he came back to London with me. But he was weakened by the whole thing. Pneumonia was what finally killed him, but it was the war, all right. It broke his heart. He hated to do—cruel things, pointless things. He was such a gentle, sweet man. Innocent."

I sat back, flabbergasted. Then I thought of Jeremy. "For heaven's sake, Aunt Sheila," I said, exasperated. "Why didn't you ever *tell* Jeremy who his real father was? Especially after Uncle Peter died? People do tell their kids such things, when they're old enough to handle it. Don't you think he had a right to know?"

She paused, flicking ash from her cigarette into the ashtray.

"I always meant to," she said mildly. "There never seemed to be a good time."

"Oh, geez!" I said. "You've got to be kidding!"

Her mouth dropped open slightly, wonderingly. She'd never really seen me behave this aggressively; to her I'd always been her meek, slightly awed American niece.

And that was another thing. "Jeremy's part American!" I said somewhat accusingly. After all, she'd taught him to be a snob, against, as it turned out, his own roots.

She smiled at me tolerantly. And now I observed tiny age lines at the corners of her eyes and mouth that I hadn't noticed at the luncheon meeting, when she seemed so dazzling and youthful to me. But perhaps I was always prepared to be dazzled by her. Maybe I needed to have a slightly snobby aunt whose approval, so elusive to get, was a way of setting goals to make myself more chic, more worldly, more grown up.

"Yes," she said gently, "Jeremy is American, too. But thanks to Peter, he grew up as any other Englishman. Peter never made Jeremy feel adopted, but always part of his family. And you see, I'm rather the black sheep of my family, so Jeremy didn't get to know them very well. It really meant a lot to him to be part of your family. He identified with Peter much more than you'd think, in spite of all their fighting. He was very fond of your Grandmother Beryl. And he got to know your Aunt Penelope a bit, at the end of her life, when she put him in charge of her estate. Don't you see how much this family means to him?"

I couldn't argue with that. I knew that it was all a big part of Jeremy's identity. "How come you didn't have any children with Uncle Peter?" I said cautiously. I knew I shouldn't ask. But she was in a mood to tell.

"I had to have a hysterectomy," she said simply. "And Peter, I want you to know, was wonderful during that time. And he was wonderful about adopting Jeremy. It was his idea. He said he never wanted the boy to 'get caught short in the world.' He wasn't just talking about money. Upbringing, he said. He wanted Jeremy to have what he called 'a good foundation' in life. They really were like father and son. Why should I take that away from either one of them? They worked out their differences, which they might not have done, if I'd given Jeremy an excuse not to take Peter seriously as a father."

"Did you love Uncle Peter?" I asked bluntly. That really wasn't fair. She gave me a look that might have been followed by a "tsk-tsk" but wasn't.

"Yes," she said. "But in a calmer way. I loved his whole family, because they were so much more tolerant than my own. And keen for Peter to marry me. Perhaps they thought he'd end up a solitary old bachelor. I was fond of them all. But Tony was—he was—"

Well, she didn't have to finish that one. She returned to her cigarette. And then I realized that I'd never seen her smoke before. Not in the past, and not at lunch the other day. Yet here she was, in her silk caftan and her cute little velvet slippers, with her hair perfectly done, looking so self-possessed—but she was probably a nervous wreck inside.

"Have you talked to Jeremy at all?" I asked, more sympathetically now.

"Oh, God," she groaned. "That French girl he works with put him on a private plane that made three stops before he landed in London. So naturally he was fit to be tied. He came roaring in here, firing off questions. I'm nearly prostrate with answering questions."

"I'm sorry," I said, momentarily reverting to my apologetic self.

"Oh, I don't mean *you*, dear," she said in amusement. "Yours are a relief compared to the way he behaved. I thought he was going to wring my neck. He'd barely let me answer a question before he'd fire off another. He really didn't want to listen, I think, beyond just obtaining his lawyerly facts. I tried to tell him how dreadfully sorry I am that it came out like this, but of course . . ." Her voice trailed off again, but this time she stubbed out her cigarette briskly and leaned forward, looking into my face searchingly.

"Maybe you could tell him what I've told you," she said urgently. "He listens to you. But then you two were always a little sweet on each other, I think."

A sudden hot flush engulfed me. Any time an older woman tells you that she's noticed you being dopey about her son, it's bound to make you feel like the world's biggest fool.

"You haven't really told me everything," I said hurriedly. "Was Tony in London when Jeremy was born?"

"No, Tony was already in Vietnam," she said. "We'd been living in a little house with the drummer from the band and his girlfriend. Jeremy was born there. Later, I had it converted into a home for veterans. It's still a soldiers' home today." She sighed. "Unfortunately there are still war veterans in this day and age. They seem to me to get younger with every war. I help raise money to keep it going, and I still look in to see if the volunteers need anything."

"Were you and—the drummer—romantically involved, later on?" I asked.

Aunt Sheila looked truly shocked. "Of course not," she said. "He got married and had a family of his own. He took a job composing music for TV, and he still helps me raise money for the home and look after it, that's all. Good heavens, wherever did you get such an idea?"

So, I realized, Aunt Sheila's weekly "tryst," as Jeremy had bitterly described it, was in reality a charity visit, the very "good works" he ridiculed.

"From Jeremy," I said. "He knows that you went there every week. If you'd only told him why . . ."

"One thing about you Americans," Aunt Sheila drawled, "you do have a tiresome habit of telling people that they should discuss their feelings more. Why is that? Is it all the therapy you go in for? Or is anything less than a happy ending such an unbearable failure to you?"

"Your American son is up a creek without a paddle," I said a bit tartly. "He could even lose his inheritance now. If you keep being secretive, you're only helping Rollo. So will you please give me Jeremy's address and telephone number? I'd like to help him, if I can."

I was tired and cranky now, and she responded by quickly giving me the information I asked for. I wrote it down, and then something occurred to me.

"Aunt Sheila," I asked, "did Jeremy's father ever—see—Jeremy? You say he returned . . ."

She looked up sharply. Then, without a word, she rose from the sofa and disappeared briefly. She came back with an old-fashioned photo, slightly crinkled, with scalloped white edges, the way they used to develop film in the 1960s.

"Keep it for him, will you? Show it to him when you think he's in a receptive mood. But please don't lose it," she said in a heartfelt tone I'd never heard from her before. "And don't let Jeremy tear it up in a fit of pique. But if you can calm him down, he may want to see it."

It was a black-and-white photo of a slim man, about nineteen years old, with longish dark hair worn shaggy, like a rock star. He was wearing bell-bottom blue jeans and a white shirt with embroidery on it, and was sitting at a dinky but clean kitchen table. Despite his shaggy style, he was one of those clean-looking, open-faced, cheerful American males; but he also looked a little thin and pale, his eyes a bit sunken and weary, as if he had indeed been ill. Still, he seemed happy. He was balancing an infant on the tabletop, holding him in a standing position, and they gazed at each other, profile to profile, in mutual fascination.

"This baby is Jeremy?" I asked in delight, after peering at the infant. Then I glanced up quickly at Aunt Sheila. Her eyes were unmistakably misty, but her voice was steady.

"With Tony," she said. "He was absolutely smitten with Jeremy. He died two weeks after that picture was taken. Jeremy was only a year old."

I kept looking at the photo in the cab as I rode to Aunt Penelope's apartment. Aunt Sheila was a little concerned when she heard I was spending the night there. She said she thought all the utilities were left on, but if I discovered that anything had been disconnected, I should not hesitate to call her.

The house was dark when the cab pulled up. The keys that Rupert had given me slid into the locks perfectly and turned without a struggle. I pushed open first the main mahogany door, then the inside one, and fumbled in the dark inside the flat, until I found a light switch on the wall that caused a wall sconce to cast a soft glow. I went from room to room, snapping on more lights.

I saw that, in her old age, Great-Aunt Penelope had been neat and well-organized. There were clean sheets and towels in the linen closet, and her dishes were stacked in orderly rows in their cupboards. There was a modern coffeemaker, a new bottle of white wine, a pantry with unopened packages of tea, sugar, crackers, tinned ham, marmalade and jam.

I'd thought I would feel faintly ghoulish, pussyfooting around there, but instead I felt as if I were being looked after by my aunt, and given shelter at night in a strange city. I made tea and crackers with jam, more as comfort food than from hunger. I ate it all gratefully at the little kitchen table. Then I tidied up, using the clean white dish towels with their stitched design of blue trim and red cherries. By the time I was done, it was midnight, and I was so tired that after making up Aunt Penelope's big canopied bed with new sheets, I tumbled into it and fell deeply asleep, not waking once in the night.

Chapter Fourteen

A T NINE THIRTY THE NEXT MORNING I DISCOVERED THAT THE TELE-
phone worked, because it shrilled from its odd place on the
dressing table. I stumbled across the room to pick up the alabaster-
colored receiver, and I heard Harold's voice in my ear.

"Jeremy's partner," he said. "You remember."

I recalled the silver-haired gentleman who'd read the will. "Just
to let you know that I'm sending you some papers to sign," he said
briskly. "A formality, regarding the English estate, because your mother
wants you to have the apartment. I e-mailed your father's lawyer in
the States, and your parents have signed off on this. Rupert will bring
the papers by, along with his preliminary assessment, which you can
use to evaluate what's in the apartment. Okeh?" he concluded, with a
note of finality, as if he were eager to ring off. I stopped him.

"Where's Jeremy?" I demanded. "I need to talk to him."

There was a pause. "Ah. Well. Jeremy won't be coming into the office today. Feeling a bit under the weather. You understand. He thinks
it's better for all concerned if I handle this matter from now on."

"Harold," I said quickly, fearing he'd hang up too soon, "what's
going on with the French will? Is it true that Jeremy can somehow
lose his inheritance?"

Harold said carefully, "The whole thing's absurd, of course. People update and change their wills all the time, especially the elderly, when they outlive the people they'd originally left the estate to. But there are many ways to make trouble among heirs. French law is very complicated and a bit archaic, especially, for instance, in divorce cases. A second wife, for example, could be challenged by the first wife's children, and end up with practically nothing."

"Yes, well, there are no wives here," I said rather crisply. He was generalizing, as lawyers and doctors do when they think you're getting too curious, as if too much knowledge is bad for you. "What's Rollo up to? Is he trying to take the villa from Jeremy? Can he do that?"

"They're trying everything," Harold said. "Including saying that Jeremy ingratiated himself with your great-aunt at the end of her life when she was vulnerable, and talked her into leaving the bulk of the French estate to him."

My mind was working on it, turning it over and over like a dog, trying to get a grip on it. "Does it matter that Jeremy's real father—isn't—" I asked haltingly.

Harold said, "It shouldn't—but it doesn't help, either. People contest wills for all kinds of ridiculous reasons, and even if it doesn't stick, it can be a damned nuisance and delay what could have been a very smooth process. Look, it's all very complicated, and nothing's been decided yet, and I certainly will keep your parents up on every development as it occurs—"

"Correct me if I'm wrong," I said, "but my parents have nothing to do with the French estate. I'm the only other heir in this fracas, other than Rollo. Right?"

"Yes," said Harold, "unless your mother wants to sue for a share."

"Ho, ho," I said. "Look, I'm just trying to help Jeremy hold on to what's his."

"As we all are," said Harold. "We won't let it go without a fight,

I assure you. And your own inheritance in France, too, of course." I caught the irony in his tone. He was making fun of my rusty little car and snake-infested garage.

"Rollo must think that car's worth something, if he tried to steal it," I said stoutly.

"We think he was trying to remove it before anyone else knew it was there and could list it as the 'contents' that you're entitled to. He's fond of antiques, I'm told. Believe me, Severine has the whole thing under control," Harold said in his best leave-the-driving-to-the-professionals tone. "Jeremy trusts her eminently, and has left the matter in our hands. Of course, if you wish to hire your own solicitor—"

That's another thing lawyers and doctors do. Threaten to quit on you if you question their methods. "I would be remiss if I didn't ask these questions," I said calmly.

"Oh, of course, of course," Harold said smoothly. "In the meanwhile, the best advice I can give you is to get back to business-as-usual in your own life. All too often, people make a mistake of dropping everything they normally do, to devote their entire time and energy to the legal aspects of the estate settlement. But you don't want to neglect your other personal and business affairs. Best not to over-focus on this." I'd listened patiently but concluded that yes, he was patronizing me for being young and inquisitive.

"As for Jeremy," I persisted, "I still want to speak to him. It's personal," I added.

"I shall convey that to his secretary, who will certainly see that he gets your message," Harold said in a slightly reproving but polite tone, and we hung up.

I was already fumbling around in my handbag for Jeremy's home number. I dialed it right away, and his answering machine picked up on the third ring. Very unceremoniously it said in Jeremy's recorded voice, "Leave a message at the tone, please. I'll get back to you."

At the beep I said, "Jeremy. It's Penny." I stopped short. I had the most uncanny idea that he was there, listening. I tried to brush it off, but it was a powerful impression, based on absolutely nothing except a feeling.

"Jeremy," I said again, "are you there? Harold says you're not feeling well. So where else would you be?" I waited. Honestly, I could feel him listening. I said, "Look, Jeremy, I've got some information you need, about a lot of things. And I need to hear from you. Please call me at Aunt Penelope's." I left the number and my mobile phone number and e-mail address, even though I knew he had it all. I hung up, feeling unsatisfied.

Chapter Fifteen

Something stupendous occurred to me in Aunt Penelope's old-fashioned bathtub, after I'd been experimenting with the water taps. The tub was huge, took forever to fill, and did not have a metal shower overhead, but instead had some archaic rubber-showerhead-with-tube contraption, attachable to the spout of the tub, which you had to use by hand like a garden hose and which kept popping off just when you thought you were up and running. I cursed a great deal because I got shampoo in my eyes. Finally I calmed down and lay back meditatively. And then it hit me, genius that I am.

"Jesus Christ," I said. "Jeremy's not my cousin."

I sat bolt upright, and sloshed water all over the floor. Very rapidly, I flashed through every memory I had of him, as if I were flipping a deck of cards that formed a moving-picture show. I felt several stabs of acute embarrassment along the way, blushing deeper and deeper with hot waves of mortification.

First of all, those childhood games of Secret Agents, which had lulled me into a false sense of security with him. He'd seen me at my most gangly, dopey self. However, this was mild compared to the utter anguish that swept over me at the recollection of recent conversations we'd had, about my love life, my track record with guys, the breakup with Paul, etc. These were harmless enough conversations to have with a cousin; like strangers on a train, you could confide and be sure that everything you said would not be used against you in a future romantic situation. But they were not the kinds of things you told a *guy*, a regular man, for heaven's sake.

"Ah, nuts," I said aloud each time I remembered things I'd said about my love life. "*Ah, nuts*," I'd repeat. For it wasn't so much what I'd said as *how* I'd said it. The tone, the gestures. "Loserville," I said aloud, and my tone of agony reverberated in Aunt Penelope's elegant hallway. Hearing the echo, I straightened up, wrapped a towel around me, and padded into the bedroom, damp and miserable.

There was a silver-framed, very stylized photograph of Aunt Penelope's younger self on the boudoir table. The photo looked as if it had been shot in a studio, for she was posed like a thirties glamour girl, in a slinky evening gown, wearing diamond earrings. She seemed to be looking straight at me.

"Pull yourself together, ducky," I said aloud, in my best imitation of Aunt Penelope's accent. I drew a deep breath. It was time to change my attitude, if not my life, and to stop tiptoeing around like Goldilocks playing in a house I'd broken into. Aunt Penelope had left this to us, to live in. My mother wanted it to be mine. I'd never had the lap of luxury before, but the least I could do was be grateful and make an effort. So the first change I was going to make in my own life was to stop being frantic and frazzled. I opened my suitcase and dressed.

And just in time, too. The doorbell rang, solemn and sonorous. For a wild moment I thought it might be Jeremy, come to apologize for dumping me in France so unceremoniously. But it was Rupert, who'd showed up dutifully with the papers Harold wanted me to sign. I showed him into the library. Because for once in my life I had a library to show somebody into, with a desk for me to write at, and nice chairs for a guest.

"It's all got to do with the transfer of the property," he explained. "From the estate to your mother, and from your mother to you. It won't be official until we attach the tally you're making. I've enclosed a preliminary assessment to start you off."

"Great," I said. "Want some coffee?" But he shook his head and sat down patiently to wait. He'd brought in the newspaper from my doorstep—it was still being delivered to Aunt Penelope—and he glanced at it casually, but I suspected that he was the kind of go-getter who's already read all the world papers by seven in the morning.

I sat at the desk and read everything carefully. My parents had e-mailed me a note assuring me that their lawyers had reviewed the documents and they were okay, and that Mom indeed wanted to transfer the property into my name, so that when she died there wouldn't be any problem inheriting it. I calculated that I could phone them later, at afternoon time in London, when it would be morning back home. I was dying to tell them personally about Jeremy.

Somebody—Rupert, no doubt—had placed tabs at all the places where I should sign, so, with Aunt Penelope's pen, I did. "I'll send you my estimate soon," I promised Rupert as I handed back the signed papers.

"Terrific. Harold says don't feel too rushed; it's more important to be accurate than quick," Rupert said, reaching into his briefcase. He handed me another envelope. "By the way, here's a telephone list you may find useful. And there's a cleaning woman who worked for your great-aunt. She comes tomorrow, unless you cancel her."

I thought that airing out the place of its sad-dust was a good idea. Rupert's telephone list included taxi, grocery market, hospital, police; and he'd enclosed a London street map and another of the Tube routes and train schedules. I thanked him, and he beamed with satisfaction.

"A pleasure," he said.

I showed him to the door and watched him climb into his tiny but expensive-looking German car. Jeremy would know what kind it was, I thought morosely to myself. What a rat to disappear like that, even if his whole life had just tumbled to pieces.

The house was deathly quiet after Rupert left. There were only two other apartments, one on the ground floor and one above me. Rupert had informed me that each was inhabited by an elderly couple, and I assumed that they all rose and retired at earlier hours than I did. The house was so soundproof, with its thick walls, that I never heard them stirring. I could hear only my own footsteps echoing on the polished wood floors, and the faint ticking of the clock in the library. I went very solemnly back into the library and sat at the desk to read Rupert's assessment of the contents of Aunt Penelope's apartment.

It really was a beautiful room when filled with morning sun, and her small walnut desk had everything you'd need to write letters—pale pink linen stationery, modest but nice pens, leather-trimmed blotter and matching notepad, gold letter-opener in a maroon leather sheath, even some stamps in a little gold cup. The lamp was black and gold, and cast good light. The matching chair was comfortable and supportive, and had a soft cushion. Whenever I looked up from the papers that I was reading, at the view through the bay windows of old trees and a pretty street, I felt as if I were already fulfilling an old dream of mine, having wandered into a time warp of London between the two world wars.

I soon became totally absorbed reading Rupert's assessment of the estate's value. He'd listed most of the possessions Aunt Penelope had left in the apartment. He was very thorough, right down to the comb-brush-mirror set on the bedroom dresser. In addition to the furniture, china, and kitchen stuff, he'd listed "assorted clothing" and "an album of pictures and personal memorabilia." He left the clothing, furniture and memorabilia value blank for me to fill in, but he'd put a stick-on note telling me that he estimated the total of her posses-

sions, including that stuff, to be about 150,000 pounds. Jeremy and I
had roughly calculated the furnishings in the villa to be worth about
350,000 pounds. The garage and its contents—a car and gardening
tools—were "at a value to be determined." And then there was the
villa itself, which, despite its need of repair and "mod-cons" (modern conveniences), because of its location was estimated to be worth
2,090,000 pounds—nearly four million dollars. No wonder Rollo
had contested the French will.

I sat back in the chair and gazed around the quiet apartment.
There was something a bit chilling about summing up a life with a
grocery-style list of possessions. Strangers coldly assessing their value,
looking at your favorite things when you weren't there to object.
And although Jeremy had warned me not to romanticize the whole
thing, I couldn't help feeling that there was some deeper meaning in
Aunt Penelope's quixotic gesture of giving me her old car and, via my
mother, this beautiful London apartment. She hardly knew me, really; yet I could imagine that if I were a woman of the world with no
children of my own, I might wish to impart wisdom to a dopey little
great-niece of a namesake. What was she trying to tell me?

I glanced at the window-seat. It reminded me of a window-seat
at Grandmother Beryl's house in Cornwall. I'd been curled up there
one rainy afternoon that summer we visited; for some reason, I was
the only one in the house that day. I'd pulled down a book of rather
dark fairy tales, and landed on a truly sad one about a poor girl who
got all excited because she received an invitation to the prince's ball.
So she made a beautiful dress and prepared to go. But her family was
jealous and said that she probably got invited by mistake, and they
wouldn't let her take the horse and carriage, so she set out on foot
and walked the whole long way to the city where the castle was. She
got her pretty dress all dusty and her shoes ruined in the puddles, but
that wasn't the worst of it. The journey took so long that by the time

she arrived, she was no longer a girl but an old lady. It had taken her all her life to get there, and the prince had married and was throwing a ball for his son now. The old woman, still clutching her tattered invitation, which the guards laughed at, collapsed on the steps of the castle; and when she heard the music from inside, while staring up at the night sky with its twinkling stars and moon, she thought she was being invited by the prince to dance, when, clearly, she was probably being summoned by death out in the ether, whilst the ballroom music filled her ears.

I was at an age when you're easily given to dramatic stabs of melancholy because you've just figured out that life indeed has its forlorn, darker side. Maybe it was the rainy day, or a jolt of loneliness in a strange windswept house in a foreign country, but that day I was moved to tears at the thought that life could play such a cruel joke on an innocent person.

And that was where Aunt Penelope had found me, at the window-seat, sniffling. At first she looked amused, curious, and I didn't want to discuss it. But I was in such a state that she easily pried it out of me. And unlike most adults, she didn't tell me that it was only a story. She listened thoughtfully, then said quietly, "I hate when they do that in fairy tales, don't you? Grant a heartfelt wish and then punish you for wanting it? Don't worry, Penny, dear. Yours is a very different fate, I'm sure." I looked at her doubtfully, and she said lightly but firmly, "Darling, I am never wrong about these things. You won't have to walk to the ball."

She said it so matter-of-factly, without any solemnity, that the day went right back to its normal insignificance, as it can only in childhood, and I never really thought about it again.

But I was remembering it now, with a startled shiver. It was almost as if she'd spoken out loud to me, because I was sitting there so quiet and still, in her home.

"Thanks, Aunt Penelope," I said aloud with real gratitude. My own voice echoed hollowly, sounding a little breathless. The thought came to me, strong as ever, that I'd been given an extraordinary new lease on life, literally. It seemed to me that the only proper way to be grateful was to appreciate every day of it. I recalled Harold's words about not neglecting your real life. It reminded me that I had some work to do, and I could actually conduct my research more easily from London than from my tiny rat-trap apartment in New York.

For instance, I'd been trying to hunt down a particular portrait, attributed to a painter named Bartolomeo Veneto. It was once thought to be of Lucrezia Borgia, but later experts believed that its subject might be another woman entirely. Still, it was the lingering image of Lucrezia that everyone has. I'd tracked it down to a special exhibit in the National Gallery of London. I wanted to go and see it with my own eyes. A moment like that could be worth weeks of poring over photo slides, light tables, research material. And Rupert had made it so easy, with his maps and directions. I rose, feeling inspired, and collected my notebook, handbag and jacket.

I went outside, down the leafy, sunny street, and took the Tube train to the Charing Cross station, then walked straight to the National Gallery, studiously avoiding all the other tempting London landmarks and tourist sights. I marched over to the Renaissance Collection, forcing myself not to be sidelined by other fascinating wings, rooms, and galleries.

But of course I had to stop and stare at the Leonardo da Vinci section; after all, he'd been a military engineer for Lucrezia's scary brother Cesare. I knew that this museum had Leonardo's famous *Cartoon*, which actually was a big chalk sketch for his painting *The Virgin and Child with Saint Anne and Saint John the Baptist*, commissioned around the time that Lucrezia's portrait was painted, 1506. Leonardo's chalk masterpiece had survived for centuries, only to be assaulted here, years ago, by somebody who came into the gallery and actually fired a gun at it. But the piece had been restored, and it was one of those works of art that critics like to argue about—was it really Saint Anne, the mother of Mary, when Anne looked barely older than Mary? Or could it be Elizabeth, the mother of John the Baptist? I stood there gaping awhile with all the other admirers, tourists and students. Then I dutifully located my image of Lucrezia.

There she was, wearing a cloak of black velvet with gold embroidery and a sparkling jeweled necklace of red and gold. On her forehead she wore a diadem of precious gems, and on her golden head were a turban and a wreath of leaves, evoking a goddess of spring from a mythological past. One little breast was provocatively exposed from its pale tunic; one hand daintily held up a delicate cluster of flowers. She stared at me. I stared back.

Maybe she was Lucrezia, maybe she wasn't. But she had a sly sidelong gaze, indicating that she knew a thing or two about how to survive in a treacherous world of secrets and lies. I was learning about Lucrezia in these small ways, and already she was like a girlfriend to me, one who could be admired for her courage, scolded for her errors; so I was glad to see her "alive" again, enigmatically watching over her admirers.

I stood there alone, quietly spellbound. I couldn't know, of course, that the telephone on Great-Aunt Penelope's boudoir table was ringing at that very moment. The caller waited three rings, four, even five, then gave up.

Part Six

Chapter Sixteen

HOURS LATER I STUMBLED HOME, DAZED AND BLEARY-EYED. OF course I'd overdone it. My first day on the loose in London—how could I help it? I should have left well enough alone after I exhausted myself wandering through the National Gallery. I contemplated darting into the nearby Portrait Gallery but wisely chose to have tea in a little shop nearby. The infusion cleared my head and brought me back to the present. I should have gone home after that. But no, all jazzed up on English-brewed tea, I had to greedily dash around, gazing up dizzily at every tourist sight I could find: Trafalgar Square, Nelson's Column, the statue of Eros at Piccadilly Circus . . . on and on, with traffic honking in my ears, and all the noise and soot of centuries of London whirling about my dazzled eyes. Furthermore, I'd got it stuck in my head that I needed an answering machine, so I stubbornly wandered around until I found a store that sold one. Then, feeling hungry, I went to the food market and stocked up on fresh provisions.

After I finally got myself back into Aunt Penelope's apartment, I just flopped onto the bed, drowsily wondering what day it was, what time it was, what year it was, what century I was in. When I woke, it was eight o'clock at night. I felt wide awake, and I was hungry again.

I ate a take-away roasted chicken and string bean salad, and I even opened that bottle of white wine in Aunt Penelope's cupboard—it was just sitting there reminding me to seize the day, and all that. The wine soothed away that slightly unnerved feeling you get when you are alone and far from home. Aunt Penelope's television set was in the kitchen, so I watched the news while I ate. Then I set up the answering machine and telephoned my parents, but they had gone out.

I decided to start my little job of going over the contents of the apartment, which was my excuse for hanging out here. Then I could give my mother a more personal report. So I went to the bedroom and bravely hauled open the closet to really look at the stuff on the list this time.

Great-Aunt Penelope had the good taste of an older European woman who isn't trying to look younger than she is but has a sharp eye for fine fabric and detail. There were winter suits in a size I hoped I'd never become, but of cloth quite pleasing to the eye and the touch—wintry blue and black wool, tweedy autumnal shades of olive green, brown, and gold, and soft, demure cashmeres of gray and black. Ahh—a spectacular mink shawl (not a stole but a shawl, which was sweepier, more luxurious) in a dark gold-and-brown honey color. It was the only item in the closet that wasn't old lady–ish.

On the top shelf, I found a few hatboxes and the aforementioned "album of pictures and personal memorabilia." But when, in a fit of sentimentality, I pulled down the album, it dumped dust motes on my head. Just what I get for being such a curious cat, I thought. I left the album on the dressing table and went through the bureau drawers. I'm doing this for Mom, I told myself, although my mother is so slim and delicate that these matronly clothes would not fit her, either. Pajamas and silk underwear. Socks and stockings. Old-fashioned starched handkerchiefs with Aunt Penelope's initials embroidered on them.

The bottom two drawers of the bureau were wide and deep. And there I hit the jackpot. Now, I am not an expert in couture, but I do know a thing or two about period costumes, and I'd just found, layered amid lavender sachets and blue tissue paper, vintage clothing worth writing home about. Great-Aunt Penelope had carefully preserved the most beautiful dresses of her youth, which meant silver and gold and violet and pale pink short sheath dresses from the twenties made of the softest, most gossamer silk and chiffon, painstakingly sewn with beading, glass "bugles," fringe, and all those beautiful shimmery things that made flappers seem as if they were always in motion.

Astonishing as they were, what really took my breath away was what lay in the last drawer—gowns from the thirties, in lovely silk-satin fabric with that fabulous bias cut. Unlike today's underslip-sausage-skins that cling rudely where they shouldn't—these vintage beauties just skimmed over the body closely but freely, like a whisper.

"Oh my God," I kept saying as I reverently unfolded one after the other. Some were invariably faded, but she had taken great care to preserve them and I found myself actually thinking, "I could wear this" or "Mom will freak over that." House of Paquin, Worth, Chanel. "Ohmigosh," I said aloud. Erik and Timothy would die just to see them, touch them, identify them.

Finally, after I'd overdosed like a glutton on glamour, I reverently folded them all back and put them exactly where they'd been. Great-Aunt Penelope had attached more value to these years. Nothing remained from the forties through the nineties. The closet held only the last years of her life, pared down to spare, simple, well-made but functional pieces.

Now I couldn't resist that photo album. I dusted it off, hauled it to the bed, and sat there turning the pages and squealing with delight. Because there was Great-Aunt Penelope in her splendid youth, modeling all the clothes I'd just seen, looking fabulous, so I could see how they were supposed to be worn. And she wore them with gusto. There she was in what looked like a Molyneux gown, in her big drawing room at the French villa, having what appeared to be a riproarious time at a cocktail party, with a dapper young man playing that cute grand piano, and other glamorous guests milling around holding cocktail glasses that were small and manageable, not like today's where one oversized cocktail can knock out a horse. The men in their evening clothes looked so spiffy and virile, and the women so slinky and spirited, laughing with mischievous, conspiratorial expressions.

The only subdued-looking photos, actually, were of Grandmother's wedding. Aunt Penelope was standing outside the front door of this very apartment, posing in a pale organdy gown, carrying a spray of roses and wearing the kind of hat that English girls wear to weddings. Only in these shots did she look a little dowdier and somewhat glum. Especially at the church, when she was glancing off-camera, looking as if her thoughts were miles away, even when she was posed next to Grandmother Beryl, who looked very solemn in a lovely white crocheted gown with a halo of white flowers and a spray of veil. Weddings weren't so much fun for single people back then, either, I supposed.

I flipped the page. It was fun to identify young Aunt Penelope in the familiar rooms in either this apartment or the villa. There were lots of landscape pictures of the seaside, too. I especially liked one with her in a white bathing suit, standing ankle-deep in the surf, smiling back at whoever was taking the picture. She looked happier in that setting, more relaxed.

Then came a snapshot of her in a fancy-dress costume and positively loaded down with spectacular jewelry—an elaborate necklace that looked like diamonds and other precious stones, with matching drop earrings. Her costume was a Venetian masquerade ball gown of patterned brocade, with a golden firebird eye-mask on a stick that she held just away from her face. The dress was an off-the-shoulders af fair with puffy sleeves, and she was sitting in a chair in the library, the one against the wall with a window on one side and a painting of a Madonna and Child on the other. Light coming in from the windows made her jewels sparkle.

And lo and behold, in the very next photo, there she was in the car! The old Dragonetta currently rusting in the garage. Only here, it wasn't old and rusty at all, it was new and shiny, and she was wearing a jaunty cloche and touring coat and gloves, but she wasn't driving the car. She was sitting in the passenger seat, parked in that circular driveway at the villa. A dark-haired, uniformed chauffeur with a dashing little moustache and a lean, elegant physique was standing just outside the driver's side, with his foot up on the running board, as if he were about to climb in the car and drive her off. There were lots of pictures of other men, especially an older guy with gray-black hair and a matching handlebar moustache. He showed up again and again, very well-dressed in dinner jackets, morning coats, silk top hat. He seemed older than the others in Great-Aunt Penelope's crowd—a bit severe-looking, often holding in his well-manicured hands a plump, expensive-looking cigar, whose plume of smoke rose visibly alongside him, making him look sophisticated and mysterious.

As I turned the pages I also found many photos of the elegant piano-player, who clowned a lot for the camera; he was slim, wiry, and a fastidious dresser. He was photographed in lots of exotic settings, wearing a wide-brimmed Asian hat in one, wearing a solar topee while sitting atop an elephant in another, and taking a touristy rickshaw ride in another.

Then there seemed to be a gap in time, and *voilà!* Color photos appeared. Snapshots of my parents, looking young and newly wed. A few kiddie shots of me. And Jeremy with Uncle Peter and Aunt Sheila. The ladies had been exchanging photos for years and years. Then, later, a picture of Great-Aunt Penelope sitting in her library again, looking older, gray-haired and sadder, gazing back at the camera almost as if challenging it.

Eventually the album ran out of pictures. But there were yellowed newspaper clippings that were truly astonishing—for apparently Great-Aunt Penelope had done a fair bit of acting in her time, in small theatres, and received some good, respectable notices on her performances, mostly singing and comedy bits. The newspaper had black-and-white reproductions of the framed picture on her boudoir table, so it must have been her publicity photo. The whole thing got me so excited that I felt a momentary pang of regret when the phone shrilled to interrupt me, even though it was the call I'd been waiting for from my mother.

Harold had already beaten me to the punch about Jeremy's real father, by e-mailing Dad's lawyer. Mom told me that my father would join us in a minute, so I should wait for him to discuss the will. I was only too happy to quiz her about Aunt Penelope's life, under the guise of trying to shed light on what I'd been sorting out here. I bubbled over with excited questions that she answered obligingly.

"Why didn't you ever *tell* me Aunt Penelope had this great life and did all these things?" I rhapsodized.

My mother was amused at my wild enthusiasm for Aunt Penelope's world of the twenties and thirties, and she gamely tried to fill in the details when I peppered her with more questions. But her tone changed when I hit pay dirt.

"It's funny that she never married," I said. "With all these fascinating men milling around her villa. Wasn't she ever even engaged?"

"Yes," my mother said, pausing delicately.

"Really?" I said, flipping the pages. "What was his name?"

"Well, darling," my mother said after hesitating again, "actually she was engaged to Grandpa Nigel."

"*What?*" I shouted. "Your father?"

"But it was only for a week. Really, he lost his head momentarily. He and your Grandmother Beryl had already been courting for a year, so of course he married Mother."

"Ye gods," I said. "You mean Grandma Beryl and Great-Aunt Penelope duked it out over—*Grandpa*?" It wasn't possible. Mild-mannered Grandfather Nigel, in his moth-eaten blue cardigan, pottering around in the garden watering the petunias, falling asleep in his lawn chair after lunch?

"Oh, Aunt Penelope was a terrible flirt in her day. She didn't mean it seriously. She wanted to teach her little sister Beryl a lesson for flirting with *her* beau, and the whole thing got out of hand. They fought like cats, then didn't speak to each other for a whole year, and after that it was tense for a time. Sisters can be like that, you know. But they reconciled and settled down. Well, Aunt Penelope never 'settled,' but she had a serious beau for years and years."

"Who?" I demanded.

My mother sighed. "I remember one man in particular, because there was always a flurry when he was around. After all, he's the reason Aunt Penelope got the money to buy all her nice things—the apartment, the villa, the clothes."

She stopped, as if that ended that. "What do you mean?" I prodded.

"Oh, darling, you know," she said evasively.

"No, I don't," I said. I knew she had to be helped along. "Are you saying Aunt Penelope lived in sin with a rich guy or something?"

"How funny you are, to talk about it in those old-fashioned words," my mother said in that tone she uses when she implies that she can't quite believe I'm her daughter because I'm being so tactless. "No, they never 'lived together.' People didn't do that in those days, especially a man in his position. He was very important in politics, I think. Much older than her. He was married, I'm afraid, so they had to be discreet, but he took good care of her."

"Mom," I said, "are you telling me now, after all these years, that Aunt Penelope was a 'kept' woman? I mean, took money to be a man's mistress?"

"Of course she didn't *take* money!" my mother exclaimed. "But in her day, the hostess of an important man had a lot of power and responsibility—and expenses, which naturally he covered—to help him entertain famous people, you know, heads of state, influential businessmen and journalists, sought-after artists, musicians, scientists. Her house, her clothes, her table setting—all this must be done correctly."

"Ho-lee cow," I said. "Was this guy famous in history?"

"No. A financier, a behind-the-scenes man. I don't even remember his name. Now stop being silly," she said. "Remember, it was a different era then. And the wars meant dreadful shortages of food, fuel . . . and men. Women worked, but they didn't necessarily have 'careers' like now, and they still needed financial and social protection from men."

"Hey, I bet I know who he was!" I shrieked, flipping the pages of the book back. The older man with the handlebar moustache. The one who looked so sure of himself. I described him to my mother and she said it sounded right.

"It's odd," my mother mused. "I thought she'd sold that villa years ago. In fact, I always got the impression that she'd spent all her money. Looks like she managed it rather well. Ah, here's your father now," she said pleasantly, as if we'd been having an ordinary old boring chat about the weather.

My father was in a business mode today, having dug out his royalty files and publishing contracts to have lunch with his publisher, so he was less interested in Great-Aunt Penelope's love life and more concerned about what was going on with the will. And I, after all, was the only one who'd talked face-to-face with Jeremy's mother. I explained all about how Rollo had dug up the truth about Jeremy.

"That Rollo is a bad apple," my father said unexpectedly. This surprised me. It wasn't like him to criticize his in-laws, or anybody, for that matter. He generally had a live-and-let-live attitude.

"What does he do for a living?" I asked. There was a pause.

"Nothing," my mother said. "Well, he's a collector. He buys and sells antiques."

My father coughed. "Whether they belong to him or not."

"Well," my mother said quickly, "that *can* be a hazard of the trade. They can't always authenticate things . . ."

"You mean, stolen stuff?" I demanded.

"It wasn't exactly stolen. It's just that they couldn't trace the ownership all the way, and it only happened once, and he gave it back as soon as he found out," my mother amended. "It happens to museums all the time."

"I didn't know what to make of him," I admitted. "Sometimes he seems sinister, and sometimes he seems vulnerable and a little pathetic."

"He's all of that, I'm afraid," my mother said. "Just be diplomatic with him." When I described that whole scene at the villa, they tsk-tsked about Rollo's shenanigans. They fell silent when I told them what Aunt Sheila had confessed. Then they asked careful, circumspect questions. My father kept saying about Jeremy, "Poor boy. Poor boy, what a shock."

Something suddenly occurred to me now. "Mom," I said slowly, "Jeremy was born before Aunt Sheila and Uncle Peter got married. How come you never told me that?"

My mother cleared her throat, and under her usual vague tone I detected a guilty note. "Oh, darling, I was in New York when Peter told me they'd eloped, with only a few friends at the ceremony, since she was so estranged from her family. He was always fuzzy about the date, so I suspected they'd had the child before they married. To be honest, I was rather pleased that my stodgy brother had done some-thing romantic for once in his life."

I couldn't believe it. Parents seem so nice and dull, but then it turns out that they've been harboring the most astonishing secrets, which you find out about only by accident.

"Now, Penny," my mother said, "you must let Jeremy know that we don't care a fig about such nonsense, that he is still one of us and we will help him fight to get what Aunt Penelope wanted him to have. You must go out of your way to let him know that all this makes no difference to us whatsoever."

"But you must also expect it to make a great deal of difference to him," my father warned. "It's only natural."

"Okay," I said, then added daringly, "I'm thinking of staying on here in London awhile longer. In Aunt Penelope's flat. At least until this will business gets a little more sorted out."

I explained that I could keep working from here. My parents lis-tened attentively and exclaimed that they thought it was an excellent idea. My father then asked me when I'd last spoken to Jeremy, and I said, rather awkwardly, that he wasn't taking my calls.

"Keep trying, dear," my mother counseled.

After we hung up I carried the photo album into the kitchen with me. I made some hot cocoa, which always helps me sleep, and I took it and the album into the library, where I sat on the sofa and had another look at Aunt Penelope's sugar daddy—the older man with the handlebar moustache and the proud look of a dignitary. Yes, he looked like the kind of man who would use money and influence to solve most of life's problems.

But now I felt less inclined to envy the dead. They had become too real, I suppose. I felt strangely excited and yet scared somehow. This business of dabbling in another person's life was fine when it was just history, but when it was somebody you were related to, it was a lot more intense. I wanted to be with someone young and alive, as I was.

I dialed Jeremy's number again, and got the same message. And still the same feeling that he was at home, listening. I tried to sound patient and sympathetic, as instructed by my parents. "Jeremy, it's Penny," I said. "Please call me. I'm staying on here in London. And I spoke to my parents. We're all on your side. Let's fight this fight together." Since it sounded so dumb, I ended my message there.

He didn't call that night. I put the album away and climbed into bed, but I was still too wide-awake, and I tossed around for hours, waiting to fall asleep.

Chapter Seventeen

THE NEXT DAY DAWNED ONE OF THOSE MISTY MORNINGS THAT LONdon is famous for, chilly enough to make you wear layers of clothes even though it's summer. I put on my raincoat, took one of Aunt Penelope's umbrellas from the umbrella bin in the hallway, and set out. I'd found a cute little café not far from the apartment, where the coffee was spectacular. But no matter how early you arrived the tables were always occupied, so I picked up a cup-to-go and a croissant. These I brought home, planning to eat while reading the newspaper.

I was already becoming accustomed to the fact that there never seemed to be anybody else out walking on this lovely, tree-lined street. Yet whenever I went out I had the strange feeling that somebody was watching me, even though I saw no one, not even at the windows.

Upon my return I charged right over to the answering machine I'd installed, hoping to find a blinking light indicating that Jeremy had finally returned my call. But there was nothing. I began to feel truly annoyed. Common courtesy and all that. I sat at the kitchen table and chewed, feeling lonely for the first time. I wished Erik and Tim were around. London would be fun with them. But the coffee revived me, so, feeling very brisk, I decided that I would spend the morning at the library.

The doorbell rang, and I rushed to it, thinking it might, after all, be Jeremy popping in for the moral support I'd promised him in my last message. But it was the cleaning lady Rupert told me about. I'd forgotten about her, but there she stood on the doorstep, smiling expectantly.

"Pleased to meet you, miss," she said. "I'm Elsie." She was small and neat, with light brown hair held back by a black band, and twinkly hazel eyes behind wire-rimmed eyeglasses. "Your great-aunt was a marvelous person, and she will be missed by all who knew her," she assured me.

Then, when she was certain that I still wanted her to continue working here, she set about, very businesslike, as a person who knew this apartment better than I did. She told me that she had a key, but did not want to use it unless she had permission from me. I told her that was fine, yet I hesitated about leaving her alone this first time. I tentatively mentioned that I was on my way out, and she said encouragingly, "Have a good day, miss."

When I returned it was past noon and raining lightly. I was preoccupied with my research, so I came in quietly. Elsie was in the bathroom, running water to clean the tub, and humming to herself. So I did not notice the man who was sitting in one of the wing chairs in the library until he spoke and nearly scared the daylights out of me.

"Penelope, hel-*lo*," he said, rose and came loping purposefully toward me. It was Rollo. His clothes were expensive, yet they had a shark-like sheen to them, the kind that crooked politicians, arms dealers, and other dubious moneymen wear. But he also had a rumpled, sad-sack, slightly alcoholic quality that made him seem like a stray dog scrounging for scraps. His eyes had those great pouchy bags under them. He was carrying a large bouquet of flowers, like an anxious suitor.

"Mum asked me to pay a call," he said, holding out the flowers to me. Twelve beautiful pale pink roses, the antique kind that are so hard to get now, delicately fragrant. "Your charwoman was good enough to let me in out of the rain."

Elsie in fact appeared right now in the hallway and took the flowers from me, to put them in a vase. "I'll be off, dearie," she said. I followed her to the kitchen and asked what the "payment arrangements" were, and she smiled and said, "End of the month, love."

I returned to the library, where Rollo was comfortably ensconced in the wing chair again. I wondered how on earth I would dislodge him. But I was mindful of my mother's advice to be diplomatic, especially when he winked and said, "So you're occupying the apartment already, eh? Don't worry, darling. We don't mind in the *least*. But Penny, dear," he said pleadingly, "Mum and I don't live far from here. Won't you please stop in and say hello to her? I'll explain that you're in a tearing hurry. Then it's over and done, and you won't have the visit hanging over your head, filling you with dread." He lowered his voice. "My life will be a living hell if I can't convince you," he confided.

"Do you promise to stay out of my garage over there in Antibes?" I said a trifle tartly. He stared at me at first, then decided it was a joke and guffawed.

"Ah, certainly, darling. Don't hold that against old Rollo," he said with a wink.

"Good," I said, making a mental note to tell Elsie never to let anyone in again. But she had already gone out. The main thing was to get Rollo out of the apartment. Then I could make my excuses. I picked up my jacket and put it on again. He followed me out.

An elderly couple was coming up the steps, nodding politely to me as if they knew who I was, but giving Rollo a doubtful look as they passed. I didn't want to stand there and have an argument with Rollo about going to see his mum, under the watchful eyes of people who lived in the building. Yet I felt like a teenage girl who desperately doesn't want her neighbors to think that the guy she's with is her date. Rollo took advantage of my embarrassment, quickly seized me by the elbow rather roughly, with a surprisingly firm grip, and speedily propelled me into the backseat of a waiting silver car parked at the curb.

"Won't take long. Mum is old-fashioned, and she wishes to see you once before you leave London," Rollo said, looking visibly relieved. He really is afraid of his own mother, I realized.

There was nobody else in the car except the driver, who wore a chauffeur's hat pulled low over his eyes. Rollo, strangely enough, sat up front with the driver and left me alone in the backseat. He acted as if it had been his mission to pick up a parcel for his mother from Harrod's, and the job was done. From time to time the driver stared hard at me in the rearview mirror, as if he was checking to make sure that the parcel didn't jump out. Which I was actually considering doing. By now, however, I had concluded that I should find out what Rollo and Dorothy were up to. They'd exposed Aunt Sheila's secret; perhaps I could figure out their next chess move.

Great-Aunt Dorothy's street was narrow and therefore a bit shadier and gloomier, but quite obviously moneyed in a smug, austere way. We pulled up before a fairly tall, dark building ringed by lots of black wrought-iron fencing with arrowlike, spiky tops that made me think of somebody in a horror movie falling out a window and being impaled. The front doors had windows laced with wrought iron, too, and heavy iron handles turned by a wizened old uniformed doorman who looked as if he'd been working there forever and was going to perform his one repetitive task slowly and deliberately until the end of time.

The elevator operator, also elderly and uniformed in navy blue with gold braid, had to haul heavy layers of wood doors and iron cages before the elevator took off with a rude lurch. Rollo just stood beside me, looking straight ahead, with an air of resignation, until we arrived with a thump. Then he led me to the apartment at the end of the hall, walked in ahead of me, and I followed him.

Great-Aunt Dorothy was seated regally in her parlor, perched literally on the edge of her high-backed chair with its padded armrests, which looked more like a throne, in gold and brown. All the pieces of furniture—three other chairs, two tiny flowered sofas, and various long, narrow tables littered with expensive knick-knacks—were placed well apart in this enormous room, like independent islands of free-floating opulence. The parlor was big and imposing and quite dark, since the heavy curtains were drawn. As my eyes adjusted I saw that the room was decorated in sunless tones of brown, beige and a rather mustardy yellow.

My great-aunt's hand trembled a little as she gestured for me to sit in the chair opposite her. It was upholstered but hard as a rock, placed out in the open without a table nearby where I could plunk my purse or jacket, which nobody had offered to take from me, until a very old, tall female servant shuffled in and unceremoniously yanked my jacket away from where it lay folded over the arm of my chair, then shuffled off with it to another room. She was the kind of servant who didn't bother to hide her resentment.

"Dear girl," Great-Aunt Dorothy chirped in a high voice that someone might use with a little girl. Not being English, she had no accent. Just a slightly nasal purr of the American upper crust. "And how are you today? Good. And how do you like London? Good."

"What can I do for you?" I asked politely.

She laughed a high, tinkly little laugh and said, "Why, darling, it's what *we* can do for *you*. I feel so *very* badly about the way I behaved when we last saw each other. I am an old woman, and I tire easily, so you must forgive me. How very pretty you are. I hope you never have to suffer the ailments I do. Be young and healthy forever, dear girl."

The servant shuffled back in, carrying a small black tray with a cut-crystal decanter of sherry and matching sherry glasses, and a plate of dry, unappetizing biscuits.

"Do join us for a drop of sherry, there's a good girl," Rollo said encouragingly.

The tray was placed on the longest table in the room, which was against the wall where Rollo had parked himself, as if he were holding up the wall. He poured one glass at a time, carrying the first to Great-Aunt Dorothy, who reached for it quickly. He handed the second to me, then kept the third for himself as he returned to his post of holding up the wall.

I sipped a bit of sherry after they raised their glasses to me, but it had a sweetish syrupy taste, like cough medicine. I was wondering uneasily how Dorothy would broach whatever it was they'd brought me here for, and she seemed to sense this, because she looked me straight in the eye now, waiting only for the sullen servant to shuffle off in her backless slippers, out of earshot.

"You can rest assured, Penny dear, that we all want to be fair. We feel it was right that your mother have the apartment. We *wanted* her to have it," Dorothy said quietly. "Penelope always said that Nancy was such an intelligent, considerate girl. As you are, my dear. Please let your mother know that we feel that way. Beryl and Penelope weren't crazy about having me for a sister-in-law, but then, nobody ever thinks any woman is good enough for her brother."

I gulped, feeling unexpectedly disarmed. I didn't know she was aware of how the elder ladies felt about her. But she seemed calm, without a grudge, delicately sipping her sherry and frugally gnawing at those indigestible biscuits as if these were her sweet treats of the day.

I start feeling sorry for people at the most inopportune times. I did so now, because there was something distinctly lonely in this atmosphere. It was suffocating and dusty, like an old folks' home where the residents are not expected to live long enough to complain about the slipshod housekeeping.

Rollo came toward me, extending a cigarette case. "Smoke?" he asked suavely. I couldn't help staring at the cigarette case. It was the ugliest, most ornate one I'd ever seen, gold, painted with a man in a turban riding an elephant. Both he and the elephant had eyes and drapery studded with gems. Rollo's eyes were on me, and he smiled and said, "Fascinating, isn't it? Bought it at auction. Unbelievably rare, but I had to have it."

He pressed the latch and as it sprang open, a mechanism made the interior of each half, which contained cigarettes, rise up automatically to offer you a smoke. He beamed like a kid, looking proud. I realized that he was waiting for me to react in delight.

"How interesting," I murmured, because he seemed so oddly vulnerable. Rumpled and paunchy as Rollo was, he was still too young to be stuck in a dark, smelly old-folks' home, even if it probably was an expensive flat. And it seemed so important to him to have his trinkets admired. The thought flashed through my head that if I wasn't careful, I could end up this way, lost in the past, drooling over crazy antique possessions, out of touch with the rest of the world.

"Are you sure? They're handmade specially. My personal blend of the rarest tobaccos," he said encouragingly.

"No, thank you, Rollo," I said as gently as possible.

"Oh, for God's sake, Rollo," Dorothy said reprovingly. "Don't bother the girl. She doesn't want those dirty things." Rollo's happy expression visibly collapsed, and he obediently slunk into a chair. After this lapse of good cheer, Dorothy turned back to me, her tone calmer.

"So please tell your mother that I have only the family's best interests at heart," she said. "We simply think it's awful that you and Rollo didn't get a share in the villa."

I'd been futilely searching for a place to park my sherry glass. "I don't really think it's wise for us to discuss these matters without our lawyers," I said cautiously, not wanting to say something that the lawyers would scold me for later. "So if you have anything to tell my mother, you should probably do it through her attorneys—"

Dorothy laughed her tinkly laugh but turned to Rollo. "Did you hear that, Rollo?" she cried. "Isn't she sweet? But Penny, this is about *your future.*"

"You're young. You may not realize it, but this could change your entire life," said Rollo in a kindly tone.

"We've seen this sort of thing happen a million times, particularly to women," Dorothy warned. "The whole point, dear, is that we don't want unscrupulous lawyers taking advantage of our own blood relatives. That young man Jeremy may mean well, but perhaps he's fallen under the influence of his colleagues. If he *really* cared about this family, he wouldn't object to having the estate divided up more fairly amongst *all* of you kids."

"I think Aunt Penelope knew how she wanted her estate divided," I said frankly.

"She was *old*," Dorothy said bluntly. "Take it from me, old people do foolish things. Because we lose track of time . . . and money." She smiled encouragingly. "So you and Rollo shouldn't be fighting *with* each other; you should be fighting *for* each other," she emphasized.

Rollo nodded and said in a milder but equally urgent tone, "Do let us help you. My lawyers could represent both of us together," he offered.

I knew it was time to go, before anything more was said that could later be misquoted or misconstrued. "That won't be necessary. Thanks very much for the sherry," I said politely, relieved when the maid came in and picked up the tray so that I could hand off my glass to her.

Rollo looked at his mother and shrugged. But she was watching me. "You must come again very soon," she called out in a quavery voice. "We want to get to know you better."

"Thank you," I said quickly. The main door opened now and a butler entered, carrying some dry-cleaning. With the door ajar, I saw a clear escape path, and I took it.

It wasn't until I was in the elevator, halfway down, that I realized I'd left my jacket behind. "Damn!" I murmured aloud.

The startled elevator operator turned to me and said, "Sorry?" in that way that anyone and everyone does in England when they want you to know that they believe you are not conducting yourself properly. But I couldn't help it. I liked that jacket.

So back up I went. Once the elevator operator dropped me off, and the elevator doors had rolled shut behind me, I screwed up my courage and approached Great-Aunt Dorothy's door. I was searching for a bell to ring when I heard that little old lady hollering in a tone I'd never heard from her before. I paused.

"You *idiot!*" she was saying with unmitigated fury. "You might have *said* something to keep her here!" The contrast in her voice now, compared to earlier, was downright shocking. "Instead you go and offer her those filthy cigarettes!"

"Thought she might like a smoke to relax. Oh, Mother, what's the point?" Rollo answered in a weary but annoyed grumble.

"The point is that *I* told you to contest both wills, but no, you couldn't resist laying your miserable hands on that cash, every pound of which will only just pay off those thugs you call friends who keep *staking* your damnable trips to the casino. There won't be anything left once you pay them off and you know it. And that insufferable girl is *never* going to be on our side!"

"Never mind the wretched girl! We don't need her on board,

and she's no threat to anybody," Rollo roared with unexpected vigor. "*She's* not the problem. It's Jeremy. He's got her dazzled, same as he did with Aunt Penelope."

"Listen to me, you lazy fool. That girl is going to be trouble. If you can't convince her to do what we want, then you've got to dispense with her! Let the people we've hired take care of it for you," Great-Aunt Dorothy said emphatically. I could feel the hair at the back of my neck stand up on end. I mean, it was a figure of speech, right? She was talking about the lawyers, surely? That old lady wasn't actually talking about, you know, *bumping me off*, was she?

"Oh, Mother, for God's sake, leave this to me," Rollo said wearily. "I've already got the ball rolling."

"What?" Great-Aunt Dorothy said skeptically. "What's your plan?" I leaned in closer, holding my breath.

But Rollo was being cagey with his own mother, and relishing it.

"You'll see. When all is said and done, I'll get the big kettle of fish. And once I get it, I'll never let anyone near it, not even you," he added bitterly.

"You're a *child*!" she cried. "You want to have your cake and eat it, too! These ne'er-do-wells of yours will get you into real trouble one of these days, and then where will you be? Oh, will you *look* at what that stupid maid did. *Now* she waters it. She's useless. Where's Clive?"

I didn't think it was possible for Dorothy to raise her voice further, but she did.

"Clive! Clive!" she hollered. Footsteps hurried from another room. Dorothy said, "Clive, get that disgusting thing out of this room at once, now that Mary's killed it dead. I told you to dispose of it this morning and it is STILL here and I hate it! I *hate* it!"

At this unlucky moment I heard quick, heavy footsteps coming toward the front door—and me. I reached out and rang the bell, just as the butler opened the door. He was carrying a dead potted plant.

Behind him, Rollo and Dorothy had gone so suddenly silent that they looked as if they'd murdered someone, stuffed the body in a lump under the carpet, and were trying, unsuccessfully, to be casual about it.

"I left my jacket," I said quickly. "The maid took it. I'd like it back, please."

Dorothy looked relieved, and waved her hand at the butler, who put down the dead plant, turned and went off, and came back with my jacket, which he held away from his body, as if it were a dead mouse that he was holding by the tail. I took it quickly and turned to go. This time they didn't try to stop me as they chorused another fond farewell.

When I returned to Aunt Penelope's house, it was cold, because the sun hadn't warmed it today. I peered at the phone. No calls on the answering machine. Shivering, I made a pot of tea and tried to decide whom to call about my visit with Rollo and Dorothy. I phoned my parents, but they were out. I knew perfectly well where they were. Out shopping together, buying food they'd cook side by side, making each other laugh at silly, private jokes.

I unwrapped my own groceries, sat at the kitchen table, and ate a nice little quiche-for-one with a salad, wondering if this would be my last meal before I was murdered in my bed in London by Rollo or Jeremy or both of them. Then I wandered into the library and sat there perusing Aunt Penelope's photo album again. I wanted a cup of coffee, and I remembered the peach tarte I'd bought for dessert, which was really too big for one person to eat alone.

Maybe I'd have it later. I supposed I could, and should, call Harold. I didn't want to call Harold, with his frosty, condescending attitude. I felt I needed a friend, not just a lawyer.

Or a cousin—or the guy you thought was your cousin. For all intents and purposes we'd grown up as cousins. Who cared if he got thrown out on a technicality? My parents believed in him. That was enough for me. I decided I must tell him so in person. I would bring the peach tarte, and command him to make coffee and eat it with me and come to his senses.

I picked up the phone and dialed Jeremy's number. Once again, I got his recorded message. Maybe he really was out. On the other hand, maybe he was lying unconscious in his apartment, having slit his wrists after being exposed by Rollo in front of all his colleagues at work. I didn't get the idea that Aunt Sheila was going to look in on him, in that detached way of hers. Especially after he'd hollered at her.

"Me again," I said.

I was staring at the framed picture of Aunt Penelope in her movie-star pose, gazing upward beatifically, as if rapt with inspiration and overcome with passion, like Garbo. Such luminous movie photos are meant to be sexy, but if you look at them closely, you can see that they are actually imitating the radiant faces of saints on holy cards and paintings. Perhaps that's why they called Garbo "divine." Aunt Penelope was looking particularly enigmatic to me today.

"Jeremy," I said in a deadly tone, "I need your help. And don't tell me to call Harold. This is a family matter, and that means you."

I hung up the telephone. Then I made a decision. I packed up the peach tarte and an unopened can of coffee, got Jeremy's address that Aunt Sheila had given me, called for a taxi, and headed for Jeremy's apartment.

Part Seven

Chapter Eighteen

JEREMY LIVED IN SOUTH KENSINGTON, IN ONE OF THOSE SUPER-MODERN high-rises outfitted with the latest technology and design, all glass and chrome and steel and zippy parking garages, and doormen who sprang forward with alacrity, and revolving doors that the tenants kept whirling.

"Jeremy's expecting me," I told the polite doorman with my most confident smile. "I'm his cousin from America."

I must have sounded convincing, because he told me where the "lift" was, and said he'd just call Jeremy and let him know I was on my way up. But then a deliveryman momentarily distracted him, and I saw my chance. The elevator doors had rolled open. I went in and up.

I wondered if the doorman would send a security guard after me. So I rushed down Jeremy's hallway and went boldly up to his door and knocked three times, loudly and firmly, and called out, "Telegram!" for no other reason than that I've seen too many movies. I would have hollered again through the door if I'd had to. But I didn't have to.

Jeremy opened it instantly, and stared at me briefly. "Telegram? Are you insane? Jake told me you were in the lift, so I knew it was you. What are you doing here?" he asked, a bit roughly. "I'm indisposed. Didn't my office tell you so?"

I stared back at him. I'd never expected to see him this way, so tousled, askew, and evidently hungover. For the neat, self-controlled Jeremy it was truly surprising. He was barefoot, unshaven, eyes murderously bloodshot, breath telltale, mouth in a combined expression of sad and mad. His hair was quite disheveled, and so were his expensive but rumpled pajamas and robe. His robe hung open, revealing that he wasn't wearing the top part of his pajamas, just the pants. I realized I hadn't seen his naked chest since he was a skinny kid; now it was a man's chest, lean and taut and nicely sculpted with a sprinkling of dark hair on it. He looked a bit dangerous, and moody, as if he'd been working himself over psychologically and, judging from the booze-breath, physically as well. There was only one way to deal with this. I was part English. I could be no-nonsense.

"Don't be absurd," I said. "Back off and let me in." He laughed without mirth, threw up his hands, and walked into the apartment, trying to look as if he didn't give a damn. But habits die hard, and he was watching me, a bit embarrassed, to see if I'd react to the mess.

Of course other men were capable of making a worse mess than this. For Jeremy, however, it was shocking, because his apartment, so modern and shiny and spare, looked as if he had, until now, kept it very meticulously uncluttered. But recently he'd left every carton of Chinese food (hardly anything eaten from them), every bottle of booze (all empty), every cup of coffee he'd choked down (halfway), every newspaper he'd glanced at, every shirt he'd hurled off himself in a huff, every piece of paper he'd crumpled, every book and magazine he'd tried to distract himself with—on every surface imaginable. The floor, the glass-and-chrome coffee table, the windowsills, the sofa . . .

"Wow," I said. "Congratulations. Usually it takes weeks to make a mess like this, but you've done it in record time." This seemed to please him, as I'd calculated it might.

But then he tried to convince himself that he didn't care, as he slumped wearily onto the sofa. "So," he said in a dry voice that cracked with fatigue, "Penny Nichols, to what do I owe this unexpected and, I might add, unannounced social call?"

"You've been home all this time, haven't you?" I said. He looked back at me defiantly.

"You might have answered my calls," I accused.

"Ah, yes, yes, those cryptic messages," he said, squinting as if he had a headache and the light hurt. He'd perhaps been sitting in the dark until alerted to my impending arrival. Always so cool, he now looked quite agitated, as if he were seething inside.

He said, "I hate to break this news to you, but frankly I'm no longer interested in what you Laidleys are up to. One would have thought that you'd consult with Harold—"

"Harold's a condescending prick," I said, hoping to shock Jeremy back into his old self. "A helpful one, perhaps, but not a man I can really talk to. I can hear his meter running the whole time."

"Mine's running too, from now on," Jeremy said, unexpectedly bitterly. But I didn't believe him. He looked curious, in spite of himself.

"Fine. I'll pay you a consultant's fee," I said sarcastically. "If that's what it takes to get you to have a simple conversation with me. It's important, damn it."

Jeremy gestured broadly. "I'm all ears," he said.

"Rollo wants the villa—" I began unceremoniously. But he waved me off immediately.

"Of course he does. But I suggest you leave this fight to your lawyer and your family," he said, "as I am no longer either . . ."

"Aw, quit feeling sorry for yourself," I said. "I'm alone here in London. You can't just abandon me to the wolves. I was kidnapped today by dear old Rollo himself."

Jeremy straightened up a little, looking annoyed. "What can you mean?"

"I mean he shoved me into a car and forced me to drink sherry with Great-Aunt Dorothy, that's what I mean," I said.

"What did they want?" he asked, alert, and I was glad to see that he still cared. But I felt uncomfortable telling him. I tried to find a way to say it that wouldn't hurt.

"First they tried the gentle, caring approach. They want me to think of them as family. Essentially they want me to join up with them to cheat you out of it, but that's not the point. I overheard them when they didn't know I was listening. Dorothy told Rollo to 'dispense' with me. She said they'd hired people to 'take care of it' for them. So if I end up floating around dead in the River Thames," I concluded dramatically, "it'll be all your fault for not looking after me, like you promised my mother." When I mentioned his promise, he looked a bit guilty.

"What's that bruise near your elbow?" Jeremy interrupted. I glanced down in surprise at a black-and-blue mark I hadn't seen before.

"Huh!" I said, momentarily distracted. "You know—I'll bet Rollo did that when he grabbed my arm and shoved me in the car, that bastard—"

The word actually made Jeremy flinch. I was so sorry I'd used it. Especially since he now turned all his bitterness on me, glaring like an oncoming train. "Ah. Well, darling, if you deplore the company of bastards, you're wasting your time with one right now."

"No, you're not," I said quickly, but he wasn't listening.

"And what's more, I'm an American," he said incredulously, his face full of horror, as if the word itself tasted like vinegar on his tongue.

"Woo, perish the thought," I said sarcastically. "You'll survive like the rest of us."

"Perhaps you all can give me lessons. I'll have to practice night and day, to speak those tortured vowels and be an ill-mannered, fat-assed, loudmouthed American. What a bloody joke, perpetrated on me by my hippie American father and my dear Mummy—and then what does she say? 'Sorry, darling. Meant to tell you someday.' "

He had some of his facts screwed up—especially about his father—but I didn't like this new vicious tone he was using, and it didn't seem a good time to tell him that I'd talked to his mother. I knew I shouldn't take his anti-American remarks personally, but one couldn't help wondering where the fat-ass stuff came from; I mean, I haven't got the smallest ass in town, but honestly, I really don't think that I and my kin qualify as fat-assed, per se . . .

"So you see, I'm not your dutiful cousin anymore," he said, leaning toward me with so much fire in his eyes that I actually shrank from him. "Go and collect your money and see if you can learn how to be rich. And leave me the hell alone, okay?"

It was his furious tone, rather than his words, that finally got to me, every time he bit off another hostile sentence. Somehow it's worse when men who aren't normally nasty suddenly start to vent, because you're not prepared for it. I've seen it happen with film crews. Everyone scurries to placate, and when that fails, they all freeze in their tracks, right down to the cat in the kitchen and the mouse in the wall. I swear I even once saw a spider stop cold at the sound of bellowing, when a director went ballistic on a set.

So when Jeremy turned the full force of his flashing blue eyes and angry voice on me to express his disgust, I reacted, to my abject horror, with tears springing to my eyes. To cover this up, I raised my chin defiantly.

"Oh, stop being a jackass. This isn't you," I said unwisely. This made him think that I wasn't taking him seriously.

"Don't you understand? I don't fucking know who I am anymore!" he said, in a tone that I later realized was agonized. "It turns out that I probably *am* a jackass, as you so winningly and articulately phrased it."

"You're you, the same as you always were when you were so confident about yourself," I insisted. "Nothing's changed. You think my parents and I care about any of this snotty heritage stuff? The entire human race descended from the same mother in Africa. Okay? So everything's relative. Get it?"

"Very good!" he said with exaggerated appreciation. "You were always such a clever little smart-ass, Miss Penny Nichols of Connecticut."

Now it *was* personal. "If you ask me, it's the well-bred, upper-crust English part of you that's behaving like a beast right now. You and your fake good manners. The whole passel of you. You're all very well-behaved when it looks like there's money in it for you. But boy, the minute you think there isn't, then *sayonara* to the good manners," I said hotly.

But this time I couldn't suppress a sniffle, and he heard it and finally noticed that I'd been winking away those foolish tears that sprang to my eyes. And, being Jeremy, he looked instantly sorry, and even slightly amused.

"Oh, dammit," he said. "You talk big, but you're such an innocent child, still."

"Bugger off," I said crossly, still wounded, and weary of being patronized by all and sundry. I turned and slammed the door behind me. The elevator—or *lift*, as my beastly ex-relative called it—was open and ready and I managed to slip right into it, even though Jeremy did, after a pause, follow me out, barefoot and pajama-clad.

"What is that parcel you've been clutching this whole time?" he asked suddenly. I looked down. I'd forgotten.

"A peach tarte," I said, intending to sound haughty but sounding, even to my ears, tearful and pathetic, and the elevator doors closed just as his irritated expression was changing to a slightly regretful look.

When the doors reopened I swept through the lobby, and outside there was someone just getting out of a cab, so it all went like clock-work for once, and I slid right into the cab and went right back to Aunt Penelope's apartment. It all went too fast, actually, so I didn't get to see if Jeremy had followed me out to the street, barefoot, in what was now pouring rain.

Chapter Nineteen

ONCE THE CAB PULLED DOWN MY STREET IN THE DARKNESS, THOUGH, I was acutely lonely. Until now, I'd felt protected knowing that Jeremy was out there for me if I needed him. And now he wasn't. But even I had my pride. I hated the way he'd spoken to me. You can't let a man get away with that, not even once, or he'll talk to you like that for the rest of your life. I know, because my Worst Boyfriend of late had done exactly that. It was downhill ever after.

Still, I felt gloomy as the cab reached Aunt Penelope's apartment, and I rushed to the door and fumbled to put my key in the lock and go in, relieved to get out of the rain. I put the tarte in the refrigerator, went straight to bed, and fell promptly asleep.

Hours later, I heard a rustling sound, and at first I thought I was dreaming. Then, of course, I thought of mice. But after I pried my eyes open fully, I thought I saw a darting light coming from the hallway. Like a bobbing flashlight. Then it was all pitch-dark again. Just as I'd convinced myself that it was probably the headlights of a passing car outside, I heard distinct footsteps, and a floorboard squeaked.

When you are imagining that someone might be in your house, it sounds one way. When somebody actually is skulking around in your house, it sounds quite another way. This was unmistakably that other way. I could tell that he was in the corridor, moving past the sewing room toward the stairs—and my bedroom. I held my breath, hoping he'd go down the stairs. But he didn't. A second later I heard another creak, closer now.

The telephone was not near the bed, but on the dressing table. I considered just diving under the bed. I couldn't stay where I was. Slowly, I tried to get out of bed without making a sound, but the second my bare foot hit the ground, a floorboard creaked. I froze.

The intruder froze, too, listening carefully. It's a very creepy feeling, to pause in the dark listening to someone who's doing exactly the same thing, listening to you and holding his breath. I knew I would have to try to get to the phone before he got to me.

I suppose this idea occurred to us both at the same time, because a second later a man in a ski mask came barreling into the room and seized me, bundling my arms behind me and clapping a gloved hand that smelled like gasoline on my mouth and nose. He got there pretty fast, which meant he'd been silently creeping up the corridor, farther along than I'd guessed.

"Shut up or I'll shoot," he growled. Then he shoved me into the bathroom and banged the door shut. I heard his footsteps scurrying down the stairs and out the door. I was still paralyzed with fear, but when I realized that he hadn't actually brandished a gun, I stumbled to my feet and pushed open the bathroom door, then raced to the library window in time to see the guy running toward the corner, where he turned and disappeared from sight. Seconds later I heard a car start up quickly and go roaring off.

The street was silent and deserted, as usual. Maybe I really did live in a ghost town, after all. Until now I'd thought the seclusion was charming, elegant. Now I felt like the last living creature on an earth that had been invaded by weird men in stinky gloves.

I picked up the telephone, dialing shakily. Naturally I got Jeremy's answering machine.

"Damn it, Jeremy!" I cried. "Somebody just broke into the apartment." I hung up, trembling in a surprisingly uncontrollable way. Finally I forced myself to get up and search for the police number that Rupert had given me. Jeremy called back just as I found it. It was probably only about twenty minutes, but it felt like years.

"Penny?" he exclaimed. "Are you all right?" I told him, in a gulpy voice, what had happened.

"He's gone now, but—he was here—right here in the bedroom—" I quavered.

"Did he hurt you?" Jeremy asked, horrified.

"He threw me in the bathroom. I'm okay but—fuck—I'm scared," I said.

"Could you tell who he was? Was he alone?"

This last idea had never occurred to me. "I don't know. I'll check," I said, dropped the receiver, and tore through the house flinging open closet doors, turning on the lights everywhere. By the time I came back to the phone Jeremy was saying, "Penny? Are you there? Are you all right? For God's sake, pick up the phone, Penny . . ."

"I'm here," I said breathlessly. "Nobody else is here. I was going to call the police—"

"I'll do it. Sit tight and wait for me. I'm coming over. Did anybody else see him?"

"I don't think so," I said.

"Did he take anything?"

"I don't know," I said.

"Look around carefully, but don't touch things."

"Forget it," I said. "No fingerprints. He was wearing gloves."

"Never mind. I'm on my way." We hung up. I tiptoed around as if I were the intruder. Nothing appeared to be missing. Bedroom, kitchen, library. Everything seemed exactly as I'd left it. Maybe the thief had been surprised too soon, before he had a chance to figure out what he wanted.

When Jeremy arrived with a policeman whom he knew and trusted and introduced as Danny, they made a more thorough search of the place, comparing what was there to Rupert's list. Nothing was missing. The young cop dutifully filled out a report, shook his head, and said there hadn't been any robberies in this neighborhood lately but you never could tell.

He said he found a gardener's ladder on the ground by the side of the house. And he'd figured out that the point of entry was the kitchen window, because it had been left ajar. He showed me the window, which had an old-fashioned handle that raised and lowered the lock. Had I ever noticed that it was unlocked? No, I hadn't. He demonstrated how it might look as if it were locked when it was not quite closed.

"No forced entry, you see," the cop said. "So it may have been someone who had access to the house and deliberately left it unlocked, knowing he'd return." He peered at me. "Anyone come to mind?" he asked.

I just looked at Jeremy. "Rollo," I said. "Before he dragged me off to see his mother, he got the maid to let him into the apartment."

The cop glanced at Jeremy, who explained that we were engaged in an inheritance dispute. "I could look in on him, but without any real evidence . . ." Danny said doubtfully.

Jeremy shook his head. "His mum will give him an alibi. She'll say he was there all night playing bridge with her," he predicted. "She's done it for him before, when he's been in scrapes."

"Well, I could keep an eye on him," the cop said. "And he won't know that we suspect him. Now what about this maid? Shall I check her out?" I told them I truly didn't think that she had anything to do with it, and explained what I'd overheard Rollo say to Aunt Dorothy.

"He's after something. He must think it's here," Jeremy said. It was at this point that the cop told me it was okay to touch things again, so I went through everything thoroughly, even the drawers in the bedroom. I saw that the gowns were still there, but they were not as carefully folded and their tissue-paper wrappings had been shoved around, as if someone had been searching for something in great haste.

"He's gone through the drawers," I said. "My God. That means he'd already been in this room, looking around while I was asleep." Involuntarily, I shuddered.

"Anything missing?" the cop asked.

"No," I said. "But it was a lot neater than this. That's how I know he was here." Jeremy registered this gravely, but the cop looked at me doubtfully, as if I were some dotty female obsessed with neatness. Then I saw something on the floor near Jeremy's foot, glinting in the light. I pointed it out to the cop, who picked it up with a cloth and held it out so that I could look at it. A glass cube, rimmed in metal, with a metal hinge so that you could open the cube and use either side to peer through one half of the heavy glass.

"Do you know what it is?" the cop asked.

"A magnifier," I said. "See? Each half has a different strength of magnification. People carry it around like a jackknife because it's handy, and you can use it to look more closely at newsprint or photographs, anything you want to see the details of," I said.

"Have you seen it before?" the cop asked. "Could it have been here all along and just fallen out now, when you were looking at things?"

"I don't think so," I said uncertainly. "I did go through a box of clippings and photos today, but I'm pretty sure that this wasn't in it." But Jeremy looked at Danny, unimpressed.

"Not much to go on," Danny said as he went out. He'd come in a plain car, Jeremy explained, so as not to excite the whole street, but he would still have to talk to the other people in the building, to ask if they'd seen or heard anything. As it turned out, he didn't even have to ring their doorbells. Because there they were, hanging about in the vestibule like four elderly magpies. One couple—whom I'd met when Rollo ambushed me—were in their robes and slippers; the other couple wore very formal evening clothes. With the prescience of busybodies, they'd figured out that something was amiss. No, they hadn't actually heard or seen the intruder, but they heard Jeremy arrive with the cop. The couple in the evening clothes had just come home from a party after the opera. The others had been in bed, and they looked at me as if they'd never seen me before.

All four of them, actually, were looking at me suspiciously, as if, being an American, I was the cause of this. I heard the dressed-up lady tell the cop as he was leaving, "My family has been in this building for a century and a half, and this is the first time *anything* like this has happened to people from *this* street!" And she glanced at me again. I could see that tomorrow the whole street was probably going to know about it.

On the way back inside, Jeremy took a deep breath. Apologies, apparently, don't come easy to this breed of fellow, but it appeared that one was on its way right now. "I'm sorry about the way I talked to you when you came to see me," he said hurriedly. Then he added defensively, "But you *would* show up unannounced when I made it patently clear that I didn't want you to!"

"Was that an apology?" I asked. "It sure was a stingy one."

He paused, and his voice was more penitent. "I know it. I behaved like a dog and I am sorry, really. Please just forget everything I said to you, will you?" He looked thoroughly mortified at the possibility of yet another scene.

"Humph," I said. "I suppose that will do."

"Look," he said, "I had a talk with Danny—the cop, he's a friend of a friend—and he said he'll drive by this place tonight to make sure that nobody shows up again. Still, I don't like the idea of you being here alone."

"The whole apartment house will be on the lookout now," I said, trying to appear brave but feeling scared anyway. Jeremy saw right through my bravado, of course.

"Right, well, all the same, I think you should stay at my place, just for tonight," he said. He glanced at his wristwatch. "What's left of tonight, that is. I would stay here with you, but I don't think that's a good idea with the neighbors keeping watch, as you said. Unless you prefer a hotel," he added.

"Thanks, but the truth is, I'm sick to death of hotels," I said.

"At least this way I can keep an eye on you," he agreed. "Give you coffee and breakfast. Then we can get some new locks put on these doors and windows, so you'll be okay." He paused, and added with some of his old, gentle amusement, "And bring the peach tarte."

I packed a few things and then we went back out. He led me to a car parked just a few yards down the road at the curb. "Wow!" I said when I saw it. "What is *that* beauty?" It was a sporty-looking auto, very old-fashioned but vaguely familiar.

"That's *my* Dragonetta," Jeremy said proudly. "It's a modern version, a repro of the one you inherited, my dear. Had to be on a wait list for two and a half years for it. They only make about four hundred of them a year nowadays."

"I've got the original of this car?" I asked, slipping into the pale leather upholstered seat. The exterior looked just like Aunt Penelope's auto, except the color was different; this one was forest-green. It had a manual drive, and it took off like the wind.

"I feel like we're flying instead of driving," I told him admiringly.

"That's the power-to-weight ratio," he explained proudly. "It can do a hundred fifty-five miles per hour." All the way to his apartment he regaled me with the details of how the powerful modern engine and the traditionally handmade wooden frame were a perfect marriage of today's technology to yesterday's elegant craftsmanship and style.

When we arrived at his apartment, he snapped on the lights. I saw that it was as messy as before—more so, in fact, since he'd got dressed in a tearing hurry and flung off his pajamas. "The guest room is this way," he said quickly. "I use it as an office most of the time."

"Is it as pristine as the rest of this place?" I could not resist teasing, as I followed him.

"It's quite clean, actually. I have someone come in every week, so fear not," he said. In a neutral tone, he pointed out where the guest bathroom was as we passed it in the hallway.

His "office-slash-guest-room" was really a small but pleasant room with a brass double bed, a stark modern computer desk, lamp, file drawers, bookshelf, closet, and a framed old print of the Thames. The bed had a nice dark green chenille bedspread and two pillows.

"Do you need some—pajamas or—" he paused awkwardly.

"No, it's okay. I brought my stuff," I said, nodding toward the overnight bag I'd packed, which he'd carried up and was still holding. He set it down now, and took the tarte from me.

"Let's eat it tomorrow with good coffee," he said gently. "You look exhausted." I shuddered involuntarily again, thinking of someone sneaking around me as I lay in bed. Jeremy went to the closet and reached for something.

"Spare blankets over here if you get cold," he said, then added somewhat awkwardly, "Well, good night, Penny dear. Sleep well. You can still get a few hours in."

"Thanks, Jeremy," I said.

"Least I could do," he said.

Chapter Twenty

I OVERSLEPT. IT WAS AN APPALLING ELEVEN O'CLOCK IN THE MORNING when I woke. I washed and dressed quickly. As I came down the hallway toward the living room, I could hear Jeremy's low murmur, as if he were on the telephone somewhere. He'd obviously been up and about for some time, and I smiled when I saw the living room. He had completely straightened it up, soundlessly, too. He wasn't there, but I followed his voice to the kitchen, a shiny affair gleaming with the latest silver gadgets and appliances.

When he saw me he got off the phone quickly. "You snore," he announced. "Like a logger. They could have heard you in Twickenham." Then, resuming a more businesslike tone, he added, "That was Rupert on the telephone. He's taking care of getting the new locks put on the apartment for you." He grinned. "Well, Detective Penny Nichols? You've had a night's sleep. Any new ideas about what Rollo's up to?"

"Without coffee in the morning I am incapable of thought," I said.

"Ah," he said, and gestured toward a fresh pot that was already brewing, and the peach tarte that he was carving up. I nodded, amused. Jeremy was still being rather penitent, and I knew it wouldn't last, so I was enjoying it.

But while we ate, we lapsed into total silence. I was sizing him up, and he was probably doing the same; in fact, we had reverted to a childhood habit of each waiting for the other to speak first and break the spell. He usually could hold out longer than me.

The phone rang, ending the impasse.

" 'Allo, Jeremy!" a male voice shouted into the recording. "*Oi!* Pick up the bloody phone, for Crissake. Are you there, mate?"

Hastily Jeremy picked up the receiver. "Denby," he said. "Sorry. Yes, yes, I remember. Hang on, will you?" He paused, and looked at me thoughtfully.

"What is it?" I asked. He covered the mouthpiece.

"I made an appointment with a man who used to work in the Dragonetta car factory," he said. "I'd forgotten all about it. He's semi-retired, and lives in Monte Carlo now. Remember I told you he specializes in fixing up these cars? He was going to assess its value for us."

"Perfect!" I cried. "When?"

Jeremy said slowly, "Tomorrow." He paused. "But perhaps you ought to hire somebody else to do this for you," he said gently. "Recommended by a different lawyer, you know?"

"Ummm," I said, as if I was pretending to consider his suggestion. "Look, Jeremy. Just do this one thing for me, okay? Because I don't know about old cars, and most other lawyers probably don't. If they hire an expert, they'll believe anything he says, and they'll probably get the wrong guy to do it. Who'll buy it from me and then sell it for a major profit."

And before he could argue with that, I added, "And don't tell me that Harold and Severine can do it. I want to inspect the car and the garage, and you were the only one with me who could remember what was and wasn't there. I just can't do this with them."

He must have been feeling guilty about being mean to me and

leaving me at the mercy of intruders in the night. But what he said was, "Idiot. It could be worse for you if I stayed on this case now. They'll think *you're* being led astray by me as well."

"Well, I'm stuck with you because I can't trust anybody else," I said teasingly. "So take me there one more time? You've got Denby lined up to look at it anyhow. I wouldn't even know what to ask him."

"It's clear I can't turn you loose down there alone. You're bound to get into trouble. So perhaps we should drive down together, and I could have Denby check a few things on my car," he said conclusively, as if he'd reached this brilliant decision all by himself. He returned to the guy on the phone. "Sorry, Denby. Had to check my calendar to be sure. No problem. I'll be there. It's not an easy place to find—do you want to meet in the village? Are you sure? See you at the villa, then." He hung up and glanced at me.

"How do you manage to convince me of these lurid scenarios you come up with?" he inquired. "You at the mercy of some lawyer who knows nothing about antique cars, or some unscrupulous mechanic out to take you for a ride. Or Rollo throwing you into the Thames—"

I smiled modestly. "You forget," I said. "I work in show biz. We make up damsel-in-distress drama every day of the week. Or—who knows? Perhaps it's because a strange man just broke into the bedroom where I was sleeping, for no apparent reason."

The telephone rang again. Evidently it wasn't just my phone calls he'd been avoiding. He didn't move right away, so his answering machine picked it up, and I heard Severine's voice ringing out with its rich French accent.

"Zheremy, poor boy," she said in a soothing and, I might add, intimate tone. "Don't worry. We are right on top of this and we will win. Please call me so I know you're okay, yes? Talk to you soon." She sounded much more warm-blooded than the cool, professional creature at the reading of the will. I didn't imagine this, because Jeremy blushed and ducked his head.

"I must say she sounds a lot friendlier on your phone," I said, going for the habitual teasing cousinly tone. But suddenly it wasn't so easy to pull off. In fact, it didn't come out teasing at all when I said, "Are you and Severine—?"

"Long time ago," Jeremy said quickly. "Very, very over."

"She doesn't sound so over," I observed, feeling a queer little ache in the pit of my stomach. But I tried to look worldly and amused.

"That was just her being concerned," he said. "French girls always sound sexy no matter what they say."

"I didn't say she sounded sexy," I retorted. "I said she sounded a trifle *intime*."

Jeremy grinned at me, and he, too, reached for his old familiar cousinly teasing tone. But when he spoke, softly, it came out differently, very differently, in a way that made me feel as if we'd been breezing along on a straight track on a roller coaster, then suddenly reached the edge and were about to plunge down a steep drop. I'd gotten a warning feeling in my gut, of either a great thrill or a grave danger ahead—I wasn't sure which.

"I keep forgetting," he said in his newer, warmer, and therefore more serious tone, "that you're French, too."

For a moment we just looked at each other, but when he spoke again he resumed his old attitude of teasing and slightly reproving, as if I were the one who was flirting with him and he, like a father with a daughter, must be responsible for bringing things back to where they should be.

"Well," he said, "you might want to pack a few things for the trip. Shall I drop you at Aunt Penelope's? You're quite safe now, because the men are there working on the locks."

"How did you get somebody over there so fast?" I wondered. "Back home it takes ages to get repairmen."

He grinned. "I haven't exactly been wasting my time, lo these many years. I do know a few useful people." We had returned to the guest bedroom so I could get my things, and I began rummaging around in my purse.

"What on earth are you foraging for in there?" he asked.

"My toothbrush," I said. He waited. "I usually brush after I eat," I confessed.

He shook his head uncomprehendingly. I paused, because instead of my toothbrush, I'd found the photograph that his mother had given me, and I was in a quandary about when to show it to him. I could wait till tomorrow, I was thinking, but if his mother calls and he finds out that I've had this all along and didn't give it to him, would he get angry? I went back and forth more than once, trying to decide, and he was watching me. I pulled the photo out of my purse.

"What's that?" he asked curiously.

"Jeremy, listen," I said gently. "When I got back to London, I didn't know what had happened to you and I was worried. So I went to see your mother."

Instantly his face hardened. "That was foolish of you," he said.

"Perhaps," I said, remembering what my father had advised about being sensitive to how Jeremy would be feeling, "but she told me about your father—which we can talk about more when you want to—and the thing is, she gave me this picture and I think you should have it, if you promise not to do anything temperamental with it like tear it up. Promise me."

He looked as if he dreaded seeing it. "Is it him?" he said sharply. "I don't want it."

"It's you," I said, holding it out but not letting go of it. "And him."

I made him swear that he wouldn't destroy it. He couldn't resist. Then I released it to him.

Jeremy held out his hand carefully as he took the photo. He bent his head over it and studied it very closely. Nothing in his face betrayed what he was thinking and feeling . . . except for a slight twitch of a muscle near his jaw.

"He wasn't exactly a hippie, you know," was the first thing that came out of my mouth. "He had a rock-and-roll band and was anti-war, but when he was called up he went. He came back alive, but ill, and stressed out. He died of pneumonia, but he lived long enough to see you. And dote on you and love you, your mother said."

Jeremy's throat moved as if he'd gulped silently. But although his voice was softer than he probably wanted it to be, he said coldly, "Love. Mum and her little secrets . . ."

"The point is, they both loved you, you dope," I said.

He glanced up, surprised. Then, looking as if something horrid had dawned on him, he said, "You and Mum are chums now, I suppose?"

"Since we both have to put up with you, I guess that makes us comrades," I retorted.

He muttered under his breath, "Women. You *do* always stick together in the end, don't you? For that, and other obvious reasons, none of you are to be trusted."

"Oh, go soak your head," was the best I could come up with. "But I've got dibs on the bathroom." I was still holding my fold-up toothbrush, which I'd finally found.

"To brush your teeth, of course," he said. "Fine. I'll go bring the car round. You can meet me downstairs."

"Right," I said. When he was gone I actually sighed in relief. It wasn't going to be a picnic, dealing with Jeremy's new edgy, angry tone. Well, I'd done my duty about his father's picture and I would never mention it again, if that was the way he wanted it. I brushed my teeth.

On the way out, I must confess that I peered into the other rooms. I saw his bedroom from the hall because the door was ajar. It was one of those men's bedrooms, modern furniture with a simple big bed covered with a blue duvet, a nightstand and modern silver lamp, a TV and sound setup, and a black rug on the floor.

I even, I'm sorry to admit, peered into the other bathroom, which was populated only by man-things. Razors, shaving cream, etc. No sign of a woman there, and all through the apartment no scent of one, either. I tried not to be a female sniffing around, but I couldn't ignore the fact that I was glad not to stumble upon perfume, hairpins, lingerie, or other indications of any recent visitors of my sex.

Part Eight

Chapter Twenty-one

OUR ROAD TRIP ACTUALLY BEGAN, ODDLY ENOUGH, WITH A TRAIN. And frankly, the less said about a Channel crossing, the better. You go either by ferry or, as we opted, by the "chunnel," which is an improbable undersea tunnel. Jeremy's car was loaded onto a train at Folkestone, and then miraculously we all arrived within an hour on the other side of the English Channel at Calais.

After having an early lunch in a village café nearby, we considered motoring down the coast so that we could see a little seaside town I knew about, from which Julius Caesar had supposedly sailed off to trounce Britain in 55 B.C. But the weather became ominous, with dark, threatening clouds and an unfriendly wind whipping up, so we jumped on the main highway and headed south. The traffic was heavy and relentless, and it was so late when we reached Paris that Jeremy telephoned Denby to see if we could put off our appointment until the next day. We could sleep in Paris overnight, then set out in the morning for the drive down to Antibes. Denby agreed readily enough.

The hotels were pretty full, but we managed to find rooms at a neat little private one on the Boulevard St.-Germain, where the lady at the front desk sat, rapt and absorbed, watching American TV dramas.

Her husband was a cook, and he served meals in a small, nondescript dining room. We didn't expect dinner because it was late—but this, after all, was Paris. He suggested a "light" supper—of the most superb *croque-monsieur* I've ever eaten, all the more surprising because of the modest surroundings. He was so certain that Jeremy and I were lovers that he looked horrified when we hesitated over his suggested glass of champagne.

"Okay, *bon*," Jeremy said hastily. When the man left Jeremy said, amused, "He thinks we're on our honeymoon or something."

"Don't worry. His wife will tell him tomorrow that we asked for separate rooms," I said.

"They'll think we had a row, then," he said. Then he paused. "Penny," he said, looking me straight in the eye, "I just want to say that I appreciate . . . the way you and your folks have stuck by me." This took me by surprise, but I couldn't resist a grin.

"Oh, well," I said nonchalantly, "somebody had to."

"No, actually, you didn't," he said. The champagne arrived and was opened with a nice, lively *pop!*—always a good moment whether you're celebrating something or not. We clinked our glasses, then ate our supper quietly.

Finally, we went upstairs. Our rooms were right next door to each other. We paused in the hallway, in a moment of awkwardness that betrayed something in both of us. He tried to look normal as he kissed me on the cheek, but it wasn't a totally cousinly kiss. There was that little moment of heat, and breathlessness, feeling each other's warmth and scent. I don't think we even looked at each other as we retreated into our own rooms for the night.

When we came downstairs in the morning, I heard familiar theme music from the TV and saw that the lady at the front desk was watching one of Pentathlon Productions' movies.

"Shh!" I told Jeremy. "I just want to see which one it is." It turned out to be the story of Calamity Jane. I cringed a little when she started firing off pistols. "Boy, it wasn't easy finding the right guns for her," I muttered.

Jeremy was fascinated, and stood there watching with the concierge. But soon his mobile phone was besieging him with urgent calls from his office, which he responded to tersely, sometimes with exasperation. I glanced up at the sky and saw that those pearly gray clouds were still threatening rain.

In fairness to the lush French countryside, the trip started out charmingly enough. A temporary burst of sunshine lulled us into a false sense of security. Outside of Paris, the traffic tapered off, and Jeremy piloted his modern-edition Dragonetta with ease and skill. It was definitely a car made for the open road. I leaned my head against the butter-soft leather upholstery, and I felt like a goddess being whisked through the sky in a chariot, watching the earthly scenery flash past me. Jeremy laughed when I exclaimed at the fluffy sheep and their babies, which dotted the fields just like the puffy clouds dotted the sky overhead. We stopped for lunch at an inn that served everything baked in a small pie—meat, fish, or vegetables—and I got a bit groggy on the local ale, which was more potent than it first seemed.

But by early afternoon the rain arrived in a sudden downpour. Jeremy had to yank the roof up, and of course he got soaked in the process. We pushed on, but the rain was so heavy that the windshield wipers could barely keep up. It was impossible to enjoy the scenery, which became such a blur that I began to feel carsick. The only thing that helped was for me to sleep, feeling a bit guilty because Jeremy had to stay awake; but he had that dogged look on his face, staring straight ahead as if, by God, he'd seen his duty and wouldn't stop until he'd done it. When a man gets that hunkered-down quality behind the wheel, it's best not to speak to him.

I woke to the rather alarming sound of an even fiercer rain pounding on the canvas roof like impatient fingers drumming on our heads. The roof held watertight, which I thought was miraculous and I ventured to say so.

Jeremy had a moment of pride and said, "Of course it held, you silly girl."

He pulled into a gas station and said, "I don't wish to be indelicate, but if you need the loo, this is a good time to go. I've got to pump some petrol. Looks like it's do-it-yourself, of course. How on earth did we all get suckered into this filthy habit?"

Fortunately there was a roof above the pumps and the path to the restrooms. I slid out of my seat because Jeremy was waiting, holding my door. As soon as I was out, he reached inside and actually pulled out a pair of old driving gloves from the glove compartment. What a fussbudget, I thought, glancing back at him as he slipped them on to wear while pumping gas.

When I returned from the ladies' room, Jeremy wasn't there, and I assumed that he was in the men's. I opened the glove compartment to study the map anew. Then I froze. Those gloves were back in there, and they smelled of gasoline.

I could feel the blood drain out of my head, and I felt slightly dizzy for a moment.

"Don't be ridiculous," I told myself. "There is no real motive here for Jeremy to break into Aunt Penelope's apartment in the dead of night. He had access to it all along."

Still, I must have seemed subdued as he climbed back in and drove off, because he said to me, "Everything all right?"

"Right-o," I said, trying to be jaunty, but my voice cracked.

"Are you ill?" he asked.

"Of course not," I said.

"Female trouble?" he said teasingly.

"Don't be daft," I responded.

Jeremy said soothingly, "Go back to sleep. I'll wake you when we're in Antibes."

But I didn't sleep after that. I kept watch over this ex-cousin of mine, covertly, from the corners of my eyes. For now he really seemed like a stranger to me.

Chapter Twenty-two

WHEN WE PULLED INTO THE CIRCULAR DRIVEWAY OF THE VILLA, the rain had long since stopped and the sun reigned again. At first the only sign of Denby was his car, a small sporty red convertible, parked at the turnaround. There were, however, plenty of sounds indicating his presence—clanks, clatterings, rattlings, and other metallica. The doors to the garage were flung open, and he'd hung up more than one battery-powered lantern-style light.

"Severine's assistant, Louis, let him in," Jeremy explained to me. He parked the car, and we got out and approached the garage. "Denby!" Jeremy shouted above the clanking.

Denby was lying under the car, and all I could see of him were his legs from the shins down, in tan pants, expensive brown loafers, and white socks. These did not really look like the feet of a mechanic.

Deftly he slid himself out from under the car. Above the tan pants was an impeccable white shirt. He was about fifty-five years old, good-looking in a salt-and-pepper-hair kind of way, and his skin had that year-round luxurious tan of a man who lives in Monte Carlo, owns his own business, and hangs around rich people who pay him well.

"Penny Nichols, this is Denby," Jeremy said. Denby pulled a blue handkerchief from his pants pocket, carefully wiped his hands, and then held out a big square paw to shake mine with friendly but not overpowering gusto.

"Hallo, love," he said in a working-class accent but the gentle tone of a man who had, as Jeremy told me earlier, taken care of his mother and sisters when he was only fourteen years old. The mother died, and the sisters were comfortably married off, so now he was on his own. He had a loyal wife who raised pedigreed dogs.

"Are you the young lady recently become the proud owner of this buggy?" he asked in his soft, pleasant voice. He spoke to me with particular kindness, like a tough man who automatically viewed women as smaller and more delicate creatures in need of protection.

"She is. What's the prognosis?" Jeremy asked, bursting with curiosity. Denby stood back a bit to gaze admiringly at Great-Aunt Penelope's car.

"It's a '36, all right," he said. "Body's begun to rust, but the chassis's just dandy—no cracks that I can see, no rot on the frame, which is solid ash, as you expected. No scuttle shake, and the doors aren't dropped, although one of them looks to be a bit wobbly on the hinge. She's got one of those monster engines built to live forever. Bet she was devilish quick."

"How fast will she go when you've fixed her up?" Jeremy asked.

"I'd say that engine could take her up to eighty miles an hour," Denby said confidently. "Brakes need work, bit o' this-and-that needed on the wheels. Tires and water pump should be completely replaced, but I believe with a bit o' detective work I can find the proper parts. Worst of it's the skin-deep, you know, the paint, the upholstery, but h'it's to be expected. 'At's her original horsehair stuffing in there, you know. In short, the old girl's not as bad as she looks. I expect she was kept covered most of her life and somebody kept 'er oiled and polished up. Just towards the end, I suspect, she was left 'ere lonely in the damp."

"Any idea what it'd cost to get it up to snuff?" Jeremy asked casually. Denby smiled and shook his head.

"Have to take a closer look for that." He nodded encouragingly to me.

"Um," I said, "if we did fix it up, um, what would it be—that is, how much—?"

Denby understood. "Well, darling, it depends on what I find when I look closer under her hood," he said, "but they only made about seven, eight hundred of these beauties in their day and most of them have vanished, so that ups the ante a bit. If she's got a bad cough or other trouble, she still might fetch about ten thousand pounds from a buyer who wants 'er bad enough. Now, if we could fix 'er up to modest condition, you're looking at anywhere from fifteen to twenty thousand pounds."

Jeremy was listening attentively, and Denby glanced at him when he added, "But if we can bring her back to the days of her youth, she might be worth more, say, tops, forty-five thousand quid. Of course, you'd have to invest money into 'er to bring it up to that price . . ."

I figured forty-five thousand pounds, roughly times two, less a bit o' this-and-that—I guessed it was about eighty thousand dollars. Jeremy, however, was not thinking along these lines because he was utterly fascinated with the auto, and pleased to hear that it was not as bad off as it looked. He and Denby were nattering on about car stuff, but Denby kept trying to include me in the conversation by turning to me and nodding encouragingly. When Jeremy paused in his questions, Denby smiled in a kind way and said to me, "Ah, darling, I did find a few l'il trinkets and things I saved for you. Come 'ave a look at this."

He bent to the floor on the passenger side and showed me where he'd placed a rusty metal box that was once a tool kit for tire changes, originally screwed into the "boot" at the back. He'd taken the old tools out and left them in the trunk, then used the box to collect any small items he found in the car and the garage that we hadn't already tagged. He'd kept everything he found, no matter how trivial, because, he said, he didn't take it upon himself to decide what items were of " 'ighly sentimental value." So the box had some faded postcards, old hairpins, a small gold pencil engraved P.L., a matchbook from a Monte Carlo casino with a unicorn on it, an ivory-colored cigarette holder, an old thimble, an empty key chain, and . . .

"This," Denby said, unwrapping something from a tissue.

"An earring!" I said, startled. It was beautiful, very Deco, a drop earring with wine-red stones, set in gold. I recognized it from the Venetian-costumed photo in the album.

"Are those rubies?" Jeremy asked, examining the larger cherry-colored stones that were set at the earlobe part. There were smaller, sparkly stones that looked like diamonds, too.

"Wouldn't be so difficult to find out," Denby said easily. He was a man who'd seen the rich and all the conceivable trinkets they'd come up with over the years—all the accoutrements for yachts, cars, villas, racehorses, mistresses and other assorted pets. He respected this little item enough to protect it in tissue, but he was not about to get excited and fanciful over a lone earring. In Monte Carlo fortunes rose and fell every day, like the ebb and flow of the sea.

He was asking Jeremy about his own car now, and Jeremy was describing the way the brakes and steering behaved, the sound the engine made, and other things that Denby nodded about. This gave me time to study the postcards he'd found. Some were highly amusing, from a man named Simon Thorne, who sent them from, it seemed, all the corners of the English empire. From India, for instance, he'd scrawled a jaunty rhyme, *Hotter than hell, but I do very well; at noon I just snooze, and then I drink booze.* There were a few from Grandmother Beryl, but hers were rather dull, of the "How are you? I am fine" variety.

Jeremy telephoned Severine's assistant, Louis, and asked him to pick up the earring from Denby. Louis would have it appraised and then keep it in a safe-deposit box. They would catalog everything, but nothing must be taken out of the country. There was still a combination lock on the garage doors.

"Can you leave your car here for a couple of days?" Denby asked Jeremy, and to my surprise Jeremy readily agreed. Denby would let Jeremy know when to come back and pick up his car, and he'd have a more formal estimate for me soon.

Denby wished us both luck when he dropped us off at the airport. It was the first time that Jeremy and I had been alone since we arrived at the villa, and I'd been mulling something over and working up a head of steam. After we boarded the airplane and took our seats, which were in the quiet, first-class section thanks to Jeremy's constant travel and its attendant perks, he turned to me and said, "Well? What's up? You look like the cat that swallowed the canary."

"It's that earring," I said. "It belongs to a necklace-and-earring set, very ornate, that Aunt Penelope wore to a costume ball. I saw it on her in a photograph in her album."

"Do you think it's very valuable?" Jeremy asked.

"Don't you think it's odd that none of Aunt Penelope's jewelry has turned up?" I asked. "Nowhere, not even in a safe-deposit box?"

Jeremy paused a moment, then said thoughtfully, "All women have jewelry, don't they?"

"Especially in those days, after one world war and heading into another," I said, bursting with enthusiasm for my own theory. "Women hid their jewels as a hedge against bad times."

"But darling, she could have sold them to pay the grocer," Jeremy said.

"Who sells one earring? And trust me, that was a great necklace. She would never have sold it," I insisted. "I mean you just can't *get* jewelry like that anymore. I've heard of old ladies who'd starve themselves and their cats rather than part with stuff like that. They feel safe knowing it's there. Like they'll stay alive as long as they don't sell it."

Jeremy tried not to look excited, but I could tell that my enthusiasm was contagious. "You know," he said slowly, "if the guy who broke into Aunt Pen's apartment—sorry, *your* apartment—was Rollo or somebody hired by him, perhaps he thinks the jewelry is still there. That would account for his rummaging through her clothing drawers. Perhaps you ought to have a good look around, just to see if the necklace or anything else turns up."

I was on the verge of telling him about Aunt Penelope's secret admirer, a rich businessman bound to give expensive trinkets as gifts, but something stopped me. I'd like to say that it was because I didn't want to gossip about my great-aunt's sex life, but in reality I think it was the stinky-glove thing that was gnawing at me. I'd been watching his reactions for telltale clues. But now I decided to be bold.

"Where were you that night, when I phoned about the break-in and you weren't home?" I said. In all the excitement, I'd never asked before. He looked up, startled, then sheepish.

"I took a good look at myself, and the apartment, and how it must have seemed from your perspective," he said awkwardly. "I realized how I'd been holed up there feeling sorry for myself, so I had to get out. I went for a coffee, to clear my head."

It sounded sincere, but still I was watching him closely. "What about that little glass cube that we found on the floor of Aunt Penelope's apartment? Near *your* shoe," I said. "*After* you arrived. You were kinda funny about it. Was that yours?"

"Mine?" he repeated blankly. "Why should it be mine?"

"It *could* have been used to examine gems, I suppose," I said, eyeing him for a reaction.

His eyes narrowed. "Penny," he said, slightly irritated, "get to the point, will you?"

"All right, then," I said bluntly. "Exactly what did you say to Aunt Penelope in those little teatimes with her? Rollo thinks you charmed her into dumping her old lawyer and hiring your firm, and making you the executor of her will. Now he thinks you're trying to influence me."

"For God's sake, what's this all about?" he asked, appearing a bit wounded now.

"Jeremy," I said in a burst, "is it some weird English thing to wear gloves when you pump gas?"

He looked embarrassed but confused. "What can you mean?" he said finally.

And I reminded him that the intruder had clapped a glove that smelled like gasoline to my mouth, not unlike the one I'd seen in Jeremy's glove compartment. He, actually, had as big a motive as Rollo to get the jewelry out of the apartment, if he'd suspected it was there . . .

I started out bravely enough, but ended up stuttering and stammering my half-baked theories. Jeremy saw how uncomfortable I was to think of him as a shady character, but somehow I pushed on, feeling that I had to confront him and size it all up. I figured I was on an airplane with loads of witnesses around, so he couldn't exactly murder me on the spot.

But Jeremy didn't look at all murderous. As it slowly dawned on him, he stared at me, then threw back his head and burst into laughter—great big choking guffaws that made the flight attendant glance our way and say brightly, "Everything all right here?"

"Dandy," he gasped. He actually had to wipe tears from his eyes. "My poor dear Penny," he said at last, when he could speak. "This whole affair is really taking a toll on you. I don't blame you a bit. No, it is not some weird English custom, but perhaps it's the one thing I have in common with Rollo. I'm glad he's not my relative. That's been the only good bit that came out of all this. I have no blood connection to him at all." And he smirked, implying that I, of course, did. "And no, I did not break into your apartment looking for poor old Aunt Pen's jewelry, though I may never forgive myself for not thinking of it. As for that cube, I wouldn't even know how to use the wretched thing. I can't tell a diamond from a rhinestone, anyway."

His whole reaction was so natural and innocent, and it was so annoyingly like him to find it funny, that I lost any modicum of mistrust that I may have harbored in my heart.

"Okay, okay, quit laughing and forget it," I said sulkily. He reached out to pat my hand, but at his touch we both melted a little, and he took mine in his and gave it a squeeze.

"I don't blame you in the least," he said ruefully. "Turns out I'm a total stranger to you."

"Not total," I said gently. The wound about all this bloodline stuff was still fresh. I could see that now. And I realized, then and there, that I was asking a lot of him to expect him to continue working on this case on our behalf. It would always be a thorn in his side, so of course he'd rather leave the whole thing with Harold. Now that I knew he wasn't going to kill himself, I should let him be.

The flight back to London was quiet and uneventful. Jeremy seemed tired and not too eager to talk, but he did turn to me and observe, "You seem a bit disappointed, Penny Nichols. Were you hoping that the car would be worth millions of dollars and you'd be set for life?"

He looked amused. I was tired of people being amused by me, and since he'd been the one to reopen the subject, I plunged back in. "Actually, I was hoping we could weaken Rollo's case by showing a judge that you weren't the only one who inherited a big chunk of the estate," I said. "That I got practically as much with something valuable, like the car or the earring. And that Aunt Penelope just didn't want irresponsible Rollo to get more than he could handle."

"Oh, I see. Those would have to be some rubies, to come near the price of that villa," he said. "Look, Penny," he added, "life just doesn't work out so romantically. I've seen enough of these cases to tell you exactly how it will go. At best the will may stand as it is. At worst, Rollo may well screw me out of the whole lot, but if so, he'd surely have to split the villa with you, and you can sell it. Meanwhile, you'll get a nice car in the bargain. If you don't want to keep it, Denby will probably buy it from you. Your mum and you can sell the London flat for a good sum, and everyone will go on doing what they always do. You will make movies, and now that the whole office knows my lineage, they'll probably hurl all the cowboy American clients my way, and I'll retire respectable. Perhaps you and your children will send Mum and me a Christmas card every year, until one year somebody forgets. Okeh? It may not be happily ever after, but considering the way the world is, it's not so bad."

"Then how come you sound mad as hell?" I countered.

"I'll get over it," he said shortly, opening up the pink *Financial Times.*

"Fine," I said, reaching for the *Herald Tribune.* And that's how we sat, side by side, pretending to read our newspapers. At least, I was pretending. The print just danced in front of my eyes. I was too keyed up to focus on any of it. Jeremy's words were depressingly familiar. After all, this wasn't the first time that a man was telling me that the world could never match up to my dreams, and the sooner I grew up and abandoned such hopes, and faced "reality" and all its ugliness, the better. Good old Paul had offered me just such a grim welcome-to-the-world speech, suggesting that I was too romantic and immature, clinging to my illusions of love and fate. Jeremy wasn't as gleeful as Paul, but the message was basically the same.

When we landed in London, Jeremy hailed me a cab in his gallant way, kissed me on the cheek, and said gently, "I'm around if you need me, of course, but don't be put off by Harold. He's very capable, a good man, and he'll always steer you right."

"Jeremy," I said, "I wish you wouldn't go this alone."

"Please, no psychotherapy," he said. "I don't believe in it."

Then he waved for another cab, and we went our separate ways.

Chapter Twenty-three

THE NEXT DAY I SEARCHED THE ENTIRE APARTMENT—EVEN IN ODD places, like loose floorboards and pantry tins—and I couldn't find a single piece of Aunt Penelope's beautiful jewelry. And then I remembered the letters and memorabilia in the hatbox. But there was no jewelry in there. Just a lot of notes addressed to the same man, "Simon Thorne." The same name on the postcards that Denby found in the car.

The correspondence was composed mostly of short, handwritten notes on initial-embossed paper with frantic, handwritten messages that seemed dashed off as if in a tearing hurry—usually to plot some party or lunch meeting or dinner. On the order of, *Are you going to Mary's dreadful weekend in Surrey? If you go, I'll go* kind of thing. People used to get mail delivered twice a day; I imagined these flying back and forth across town. The postcards were more fun, sent from everywhere around the globe, from Rangoon to Nome; written in thick dried ink full of exclamation points and question marks and little witticisms like, *Befriended a penguin. Drank me under the table! Please send aspirin.* But there was one serious, comparatively longish letter from Simon, thanking Aunt Penelope for consoling him when his mother died.

"Simon Thorne," I said aloud. The name sounded vaguely familiar, so I went back to the photo album that I'd left on the desk in the library. There he was, in the press clippings, as Aunt Penelope's accompanist. Apparently he sang, too, and they'd had a little nightclub act, and the reviews were mainly positive.

"Their voices, though not the stuff of legends, are overall very pleasing," one fusty reviewer wrote. "Their harmonies are perfectly matched, their point-counterpoint complementary and at times delightful. Mr. Simon Thorne, occasionally over-emotional, does infuse the male role with genuine feeling, and Miss Penelope Laidley's trills, though at times thin, are able and lively." They sang sweet, sad, romantic songs, and did some comic music-hall tunes and sketches.

I flipped through the pictures in the photo album to stare at the photographs of Simon and Aunt Penelope cavorting at the estate, where Simon was playing the piano and Aunt Penelope hovered nearby, with a cocktail glass in her hand and her mouth open as if she were singing with him. I peered more closely. She might, in fact, be wearing those very earrings, one of which Denby found in the car. And she wore them in her framed publicity photo, right here on the boudoir table. I believed there was also a necklace that matched them, which I'd seen in another picture—the one when she wore that Venetian costume with the puffy sleeves. I flipped through the album to verify it.

But there was no Venetian picture. It was gone. There was only a dark square testifying to where it had been, and those little corners that people stuck onto the pages of photo albums, which were used to hold the picture in place. Someone had stolen that photo, which showed not only the earrings but their matching necklace.

I didn't want to bug Jeremy, but I couldn't help it. I dialed his number and got his answering machine. I said, "Jeremy. Penny. I found out what the thief took. A photo. Of Aunt Penelope wearing that necklace. Has the appraiser told you what it's worth yet? Call me."

I went back to the photo album, and I stared at the picture of Simon. He and Great-Aunt Penelope were pals, clearly. He probably knew a lot of things about her. I wondered if he was still alive. There was a London phone book in the telephone table, and I actually found him listed. I hesitated a moment. But I couldn't resist dialing. He answered on the second ring, and once he knew who I was, he told me to come right over.

Chapter Twenty-four

SIMON THORNE LIVED IN BLOOMSBURY, IN A CHARMING LITTLE SQUARE ringed with well-kept, homey old houses. It's funny, but the English, who consider certain colors of flowers too garish for their gardens, will nonetheless go to hell with themselves when it comes to painting their front doors all kinds of startling colors. Bright reds, greens, blues. Simon's was purple. And it wasn't the only purple one, either. I rang the bell and gazed at the big fat doorknob plunked right in the center of the door instead of to the side where American doorknobs sit. He answered the door himself.

He was a fairly short man, but lean and lithe and powerful-looking. He moved with precise, elegant grace, like a panther. In his voice I could hear the years of cigarette smoking and gin drinking, but he was determinedly cheerful in that stiff-upper-lip, bright-as-a-button way, like a man who'd spent his life entertaining people and staying "up" even on days when he didn't feel so chipper. He had alert, bright hazel eyes, a long narrow nose, and a slightly balding head, but what hair he had was well-clipped and cared for, brown and silver. He wore a green and gold silk brocade dressing gown with gold fringe tassels on the belt, but under the gown he wore a spic-and-span cream-colored shirt and good wool brown pants, green silk socks and soft slippers of dark brown leather. He had a paisley silk scarf around his throat.

"My dear girl," he said when I arrived. "You are a Penny, all right."

He cocked his head to one side and surveyed me critically. "Not quite the spitting-est of images of your great-auntie," he commented. "She was a bit shorter than you, and her nose was different. I daresay you have a prettier, higher forehead, too. Still, the family resemblance is there. Not just the face, but the way you carry yourself. She had that habit of tripping along on her toes, not quite landing on the heels, and so do you. Did you study dance, my dear? Ah, I thought so. Yet you gave it up." His voice assumed a theatrical, slightly sorrowful air, as if ending my girlhood dancing lessons had possibly robbed the world of a great dancer. At the same time, he was smiling, so that the tragedy had the gay, airy lightness of a soufflé.

He led me to his parlor, which was a bit like an old lady's, with lace antimacassars on flowered upholstery, china figurines displayed on shelves, lamps with big heavy glass "teardrops" ringing the edge of the shades, and an upright piano tucked against the wall.

He told me with a grand wave of his hand that he owned the house but occupied the first floor only. All these years, he explained, he had been running a boardinghouse for actors, who were notoriously bad about paying their rent on time, if at all. "But I like to watch the new lads come and go," he said. I nodded toward the polished piano in the corner.

"Do you still play?" I asked, then realized that, with all the fecklessness of youth, I was reminding an older person of how old he was, which elderly people really don't want to hear. Despite his high energy, he was a bit delicate-looking, with a slight limp, and the brittle thinness of old age. But his mind was alert and playful, and he responded with a great gusty, theatrical sigh.

"Darling, it's like sex and bicycle riding," he said impishly. "Once you've learned to do it well, you never forget how, but there comes a time when you find that you do it a lot less often than you ever dreamed possible, until one day it seems like more trouble than it's worth. Now do tell—what brings the progeny of my old singing partner here to see me? And pray what is that lovely gilt-wrapped thing you're clutching in the palm of your hand? Is it a present?"

I had brought him a bottle of the nicest champagne I could afford. He clapped his hands with glee when he tore off the wrapper, and spent fifteen minutes filling a silver champagne bucket with cold water, salt and ice.

"It must be positively frigid when you drink it," he advised me. "Never trust a fellow who serves you warm champagne. Two things you must never keep waiting: a hot lover and a cold champagne. What's in that weather-beaten leather portfolio you're carrying?"

I hauled out Aunt Penelope's press clippings, and he let out a cry of recognition. I'd brought some of the photos, too. He put on his narrow reading glasses and gazed at each picture for a long time, as if staring into a mirror.

"Shades of my youth!" he cried. I had to wait for him to calm down before I could start asking him questions, but he was perfectly happy to answer all of them very patiently—especially once he announced that the champagne was cold enough to drink. He reverently poured out a glass for each of us in two antique cocktail glasses with gold stems that were made to resemble tree branches, with their leaves twining around the lower cup part of the glasses, as if they were goblets plucked from a magic shrub of golden leaves.

He drank the first glass happily, and probably would have corked the bottle and saved it frugally for the next time, like a man who doles out his pleasures to make them last because of straitened circumstances. But I encouraged him to have a second glass, because the atmosphere had become festive by then, and I am a sucker for a good storyteller. Simon loved a rapt audience, so we got on well. When he saw that I was interested in Aunt Penelope's favorite London haunts, he gazed at my London map and showed me where they ate lunch, and where she'd visit her masseuse-cum-fortune-teller, and which theatres they'd performed in.

"Was it more fun in those days?" I persisted. He smiled at me understandingly.

"Yes and no, darling. It helped if your friends were rich or clever— and I think the wealthy were a shade less *gauche* than they are now. And certainly it was a quieter, slower world than this mad noisy one. But there were too many things you couldn't speak of publicly—abortion, affairs, homosexuality, drug addiction, incest. I wish we could have talked more frankly then, and less frankly now. However, back then the food was not quite so *ersatz*." He exhaled deeply. "But nothing beats being young," he admonished, wagging a finger at me playfully again. I asked him about the villa and the Dragonetta.

"Oh, my, yes, of course I remember that car," he said fondly. "We zipped along in that baby all around the Riviera. Penelope didn't like driving in London. City traffic gave her a fright. But oh, the picnics! The nights at the seaside! And the parties, darling, the parties! You never knew just *who* you were going to find with *whom* in the back-seat when you came out into the car-park at four in the morning!"

He could tell me where she'd bought each gown, and what fabric it was made of, and which gig was the one where they both came down with bronchitis and had to croak their way through a song and the audience never knew that the joke wasn't deliberate.

"Tell me about Aunt Penelope's rich guy," I prodded.

"Belvedere Hanover Wendell the Third. I always thought he was a bit of a clod," Simon said, "but Penelope seemed to get on with him well enough. Don't I have a marvelous talent for recalling names? He was a big man in politics, so mercifully he wasn't around all the time. Had a wife and children, too, so we all had to pretend that Penelope was my date to the big fancy dinner parties in town. But nobody minded, really. We all knew how to stay out of each other's way."

"Aunt Penelope certainly was stylish," I said craftily, pointing to the picture of the two of them cavorting at the piano in the villa. "Where did she get all that great jewelry?" I asked.

But my casual tone didn't fool him in the least. He was like a cat, alert to the slightest warning of a trap. He knew all about jewelry and inheritance battles—I could tell from his sharp expression. He observed me in amusement, peering at me over the tops of his reading glasses that had slunk down on his nose. "Did you find any of it?" he inquired.

"One lone earring," I admitted. "I don't know where the mate is—" But he put his hand on mine and patted me in a fatherly way. His tone was consoling, but slightly reproving.

"Darling, don't upset yourself over it," he said. "It really isn't worth it."

I paused. "What do you mean?" I asked.

"Paste," he said sadly.

"Paste?" I asked.

"Paste," he repeated positively. "All of it."

"All of it?" I echoed.

"All of it."

"You mean, she had paste copies of her jewelry?" I asked. I knew that some rich people kept the real stuff in safes while they wore the fakes to parties. But he shook his head again.

"No, darling, all she ever had was paste," he said. "It was the thing then. Everybody had paste. Some of it was quite lovely, and today it would fetch a decent, but not astounding price in the antique markets, you know, because of the Deco. Everyone's suddenly mad for Deco, when for years they wouldn't touch it. Said it was too old-fashioned, the peasants. You can't get such detail and craft now. But the point is, he never gave her any truly priceless gems. Some peculiar morality of his—only his wife got those. Penelope didn't care; she was never one for making a big deal about jewelry. She gave most of it away. She was like that. And Belvedere didn't mind paying for a lot of those gowns."

My mother had intimated some of this, yet I must have looked surprised.

"I sort of wondered how she could afford the best fashion houses on earth," I admitted.

He smiled indulgently, then said with a chuckle, "Well, my dear, you don't think your great-auntie got all those lovely things from being a thespian, do you? And her brother Roland got most of her parents' money. Boys usually did in those days. That horrid Roland. What a gargoyle he was! Some people put energy into a room when they enter it. That was our dear Penelope. Some people just drain the living daylights out of room. That was Roland. The sister—Beryl, your grand-mama—she was somewhere in between. More of a homebody, really. It was Penelope who hauled in the big tuna when the time came."

"What tuna?" I asked. "Do you mean that the rich guy—?"

"Made a lovely settlement on your great-auntie," he summed up. "In return, she promised to keep quiet about him." He winked.

"She didn't make him—I mean, she didn't actually . . ." I asked delicately.

"Threaten him? Blackmail him? Certainly not. It wasn't her style. But things were cooling off, for her anyway, and he knew she was getting restless, and around that time there was a rash of mistresses who were beginning to get careless and cause scandals. You probably can't imagine what it meant back then to have a scandal, but believe me, heads rolled, careers tumbled, there were suicides and all kinds of things when a mistress blabbed, either to the wife or if she just let the reporters follow her trail of bread crumbs.

"So Penelope's fellow decided not to take any chances, and bought her a marvellous apartment in Belgravia and a villa in the South of France, to keep her mouth shut. I hate to be so blunt. Personally, I think a man *ought* to take care of a gal when they're both getting old. It's a perfectly civilized thing to do. He never really liked the sun anyway, he was one of those men who went to the beach wearing the same suit and shoes he wore to the office." Simon shuddered delicately at such a fashion *faux pas*.

I must have still looked surprised. "Why, darling, don't tell me the apartment and the villa disappeared, too," he said, faintly alarmed. "Together they were worth millions!"

I had to reassure him that they were in the estate, divided among the heirs. I wasn't ready yet to tell him we were fighting over the villa.

"Good," he said briskly. "I hope your legacy gives you a start in life. That's all any of us ever really needs, if you've got a pleasant face and some brains."

He returned to the photographs. "So let's see who else you've got in here on this lovely trip down Memory Boulevard," he said. He paused and sighed at the sight of the dapper chauffeur posing in front of the car.

"Oh, Giulio," he trilled. "What a dreamboat he was! No wonder the girls squabbled over him!"

"What girls?" I asked. Simon had raised the bottle of champagne over the bucket, allowing the melted ice to drip off it while he surveyed what was left inside the bottle.

"Hmmm," he said, "at this stage, I don't see the point of corking up so little of it. Do you?" And he poured out the remaining champagne, going back and forth twice, into his glass and mine, so we'd get the same amount of the last of it. "What were we saying, Penny dear?"

"You said some girls fought over this guy," I reminded him. "What girls?" I thought he was going to tell me about the scullery maid or the butler's daughter.

He glanced at me in wicked amusement. "My dear, *the* girls. *Les* girls. Penelope and Beryl, of course."

"What!" I shrieked. I'd had some champagne too, after all. "Did you just say that my great-aunt and my grandmother fancied the chauffeur?"

"Driver, dear, driver," he said. "Only the *petite bourgeoisie* use the c-word. The answer is, hell yes. They fought tooth and nail over him. For a whole year they didn't even speak to each other. Then the war came, of course—"

"Wait a minute, wait a minute," I commanded. "If you don't start at the beginning I'll scream." He grinned.

"You are *so* like her, after all," he said. "Well, of course, darling. Giulio was an out-of-work actor not unlike yours truly here. Only if I may say so, I worked my little fanny off to make a modest little success of myself, whereas Giulio, being of a rather highly born family in Italy, was not so inclined to fighting it out in the rough-and-tumble streets day after day. We all thought he'd be the next Valentino. Alas, no. He was not the type to push, and an actor must push, you know. He was flat broke when we found him knocking about London, and we took him in and gave him a hot meal and a hot bath. Penelope had her sugar daddy paying for the car, the clothes, the villa, and any staff she cared to hire, so she clapped her hands like a fairy godmother and gave Giulio a job as her driver so that he wouldn't starve.

"It was a good thing, too, because as I said, Penelope hated driving in London. She was just beastly with start-and-stop traffic and lights and pedestrians, and she'd got into trouble one too many times with the London traffic cops. I mean, honestly, out on the open road she was just fine, but—well, anyway, she needed a good driver, and it was excellent cover once they embarked on their love affair. Nobody knew for years and years, not until her bratty little sister took it into her head to fancy him. Beryl was like that, you know. If you don't mind my saying so, your grandmother was a bit of a dull gal when it came to improvising a life. All she wanted was whatever her sister had. If Penelope had a pair of gold sandals, why then, Beryl had to have a pair of gold sandals. If Penelope had dancing lessons, Beryl had to have them. Do you know that when Penelope came down with mumps, Beryl sulked for weeks and kept trying to catch them so that everybody would fuss over her, too?"

I couldn't suppress a giggle at the image of my sensible, stalwart grandmother once being a jealous young girl squabbling and competing with her older sister.

"But of course, Giulio wasn't in love with Beryl. He called her an infant, which didn't go down well," Simon explained. "However, being a macho sort of male, he couldn't help being flattered by her attention, and that was all the encouragement she needed to keep it up. Honestly, it was ridiculous after awhile. So Penelope turned the tables on Beryl by flirting with that fellow that Beryl was engaged to and finally married—"

"You mean Grandpa Nigel," I said. This was matching what my mother told me.

"Yes, I do," Simon said, nodding gravely. "To show Beryl how silly she was being, Penelope pretended to fall for your gramps, but he took it rather seriously and the whole thing got out of hand. Then, as I said before you so rudely interrupted me ages ago, the war broke out, and everything went topsy-turvy."

"Why?" I asked. "What happened?"

"Giulio got called up by the Italian army to go and fight with

Mussolini," Simon whispered, shuddering as if it had happened just yesterday. "Oh, the scenes! The intrigues! Should he go back to Italy? Should he stay in London and sign up with the Brits, and possibly shame his parents? He was their only child who survived—three other infants died at birth or from illness. Well, while he was deciding, Beryl made up his mind for him."

"Grandma? How?" I breathed, spellbound.

"She blabbed to an English soldier and inadvertently reported him as an enemy alien," Simon announced. "Revenge, darling. Sisters can be like that, you know. They seethe inside and then one day, bang! They take the first opportunity. Poor Giulio, he wasn't a fascist, but what could he do? He *had* to leave England before they interned him in some awful jail. But Penelope surprised us all. We knew she adored him, we knew they were lovers, but what we didn't know was that she really, truly loved the boy and was willing to go to Italy with him, can you imagine, when every British citizen was scurrying out of Italy on every last train, plane or hay-cart?"

"What happened to them in Italy?" I asked. "When was this? What year?"

"Oh, 1940. For a few weeks she seemed to just vanish. We were frantic, nobody knew where she was, alive or dead. Because"—here he paused triumphantly and significantly—"she drove into Italy in that car, my dear. That selfsame car. And when the time came, she drove herself right back out of there. How, I don't know. I heard it was all pretty dicey. Giulio had to go into the Italian army. But his parents died before the war was over. They were old, and the stress, I'm sure, was too much for them. Giulio was reported missing in action, and it broke them, just broke them. Then Penelope got word he'd been killed. She was ready; he'd told her what to do if he died. She took the child back to London for the rest of the war."

I nearly dropped my teeth. "Child?" I said as calmly as possible. "Did Aunt Penelope have a child?"

Simon looked taken aback. "Good God, of course not. She was much too careful for that sort of thing," he said primly. "No, no. Giulio had a ten-year-old son by an American woman he'd met in Italy, long before he met Penelope. The American gal fell in love with him as only rich Americans can, and she had his baby. But then she didn't want it. She acted like those people who go on vacation and buy a cat, but when it's time to return home they simply sail off leaving the pet tied to a fence to starve. She wanted to give it to an orphanage. Giulio, of course, wouldn't hear of it—family pride and all. So he kept it.

"He adored the child, who lived mostly with Giulio's parents in Italy but came to visit at Penelope's house on the Riviera in the summertime. A beautiful boy he was, with lovely dark hair and blue eyes. Oh dear, what was his name? It will come. I used to bring him little chocolates, too, you'd think I'd remember. Getting old is a dreadful thing, my dear, try not to do it if you can possibly avoid it. I mean, the scientists must have come up with something in their wretched test tubes by now, mustn't they? But for codgers like me, old age is the only way to go, considering there's only one other, and fatal, alternative—"

His teasing tone was meant to distract me, I knew, but I hung on with all my might to this story. "You were saying—the child's name was—?" I persisted.

He snapped his fingers. "Domenico," he said briskly. "That's it. Everyone just naturally assumed he was a war orphan when Penelope brought him to London. She positively doted on him. Bought him a darling rocking-horse for Christmas, dressed him in good wool coats in the winter, made sure he got plenty of Italian food so he wouldn't forget his papa. Ah, me," Simon sighed, and this time there was no theatricality to the brightness in his eyes. "The war made heroes and fools of us all," he said. He fell silent, remembering.

And suddenly I thought of the map in Aunt Penelope's car, and the little toy soldier I'd found on the floor. Something you might use to distract a child so he wouldn't notice the grave danger he was in on a long road-trip getaway during a war.

I had quietly hauled out my little chart of my family tree, and while Simon was talking, I began adding a branch down the middle for Aunt Penelope. It looked like this:

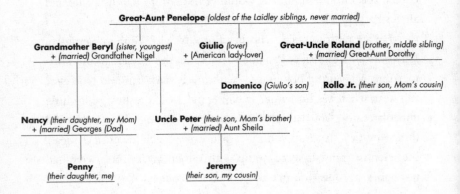

Great-Aunt Penelope *(oldest of the Laidley siblings, never married)*

Grandmother Beryl *(sister, youngest)* + *(married)* Grandfather Nigel

Giulio *(lover)* + *(American lady-lover)*

Great-Uncle Roland *(brother, middle sibling)* + *(married)* Great-Aunt Dorothy

Domenico *(Giulio's son)*   **Rollo Jr.** *(their son, Mom's cousin)*

Nancy *(their daughter, my Mom)* + *(married)* Georges *(Dad)*

Uncle Peter *(their son, Mom's brother)* + *(married)* Aunt Sheila

Penny *(their daughter, me)*

Jeremy *(their son, my cousin)*

I paused, but I had to ask. "What became of the little boy, Domenico?"

Simon shook his head. "Oh, the American woman found out that she couldn't have another child with her new American husband, so she tracked down Domenico to reclaim him and drag him back to the States. She had the money, clout, and bloodline to do so, I suppose, but certainly it wasn't fair to poor Penelope. Just broke her heart all over again, like losing Giulio. Penelope tried to keep in direct contact with Giulio's boy, but the Americans sent back all her letters to him unopened. Beasts. Anyway, we never saw Domenico again.

"But Penelope had her spies, and she found out that Giulio's little boy had grown up. Domenico married, and he ran a little grocery store with his wife, and he had a son of his own."

"What was the name of Domenico's son?" I asked.

"Now you're *really* pushing my old gray matter," Simon told me, screwing his eyes shut, recalling the name like a fortune-teller peering into the past. "Wait . . . wait . . . it's coming . . . yes. Domenico's son was called—Anthony. He actually came to live in London, and he fell in love with an English girl. But the poor boy. Then it was *his* turn for a war. Vietnam this time. Boys like him always say they won't go, but in the end they go. Point of honor and all that, can't let their country down. At least Tony managed to survive long enough to come back to England before he died, but all the same, his little English girlfriend was left stranded with *his* son. You see the way history really works, don't you, dear? Men keep siring babies and getting killed in wars, and the women and children have to pick up the pieces."

I was scribbling rapidly to keep up with Simon, adding more names down the middle:

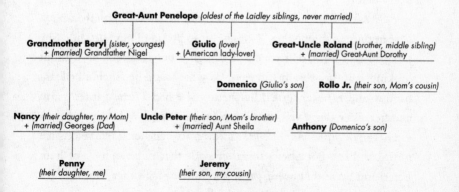

I paused, waiting for the name of Anthony's son. Simon wagged his finger at me.

"Well, your auntie was a good soul, never forget that. Cleverer and more beautiful than anyone I've seen before or since. And she knew how to make a move, and when to make a move. She simply couldn't sit still when she heard that Giulio's great-grandchild was living in some wretched one-room flat in London, with a working mama. The English girl who worked in the theatrical agency . . . her name was . . . Sheila . . . she'd had a falling-out with her own fine family, you see, and they wanted her to put the baby up for adoption, but when she refused they just cut her off."

He drew his finger across his neck. "Penelope found out about it, and came up with the right solution, of course. She always did, with that fine mind of hers."

I had a strange sensation, as if the world had stopped spinning and everything was absolutely still, as if even the furniture was holding its breath, as I was. I was trying very hard to ask the right questions in the right way so that Simon wouldn't suddenly wake up from his dream of the past and stop talking, when he was right at the point of telling me something I just had to know, yet, almost like *déjà vu*, had surely heard before.

"So, what did Aunt Penelope do about it?" I asked quietly.

Simon straightened up. "I was never so proud of her," he said. "She just had that light, deft touch of bringing people together without looking as if she were half trying. It's what made her such a brilliant hostess, and it never served her better. She had a little garden party, and her sister Beryl was there with *her* son, Peter. Well, Penelope invited Tony's girlfriend, Sheila, and even loaned her a marvelous tea gown; and she got Sheila together with that dull nephew of hers, Peter; and there they were, getting to know each other over iced tea cakes. And soon enough, Peter proposed. Even so, Penelope had to have a little sit-down talk with Sheila, to convince her that it was in the baby's best interest to accept Peter's proposal, and that Tony's child would be raised with all the advantages of a proper English gentleman . . ."

He saw the look on my face then, and his eyes narrowed and his voice trailed off warily.

"My dear girl, what a peculiar shade of pale green you've turned," he said. "Are you about to become ill? You mustn't do it here. This carpet was given me by an Arab prince—"

He stopped joking when I didn't laugh. I'd been with him all the way, but now I was doing a little remembering of my own. He noticed that I was writing, but he politely refrained from trying to peer at the chart.

"What is it, darling?" he said gently. "Tell Uncle Simon and maybe he can help."

I recovered just slightly, enough to say quietly, "I think—I think I know him. Who you're talking about."

" 'He who I am talking about?' " he repeated, puzzled.

"The great-grandson of Aunt Penelope's driver. I think I know his name," I said in a whisper.

"Wait, don't tell me. I, unlike most people, am very good with names," he said, as if trying to calm me down by making a game of it. "Let's see, let's see . . . the handsome Giulio Principe first; then his poor little boy, Domenico; then Domenico's American son, Tony, who came to London and was smitten with an English girl—and they had a son who I heard of, but never met, called . . ." He paused. He glanced away, and it took him several seconds to remember.

I'd already drawn the lines, which unexpectedly veered toward Aunt Sheila, connecting her with Anthony. Which then, astoundingly, connected with the last name on the chart:

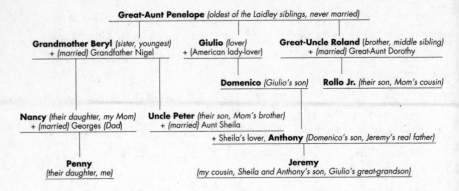

Great-Aunt Penelope *(oldest of the Laidley siblings, never married)*

Grandmother Beryl *(sister, youngest)* + *(married)* Grandfather Nigel

Giulio *(lover)* + *(American lady-lover)*

Great-Uncle Roland *(brother, middle sibling)* + *(married)* Great-Aunt Dorothy

Domenico *(Giulio's son)*   **Rollo Jr.** *(their son, Mom's cousin)*

Nancy *(their daughter, my Mom)* + *(married)* Georges *(Dad)*

Uncle Peter *(their son, Mom's brother)* + *(married)* Aunt Sheila

+ Sheila's lover, **Anthony** *(Domenico's son, Jeremy's real father)*

Penny *(their daughter, me)*

Jeremy *(my cousin, Sheila and Anthony's son, Giulio's great-grandson)*

Then Simon remembered the name of Anthony's son, snapped his fingers, and turned back to me triumphantly. When he did, we both spoke at the same time.

"Jeremy," we said together.

Part Nine

Chapter Twenty-five

Y OU WOULD THINK THAT HAVING SET MYSELF ON A HISTORY–DETECTIVE path researching my own family—I mean, this wasn't just comfortable dusty stuff about Cleopatra or the Borgias or Pocahontas—you would think that as a sober young woman who's stumbled onto, if not family skeletons in the closet, at least a few buried bones—well, you would think it would make me so utterly professional, so seriously focused, that I would abandon any previous vanities and keep my nose to the trail like a good bloodhound.

Well, I didn't. And there were two reasons why. Both involved the blinking light on my new answering machine the next morning, indicating phone calls that had come in while I'd gone out for my coffee. First there was a message from Erik, my boss. He sounded breathless.

"Penny darling, it's red-alert time," he announced. "Paul's been nosing around trying to find out what you're up to. Naturally we fudged for you, said you stayed on in London to do ultra-valuable research. But that little twit producer, Sheri, who was following us around in Cannes, blabbed about your inheritance. Paul didn't say anything, but you could just *see* the wheels turning. So, a word to the wise. As for us, we're still in Spain, so you don't have to call back. Love and kisses, darling. P.S., Are you rich yet? Hope so."

I didn't feel the usual apprehensive pang in my gut; Paul's image was fading fast in my mind. "Hell with Paul. I'm not a scared rabbit anymore," I said aloud. The next phone call was from Jeremy, returning the message I'd left for him last night. He spoke in a short, dismissive business tone that I figured he used on clients that he was telling to go to hell.

"Penny. It's Jeremy," he said, sounding irritated that I wasn't there. "Look. Severine called and said the earring isn't especially valuable. I mean it's not rubies. It's made of *paste*," he said, punching the word with scorn. "So that's that," he added flatly. "As for the stolen photo, well, let Rollo go chasing after fake rubies. Serves him right. Look, I have to go out of town for a few days. Harold will keep you apprised of any new developments." Then, as if he realized what a skunk he was being, he added briefly, "Be well. Good-bye."

He might just as well have added, "So buzz off, you dumbo with your crazy theories." I was understanding him better, though; I knew that I'd instilled some hope in his heart by suggesting that we would turn up something—the jewelry—that would erode Rollo's claim to the villa. When you convince other people to believe in some dopey theory of yours promising that the sun will come out and everything will be fine, and later, when it doesn't and it isn't . . . they will turn on you, because you made a fool of them for having false hopes. Well, I would send Harold my assessment of Aunt Penelope's London possessions, which totalled a bit higher than Rupert's . . . and that would be that.

However, I did have this new bombshell information about Great-Aunt Penelope's lover and Jeremy's own bloodlines, for God's sake. So I immediately telephoned him back, and of course all I got was his answering machine.

"Jeremy. Penny," I said. "I found out something important that you should know about. So call me when you return." I didn't mean to be cryptic, but it wasn't the sort of information you could leave in a machine message. Trying to be clear yet discreet is impossible, so you just hang up.

Only, the nice thing about talking to someone's answering machine from a place as lovely as Aunt Penelope's apartment was that I felt like a movie star, sadly but dramatically hanging up a pretty telephone on a theatrical-looking boudoir table-and-mirror, all framed in white and gold. Even being upset in this environment was an improvement over my previous life, where the rat-trap surroundings only reinforced one's sense of doom. Here, in this glamorous bedroom of a fabulous London house, I could sigh over my troubles like a heroine who's still pretty sure that things will turn out all right in the end.

"Paste," I repeated to myself, sighing theatrically like Simon. Then I had a shock. Right next to Great-Aunt Penelope's gilt-framed movie-star photo, I saw my own face, reflected and framed in the gold-and-white mirror. There we were, side by side, about the same age, but she looked glamorous and carefree, and I looked like a hunched-over, disheveled, frowning, pale, poor comparison as I squinted at the sparkling earrings in the photo, trying to see that they weren't diamonds after all—hence my furrowed brow. And believe me, it wasn't a pretty sight.

I'd been feeling like a movie star because of my charming surroundings, but in reality I looked more like a scullery maid who's just scuttled the ashes and paused to catch her breath by sneakily sitting at her ladyship's table. The lack of sleep, the dehydration from too much airplane travel, the months of cramped, crunched-up muscles from close work—it was all catching up with me. In my twenties, one night's sleep usually banished any telltale signs of the previous day. But now, there I was, eyes all squinty, hair all flat, dark sleepless circles under the eyes, mouth pressed together in grim concentration, brow all furrowed, clothes all wrinkled from travel, like yesterday's newspaper.

I straightened up, horrified. I saw that I'd been working like a galley slave for months, maybe years. I never took vacations because of the fear of dropping out of sight and not being hired ever again. Unemployed spells were not restful, because the credit-card balance mounted and every jaunt to a shop or restaurant caused paroxysms of guilt about spending more money. Not enough sleep, too much dread. It was all there, in worried little puckers and lines. I needed smoothing out, or this rumpled, mournful look might just become my permanent face.

I thought of Severine, too. Somehow she managed to work, be efficient and productive, and still look ruthlessly magnificent. But she had Louis, an assistant, and she made loads of money. Surely that helped. She didn't go scurrying around library stalls, squinting at badly projected microfilms of old manuscripts and newspapers.

I looked at Aunt Penelope's photograph again. It was a publicity shot, of course, and she'd probably pulled out all the stops to look glamorous for it, but it implied a certain lifestyle of fun and good times and carefree tossing of the head on the deck of a yacht or the balcony of a villa. She went jaunting around in an "auto," not a "car," for fun, not simply to commute to work in rush-hour traffic and then to scramble from one chore to the next.

She'd be baffled if she knew how we "liberated" women spent our days, even our pathetic little extended weekend vacations, when we bothered to take them at all. When Aunt Penelope's generation travelled, I thought darkly, they didn't kill themselves rushing to get to the airport early, only to be frisked like thieves at security checkpoints.

No, Aunt Penelope's crowd lazily sailed away on "ocean liners" that might take a month to reach their destinations. So people made a party of it, with friends coming down to the boat to gaily see them off; then they embarked upon weeks of floating champagne suppers

and dancing under the stars, in the company of dukes and ballet danc-
ers, not swarms of budget tourists looking for a cheap buffet.

Oh, I knew perfectly well that nostalgia for the past—especially
a past that isn't even your own—is like believing in fairy tales. But
maybe our rushed new century is missing something slow, sweet and
elegant from bygone eras. If we even remembered to look for charm
and elegance in our lives, could we manage to find it? I wondered.

That was why I kept trying to escape into romanticized previous
times, but I saw that as a strategy for living it clearly wasn't working. Because I'd finally got my magic wish—to have a little paid-up,
elegant launch pad in a fine part of a lively city—and now, I was the
one who had to change, and learn to live up to it, or surely it would
disappear.

The clock in the library gonged softly, telling the passing hour. It
told me that there probably wasn't much I could do about it immediately, but still I ought to do something, even symbolic, perhaps one
tiny step toward restoration that would set me on a larger path.

So, with this in mind, I rose resolutely and put on an old favorite
flowered cotton dress that had a full, flounced, fifties skirt and short
matching jacket, which I'd brought with me on the off-chance that
I'd have a day without work. Then I set out to experience the world
with new eyes, and to enjoy my own life.

Chapter Twenty-six

N OT BEING PARTICULARLY EXPERIENCED IN DOING SIMPLE, LIGHT-hearted things, and not really knowing my way around London's pleasures, I started out getting knocked about in pedestrian traffic, bus traffic, the Tube trains underground, and general everyday mayhem. I couldn't go to a museum like most people, because for me that would be a busman's holiday.

But, thanks to Simon, who'd told me about Aunt Penelope's favorite haunts in London, I was able to plunk myself on a park bench by her favorite fragrant flowered path, where I could enjoy the light, sweet air of a warm summer day in London. Then I did a little selective shopping. Mindful of Aunt Penelope, I bought a few good things that I normally would find excuses not to buy: a fine-spun silky cocktail dress with a gold satin evening coat whose lining matched the dress, and a pretty bathing suit with a cover-up. The kinds of things I always wanted but talked myself out of, by buying cheaper versions, for fear that my grubby lifestyle would wear them out and I wouldn't be able to afford to replace them. All in soft pastels and whites, too, instead of dour and durable black. It may seem a conventional way to try to improve one's life and appearance, but for me it was a major accomplishment, because I normally hate shopping and do it with grim determination, agony over money, and guilt. It's amazing how quickly you can shop when you're not torturing yourself.

When I was done, I felt triumphant, but out on the street again the rest of the world was definitely not trying to lead a calmer life, and everybody was in a frantic hurry to get past me, around me, and perhaps through me if necessary—and because of lingering travel fatigue I was at a disadvantage in maneuvering. I looked around quickly for some quiet place to duck into so I could catch my breath and get my bearings.

I'd retraced Aunt Penelope's footsteps all over London, and, according to Simon, this was the street where she went to have a weekly massage ... and to have her palm read. There were no fortune-tellers there anymore, but Aunt Penelope's little masseuse had been replaced by a full-fledged spa, right there in the very same building, with the same narrow, dark flight of stairs (although I later discovered that around the corner there was another entrance, with a fast modern elevator). It was just too appealing to my mystic sense of fate, so I went right in the same door as Aunt Penelope, and up the same mysterious staircase.

What was I expecting to find? A peaceful, leisurely Victorian spa where mildly tubercular guests clad in formal white linen were served seven-course meals on delicate china and crystal in turn-of-the-century dining rooms? Where you were bathed and gently massaged and then tucked into balcony chairs with blankets called "rugs," overlooking placid lakes and mountains, where you could be generally pampered in a quiet and dignified environment? Once again, my fatal capacity for believing what I read instead of seeing what's right in front of me did me in.

To be fair, it's not entirely my fault that I'm so gullible. I'm not the only one who goes around pretending that things are more wonderful than they really are. Somebody took the trouble to make that reception room a peaceful cocoon in earthy red, brown and cinnamon, replete with dried flowers and herbs, soft, soothing music and lighting, and a whispery high-priestess receptionist who offered me a gentle, restorative "Half Day of Rejuvenation" described with overtones of a nineteenth-century taking-of-the-waters experience.

But in the end, whammo—modern everyday reality took over. Once she knew I was on board, the receptionist's voice actually changed from soothing guru to brisk assembly-line overseer, as she whisked me off to a gym-style locker room where she padlocked my clothes so I couldn't have a sudden change of heart and bolt out of the place.

Wearing my newly issued cardboard slippers and a scratchy one-size-doesn't-fit-all, fat-lady robe with sleeves as long as the Seven Dwarfs', I padded down the hallway, which smelled of glue and quick-dry paint from the nail salon that treated hands like reconstruction jobs. I declined a complete nail replastering, and got a quick paint job, requiring me to make that tiresome request of please-don't-cut-my-cuticles-thank-you.

Beyond the nail salon was the chamber where torturous medical instruments were being used to do "scientific" things to brighten, whiten, even out, and rejuvenate the skin with poisonous needles and peels. Or you could get the "natural" option, a mud face masque for sensitive souls, which I went for. I was then parked in a waiting room among other robe-clad women with masques on their faces and cotton stuck between their toes, who coughed ominously and chatted loudly on mobile phones. At this odd juncture I was offered a "health appetizer"—stale carrot juice and soy paté that tasted of refrigerators. I was kept waiting long enough to hear the same sitar ditty come round again on the canned music.

Finally I was summoned into a dark, closet-sized room at the very far end of the hall, which was filled with a massage table and pots of creams in unmarked silver containers, making the room resemble a doctor's office. Here at last I met a tired-looking woman who introduced herself as my "massage therapist" (she got insulted when I called her a masseuse). She rattled off a swift explanation of every phase of the treatment, with mingled overtones of religious fervor, medical righteousness, and false perkiness, as she helped me onto a table so overheated electrically that I felt nauseous when I lay stomach-down on it.

I'd expected to drift off drowsily with a meditative massage, but this salon believed in pummeling you into shape to give you a smugly virtuous edge over the rest of the flabby world. In a muffled voice I explained that I wasn't interested in having my inner organs pounded and kneaded like dough. She shrugged and lightened up, but her mind seemed to be on her next meal, date, or day off, because occasionally she'd have a lapse and start vigorously shaking my arms out of their sockets as if shaking out a mop, until I squawked and woke her from her reverie.

Having next been covered with seaweed, wrapped in foil, and steamed like a fish, all to the tune of Zen zithers or whatever they were, I at least had the sense to refuse a radical haircut and asked, instead, for a light trim and a simple blow-dry. However, I didn't catch on in time to avoid the highlight of my treatment, which spas seem to be most obsessed about—the removal of body hair. The "Half Day of Rejuvenation" included getting waxed like a lemon.

During the whole rip-and-tear session I kept my mind busy by contemplating how the act of dripping hot wax on a human being would have displeased Lucrezia Borgia, who, after just one of these sessions, would surely have ordered her "massage therapist" to be summarily executed by being dropped into a vat of hot wax. And further back, our monkey ancestors would have simply bitten the arm off anybody who tried to deprive them of their body hair.

Mercifully, my skin rebelled just in time to prevent me from having the final wax job on an area of the body that only porn stars used to wax. The "therapist" stopped short and said, "Oh my God. You should have told me you were sensitive. Better not do the bikini area."

I looked down at my arms and legs, which were covered with round red welts the size of silver dollars. "What's that?" I cried.

"Hives," she said quickly. "It must be hives. Haven't you ever had hives before?"

"No," I said. It looked like I had a rare case of mega-measles.

"They'll go away in a few hours," she promised in an uncertain tone. "Your skin is *really* sensitive. You should *definitely* skip the exfoliator. I wouldn't do another thing to your face."

At that particular moment my mobile phone rang in the pocket of my scratchy bathrobe. It had been there all day, but any sound it may have made earlier would have been drowned out by the very loud Zen lutes, flutes, drums and chants that were piped in at full roar in every treatment room. They must have paused to change the tape or something, for in that blessed moment of silence I heard my phone shrilling insistently. The girl handed me my robe from the hook on the door where it was hanging, and I fumbled around in the voluminous pockets.

"Penny," Jeremy said. "Where the bloody hell are you? My out-of-town client cancelled and I've been trying to reach you at Aunt Pen's all morning. Then I found your mobile number, but I kept getting your recording. Are you all right?"

"I had an appointment," I said, trying to sound as confident as Aunt Penelope. The Zen music started up again, full bore.

"What's that music? Have you put yourself in an ashram or something?" he demanded.

"Has something happened?" I inquired in a tone to challenge his demanding one, covering my other ear so I could hear him better.

"Denby called," Jeremy said. "He said he'd found a few things in the car we might want to see for ourselves. He was funny about it, said he didn't want to discuss it on the phone. He's never like that. Besides, my car is ready, too. Severine is out of town and I don't want to leave this to Louis, so I'm going to fly down there. Do you want to come? Because I'm on my way to the airport and I can pick you up, but really we've got to move fast. Where are you?"

I gave him the address of the salon, but not the name, because it was called "The Scarlet Plume." I'd no idea why. Anyway, he said, "Fine. Because I'm only fifteen minutes away. But can you be out on the street ready to jump in? Because we literally must fly."

"All right, all right," I said. "I'll be out there ready when you arrive."

And then, after I rang off, having allowed my not-cousin to rush me like that right after vowing that I would lead a calmer, more mea- sured, ocean-liner-paced life, I saw that there were not only more red splotches on my legs but new ones emerging between my eyebrows.

"Oh, *no*," I moaned. "I can't let him see me like this. Can't you do something?"

To her credit, the wax therapist swung into action by paging the make-up expert and having him come in. He was a tall, thin, wiry Asian man with a headful of thick, wavy hair.

When he saw me, he sucked in his breath between his teeth, sized it all up, and said, "For the arms and legs, we'll use my BodyGuard Armour for Extra-Sensitive Skin—it's got skin-colored vitamin E lo- tion. Maybe a little green Sleuth UnderCover first, which I'll also use on your face so it won't be, like, the first thing that hits him when he sees you." It was then, and only then, that I understood the motif of this place, which was that it used espionage and spy symbols, as if its customers were international intriguers. For fun.

"Are you sure her skin can take it?" the wax therapist asked nervously.

"Honey, this is *not* my first time out at the rodeo," he said. "A little Agent Aloe under all of it will do the trick."

"You've now got eleven minutes," I gulped. He flung open his bag of tricks and set to work, expertly painting with green makeup, and blue, which at first alarmed me because it looked far more monstrous, but then came the next layers of ivory, yellow, and white.

"Go easy on the face," I warned. "I don't want to look like a clown."

"No clowns in this circus," he assured me. "And while I'm at it, I'll get rid of those dark circles under your eyes." When he was done, it actually looked so miraculously normal and healthy that I ended up buying the green and blue and other paints.

"Not that I expect to break out into hives like this again anytime soon," I mumbled.

"Be prepared. That's my motto," he said crisply.

I stumbled into the reception area and elevator with all my shopping bags of new clothes for a calmer life, trying not to sneeze at the mingled strong scents of hair dye, nail glue, chemical peel, and aromatherapy with wafting patchouli, fake lavender, rosemary, and camphor. There is, after all, a rather fine line between being pampered and being embalmed.

Down on the street a nice wind whipped up, all full of soot, dust, and the first plops of rain. It had been deceptively sunny when I'd gone out without my umbrella. So now I stood there while my expensive hair blow-dry wilted and I tried to shield my face-camouflage from being washed off. Mercifully my new clothes were in plastic garment bags, so they were more sheltered than I was.

Jeremy had, of course, neglected to tell me that he would be in a company car that looked like everybody else's wet black company car. He had to bellow out the window, "Penny! Yoo-hoo!" and I had to slosh through some rapidly forming puddles and take one last splashy leap into the backseat, where I landed half across his lap.

"Marvelous. Do you jump through hoops of flame as well?" he inquired, trying to help me right myself. He sniffed. "Wow. You smell like you've plunged into a barrel of patchouli," he said. "You're late. Why didn't you tell me you were at The Scarlet Plume, instead of being so mysterious with building numbers? Were you considered a hard-core case? What exactly have you been up to this afternoon?"

"Nothing," I muttered. "A man who doesn't return phone calls and then suddenly shows up with an emergency flight plan really doesn't have any business asking a lot of nosy questions no man should ask a woman. And how do you know about this place? Have you been there yourself?"

"My secretary swears by it," he said with a straight face that required absolute control.

"Oh, shit," I said wearily, and I thought I saw the driver grin to himself.

"Very well. I won't ask," Jeremy assured me, but he peered at me curiously. "Did you have a rendezvous with a suitor tonight that I inadvertently interfered with?"

"Again, it's not the sort of inquiry a gentleman makes," I said.

"Have you been reading old English novels or something?" he guessed. "You sound funny."

At this point I felt I ought to abandon my half-baked attempts to make my life more elegant and dignified. I simply didn't have enough criteria to know what to do first. It would be a massive job, I now saw, to resist the many frenzied tugs and sand traps of the twenty-first century. I'd have to postpone the task until I'd researched it more thoroughly.

Changing the subject usually works with men. So I turned to him and said, "Did Denby say anything more than what you told me on the telephone?"

He shook his head. "No. I haven't a clue what he's up to, but his clients are pretty wealthy, paranoid people who are fanatical about discretion, so he prefers to err on the side of caution. Still, from his tone it sounded pretty big."

I wasn't sure how to broach the subject of Simon and, more important, Aunt Penelope's chauffeur-lover. I certainly wasn't going to do it in a London limousine with a nosey-parker eavesdropping driver who was desperately threading his way through a maze of traffic to Heathrow but was still listening to every word, or so it seemed. I thought ahead and still couldn't see myself saying, while seated in an airplane soaring over France, "Oh, by the way, did you know that Aunt Penelope was so madly in love with your great-grandfather that she may have talked your mother into marrying her nephew Peter just to keep you under her wing?"

Yet it was information I felt he truly needed to know. Unless, of course, it was all gossip. I didn't think so, but I ought to be careful. While I'd been lying on the massage table trying to figure out my next move, it occurred to me that I ought to pay another little call on Aunt Sheila, and I'd been planning to do just that until Jeremy whisked me away so unceremoniously.

"Jeremy," I said cautiously, "when was the last time you talked to your mother?"

He glanced up, slightly annoyed. "She left a message for me yesterday," he said. "She's gone to Italy on holiday. She goes there often, whenever she feels 'a bit stressed out,' she says." He tried unsuccessfully to keep the bitterness out of his voice.

"I've been doing a little research into Aunt Penelope's life," I said quietly, "and I think we should talk when we're somewhere private."

The car was pulling up to the terminal now, and he was slightly distracted. "Hmm? Talk? About what?" But then the glare of lights from the terminal came spilling into the car and washed over us when we started sliding out of the vehicle. He stared at me in sudden shock and said, "What on earth is the matter with your legs? What's that red stuff all over them?"

My skirt had gotten pushed up while I was struggling to follow him out. He actually stopped sliding across the seat. Aghast, I saw that a few more hives had emerged.

"Oh, that," I said, trying to sound casual. "Just hives. I was having a skin treatment and my skin's a bit sensitive."

"A bit!" he said, with fascinated horror. "Whoa, those are the biggest hives I've ever seen. My God, they're positively tremendous! Are you sure you're all right?"

"Yes, yes," I said irritably, pushing him out of the car, glancing worriedly at the skycap who was on the lookout to collect luggage. "Now shut up before someone overhears you and thinks I've got a communicable disease and shouldn't be let on the plane," I hissed.

"It's a good thing that I came along and broke your dinner date," he said with mock sincerity. "Your fortune hunter might have taken one look at those hives and decided that, heiress or not, you would be too much trouble."

Chapter Twenty-seven

WELL, I CHICKENED OUT AND DIDN'T TELL HIM ON THE AIRPLANE. He's the type of man that stewardesses hover around, and I couldn't exactly say, "Guess what? Your great-grandfather was Aunt Penelope's lover and chauffeur." I felt certain he'd strangle the messenger who gave him such shocking news and, having gone berserk, be mistaken for a terrorist. We were flying business class this time, and Jeremy spent the entire flight frowning into his computer and clicking away, which was a bore.

When we landed, he glanced up briskly and said, "Severine sent a message that she's back in town, so either she or Louis will pick us up and drop us at the villa." I was momentarily distracted by that queer little feeling in the pit of my stomach at the mention of Severine; and what's more, when I saw Louis waving at us, I felt an embarrassing but involuntary surge of relief that it was he who'd showed up and not Severine.

Louis was his usual calm, polite self, but I had a nagging feeling that something serious was going to happen, even before we reached the narrow road that led to the villa. It doesn't occur often, but sometimes I get a slight premonition that starts with a cold chill on the back of my neck and makes my hair stand on end. Sure enough, we turned down the road leading to Aunt Penelope's street, swung around the curve—and there was an ambulance and flashing lights and medical attendants and a stretcher, and Denby's dashing red sports car with the side smashed in.

Louis had to do a lot of rapid-fire translating for us and for the French emergency team. Everybody seemed to be talking all at once, but somehow we managed to piece together what had happened, especially since the female medic spoke enough patchy English to help us out. Some truck had sideswiped Denby. It was a hit-and-run job. Happened so fast in the blinding afternoon sunlight that he couldn't really describe it, except to say vaguely that it was a black truck, the kind landscapers and builders use, and he never saw the driver's face. Pretty bad description for a mechanic, but Denby was dazed, and his face was bruised from the rearview mirror, which had broken off at the impact and whacked him in the head.

The medic got really fussy at that point and told us to get out of the way because they had to take him to the hospital. Louis arranged to have Denby's car towed; then he drove us to the villa, where Jeremy and I and all my parcels got into Jeremy's car, which Denby had left all fixed up and waiting for us in the villa turnaround. Then we followed Louis's car to the hospital.

"Bloody bastards!" Jeremy kept saying with feeling, and "Poor old Denby."

When we reached the hospital, they were unloading the stretcher, and Louis had to deal with most of the bureaucratic stuff and the cops. A nurse asked if Denby had any family she should call. Jeremy managed to extract from Denby several phone numbers for his wife, and he left messages at all of them. Louis had to go back to the office, but told us to call him if we needed him again.

When Denby's wife called the emergency room, Jeremy was summoned to the telephone to explain things to her in English. Denby motioned to me to bend down near his face so I could hear him.

"There was something in the door of your auntie's car, love," he whispered. " 'At's why she hung a bit crooked. A painting, packed real careful. I took it out and put it on the car seat, then locked up the garage. 'Twas a Virgin and Child, like the Catholics do." He spoke in a tired, muffled voice. The nurse came over and gave me the fish-eye and told me that the patient must be kept quiet and I should wait in the waiting room until summoned by the doctor; then she whisked Denby away behind the swinging doors of the emergency examining rooms.

Mercifully, the doctor spoke some English, and after he examined Denby he told Jeremy about fractures, bruises, etc., and he said that more tests and X-rays would have to be done, but he thought Denby had lucked out and was in pretty good shape, considering. The doctor expected him to remain stable, but he must be kept under observation for possible concussion. We were not allowed back to talk to Denby, who'd already been sent off for his X-rays. Jeremy conferred more with the nurse and then the cops. They were singularly unfazed by the whole event, and said that now that the summer season had begun, it was all too common during *les vacances* to have these hit-and-run crashes.

"Jeremy," I said urgently, as soon as I could talk to him alone, "we've got to get back to the villa. Denby said he found a painting hidden inside the door of the car. And he left it in the car. Oh, my God!" I said suddenly.

"What is it?" he said.

"*That's* why the photograph was stolen from Aunt Penny's photo album!" I whispered. "It wasn't because of the necklace she was wearing. It was because of that painting hanging behind her. Jeremy. Did you ever see a painting of a Madonna and Child listed anywhere on Aunt Penelope's list of possessions? I sure didn't. And there isn't any such painting hanging now on the library wall."

Chapter Twenty-eight

Aᴌᴌ ᴛʜᴇ ʀᴇsᴛ ᴏꜰ ᴛʜᴇ ᴡᴀʏ ᴛᴏ ᴛʜᴇ ᴠɪʟʟᴀ, Jᴇʀᴇᴍʏ ꜰɪʀᴇᴅ ᴏꜰꜰ ᴏᴜᴇs-tions at me about the painting. What did it look like? How big was it? Could I tell who the artist might be, what style, what country of origin? What time period? Did I know anything about the artist?

I shook my head. I'd never seen the painting up close, only in the background of the snapshot. But something else occurred to me. "You know, there's a later photo of Aunt Penelope sitting in the same chair in the same spot—looking older, wiser, sadder—and I don't think the painting was still on the wall in that one. That means she either took it down and put it somewhere else or sold it—or somebody else took it."

Jeremy absorbed this. "I never saw any insurance claims filed for stolen art, or any bills of sale. And she kept every scrap of paper regarding money. When were these pictures taken?"

"The first one, with the painting on the wall behind her, was in the thirties, judging by her age and the clothes," I said. "The later one, taken in the exact same spot in the library, without the painting, was much later, like the nineties."

We had reached the driveway of the villa by now, and there was a light on in the garage. "Denby could have left it on, I suppose," Jeremy muttered. I could hardly bear to wait for him to pull up to the garage, jump out, and open the combination lock so we could get inside.

We rushed to the old Dragonetta. The right-side door had been taken off and laid on the floor. Denby, with the skill of a surgeon, had carefully taken it apart, removing the leather padding. On the inside of the car door, there was space for something big and flat and slim to be nestled, well-protected by the upholstery. But nothing was there now.

"He said he left the painting for us on the seat of the car," I remembered. "Then he locked up the garage." Eagerly we peered into the car.

Nothing was on the seat. We searched the whole garage, and there was no painting at all, let alone a Madonna and Child.

"Are you sure you heard him right?" Jeremy asked, for lack of any other explanation. I nodded vigorously, then shivered, feeling a strange cool draft on my skin. Then I saw why. The evening breeze was wafting in through the garage window. Which was wide open. I pointed to it.

"Would Denby leave a window open like that after being so careful to lock this place up for us?" I asked. "I mean, he thought it was valuable."

"No," said Jeremy. "He wouldn't leave a window open. Somebody's been here. And might still be. Stay here, Penny. I'm going to look around. Keep your phone on."

Jeremy quickly took a tour of the villa and the grounds. It was a little creepy, waiting for him in the garage. The sun was already setting and casting strange shadows everywhere. But soon he came back and announced, "Nobody's here anymore. No signs of entry in the villa."

"Jeremy," I said, "there's only one person I know who could have seen that painting in the London apartment, lusted after it, searched for it, and stolen it. Someone who likes to collect, buy, and sell art and antiques. Good old Rollo. Did he know all along that it was here? Is that why we caught him trying to steal the car, with that whole dumb bobsled story?"

Jeremy shook his head. "I don't think he knew that the painting was hidden in the car," he said. "I think he just wanted the car because it looked valuable. But I do think Rollo was aware that the painting existed, and when he didn't find it among the contents of the villa that he's supposed to get, he went looking for it in Aunt Pen's apartment in London."

"And when the painting didn't turn up in the apartment the night he broke in, Rollo came back to the villa to search for it again, saw that Denby had found it, and swiped it?" I asked.

"Not quite. Rollo's been in London all this time. We've had a man watching him since the night somebody broke into your apartment," Jeremy said. He paused. "But he could have had somebody here in France working with him, keeping an eye out for the painting."

"Yes! Remember those guys who were with him but ran away the night we caught him here at the garage?" I said excitedly. "One of them could have been watching this place, especially once Denby started inspecting the car. Maybe he even saw Denby remove the painting from the door."

We made a quick search, but nothing else seemed to be missing. I picked up the toy soldier, and something made me put it in my purse, so I could talk about it later with Jeremy. I looked for the toolbox that Denby had filled with all the little oddities he'd found in the car. It was still there. Everything was the same, but something bothered me about the matchbook Denby had found. I picked it up.

Jeremy's phone rang. He spoke into it tersely, then ended the call and turned to me. His voice sounded odd when he said, "Are you ready for this? That was a report from the man who's been keeping an eye on Rollo in London," he said. "Said that Rollo's at the airport there. He bought a ticket for France."

"You were right, then!" I said excitedly. "Somebody here alerted him that Denby found the painting. So Rollo had the guy steal the painting for him before we could see it."

"It's possible," Jeremy muttered.

"Hey. This matchbook isn't old, like all the other stuff," I said suddenly, staring at the name of the Monte Carlo casino. "I don't think it belonged to Aunt Penelope. But it had to have been in the car before you asked Denby to get involved. That's why Denby thought it was something he should toss into this box along with everything else he gathered up for me that belonged to Aunt Penelope. But I think somebody else dropped it here."

Jeremy wasn't really listening about the matchbook. "I didn't finish telling you which city Rollo's flying to," he said.

"I already know," I answered. "Monte Carlo." I held out the matchbook. "Rollo, you see, is a gambling man. He must have dropped it here that night we caught him." Jeremy looked at the matchbook now.

"Is there a telephone number?" he asked. "We could see if he's checked in—"

I called the hotel, and asked if Rollo had checked in yet. There was a pause, and then the front desk said not yet, but he had a reservation. I thanked them sweetly and rang off.

"You didn't ask for his room number," Jeremy observed.

"I knew they'd never give out a room number," I said, "and I didn't want to stay on long enough for them to ask who I was and if I'd like to leave a message."

"You still could have asked."

"No I couldn't," I said, irritated. Then I gave him a sly, truly inspired look. "Listen," I said, "I've got a plan. To catch this thief and get that painting back. Care to join me?"

Part Ten

Chapter Twenty-nine

I HAVEN'T MADE MANY GREAT PLANS IN MY LIFE, BUT THIS ONE, I THINK, was my best, and Jeremy didn't actually say so, but he went along with it. And it would have worked, too, except for one little hitch.

We found the casino easily enough; it was inside an old hotel on the main avenue of Monte Carlo. The hotel looked like a big bridal cake, white with carved scrolls and curlicues as if it were iced with dollops of whipped cream. It was enormous. You drove up a private driveway that swept around the front of it, where uniformed valets and doormen sprang to your car even before you brought it to a stop, and they opened the doors and wrestled your key away from you so that they could park your car and keep the traffic moving. Which it did, with well-dressed gamblers hurrying to get closer to the money.

"Let me get this straight," Jeremy said as we pulled up to the casino. "You think that the guys who stole the painting for Rollo are going to hand it over to him here?"

"Yes," I said positively. "In a hotel room where we'd never look for him. I'll bet he's a regular here. Great-Aunt Dorothy really howled about it. He apparently has a habit."

"Drugs," Jeremy said. "That was years ago."

"No," I said. "He's a gambler. Has oodles of debts. Which is why he settled the English will. So he could get his hands on the cash Aunt Penelope left him, to pay off his pals. But he's also a compulsive antiques collector. You should have seen him, with his little antique cigarette case. I'm telling you, he can't help himself with these things. Gambling, collecting, and selling artifacts of dubious origin, according to my parents."

"Right. He got into trouble once," Jeremy recalled. "Family had to pay off somebody to keep him out of jail."

"Yes. I heard Dorothy criticize the people he hangs out with to gamble. She made it sound as if this casino was his home away from home—the perfect place for the guys who stole the painting to exchange it for cash. I just hope we can catch him before the deal goes down and he leaves."

"Steady now," Jeremy said. "And stop talking like a copper. He can't have arrived yet. Just what we'll do with him when he shows up, however—"

"I told you the whole plan," I said. "Jeremy, are you with me on this caper or not?"

"I'm just trying to keep you out of trouble, you madwoman," he said.

The hotel foyer had soaring ceilings, marble floors and pillars, a bar and tea lounge, wood-paneled gift shops and designer clothing boutiques, lots of giant potted palms, an elevator bank with gleaming gold doors, and, to the left, a large reception area for checking in and out. To the right was a well-lighted atrium, beyond which a dark, cavernous area led to the hotel dining room and, beyond that, the big casino.

Jeremy took all this in at a glance. "There must be hundreds of guests at this hotel, not to mention people who walk in just to eat in the restaurant or gamble in the casino," he said. "Even if we could track Rollo down, how do you propose to get hold of the painting?

Are you merely going to make a citizen's arrest for art theft? Possession, my dear girl—"

"Just follow the plan," I said tersely, and to my surprise, he did. We split up and communicated with our mobile phones as we cased out the hotel, looking for Rollo.

While I was checking the cocktail lounge and dining room, pretending to be thinking about making future reservations for a rather large party of guests, Jeremy went to the casino, ordered a drink, and sat at the bar to keep watch. I waited in the tea lounge for his call; I sat at a tiny table and ordered a champagne cocktail. I had my portfolio with me, but I kept it at my feet so as not to attract undue attention.

The cocktail cost more than I would normally pay for lunch. My chair was the kind that makes you sink deeply and alarmingly into it. And perhaps it wasn't the best idea to be drinking alone, because I started getting a few looks from some men at the bar, obviously on the prowl. I refused to catch their eye. It's funny, but when you are very intent on accomplishing something, it translates physically into confidence, which attracts people. Maybe they think you're on the trail of the biggest pot of gold on earth. I studied my drink, trying to look nonchalant.

Finally I got up and went back to the lobby, which had those big two-club-chairs-in-one, attached by a central shared armrest. One seat faces north, the other south, yet two people can still look at and talk to each other. I found one with two empty seats, so I parked myself on the side facing the main entrance. It was an ideal spot to watch people arriving. The waiter trailed after me, transporting my drink.

Shortly after that, my phone rang. Jeremy's voice said, "This is a waste of time."

I looked up, and there was Jeremy, walking across the lobby toward me, staring at me dolefully as he continued talking into his phone. "I see you," he said. "Do you see me? Good. Because I'm coming to take you home."

"Listen, my dear fellow," I said. "Rollo just walked in the main door, right behind you. And with him is one of the skanky guys who tried to steal my car. The guy is carrying a wrapped parcel shaped exactly like a painting. They're at the front desk now. Rollo's getting a key. Come here quick, and don't turn around." I ducked my head, in case Rollo looked up.

Jeremy dropped into the seat attached to mine. "Do you see what I see?" I demanded. I nodded toward the reception desk. There was Rollo, all right, in a white linen suit and a panama hat. Accompanied by the aforementioned creepy pal, who was wearing a dark, ill-fitting suit.

"Yep," Jeremy admitted, and he stared, fascinated, as the two men went up in the elevator together, with Rollo's pal carrying the plain, flat package wrapped in brown paper and string. It looked like the kind of package you'd see tourists carrying around when they've bought a picture at a local gallery selling views of the Riviera to remember their vacation by.

We sat there and waited, watching the elevator doors. Jeremy drank half my cocktail. It wasn't long before Rollo and his pal emerged, *sans* painting. I could barely sit still.

"He left it upstairs," I squealed.

"Shut up," Jeremy hissed. "They're heading for the casino."

"Jeremy," I said, "you follow them, and proceed with Phase Two."

"You're out of your mind. It's too risky," he said.

"It's our only chance and you know it," I said. "Go. I need you to look out for me."

Jeremy gave me a hard stare; then, resolutely, he got up. Within minutes my phone rang. "I found him," Jeremy said in a low voice. "Roulette's his game. He's settled in for a bit. Believe it or not, I think he's paying the guy off in chips. He keeps splitting his pile and sliding it in front of the guy."

"Okay," I muttered into my phone. "Proceed with Phase Three."

"You fool," he hissed. "Forget Phase Three."

"You'd better do it," I returned, "because I'm going ahead with Phase Four, regardless."

"Oh, for Christ's sake, all right. Wait for my call," he said. Phase Three was for Jeremy to phone the front desk, say that he was Rollo and that he was expecting his little female American cousin to show up and they should give her a key to his room. A few interminable minutes later, my phone rang again.

"Okay," Jeremy said. "I did as you asked. Wait for me for Phase Four, you nut—"

"Stop gumming up the plan," I snapped. "You should be getting ready for Phase Five."

So I went ahead with Phase Four by going to the desk and being my most winsome, scatterbrained self.

"Excuse me," I said in a sweet, I'm-just-a-dopey-American voice. "My cousin Rollo told me he's staying here and—at least, I *think* it's here. There's *so* many hotels on this street, gosh, I hope I'm in the right one! Mummy said it was this, but she's *so* forgetful sometimes . . . !"

"The last name, madame?" the bored man at the reception counter inquired. I told him, and another man behind the counter looked up and said, "Yes, your cousin called. He is at the casino, but asked that you wait in his room." And he handed me the key to room 719.

From the minute I got into the elevator my heart began to pound unnaturally hard and I could barely breathe. It dawned on me that I was not really cut out for this line of work—spying, stealing, what have you. I thought that everyone—the young elevator operator, the maids with their carts, and the other guests at the hotel— must surely be able to hear my racing heart banging against my ribs.

But everything went as smoothly as clockwork. I found Rollo's room, the key fit into the lock, and I slipped into the room unnoticed, because I waited for the maids to go round the corner. I'd listened at the door before I went in (I was proud of this foresight), and when I was sure that no one else was in the room, I phoned Jeremy on my mobile.

"I'm in the room. It's number 719," I said. "Proceed with Phase Five."

That meant that Jeremy was to keep an eye on Rollo, and if he got up and seemed to be heading back to the hotel room, Jeremy was to alert me. Meanwhile, it was my job to find the damned painting.

"You truly are a complete nutter," Jeremy muttered, but he hung up and continued staring at Rollo, who, he later told me, was drinking like a fish.

Rollo's room was so empty that at first I thought the man at the front desk was mistaken. The bed was still made, and there wasn't any luggage or clothing about, not even in the closet, as if nobody had checked in yet. But then I got that prickly feeling at the back of my neck again. The painting was in here. I could feel it. And I found it in the first real place I thought it might be. Under the bed.

I dragged it out and onto the bed, and my hands were shaking as I carefully untied the string and unwrapped the brown paper with agonizing care. Inside, plain cardboard lay on top, then blue tissue paper—then there it was.

It wasn't nearly as big as I'd expected. About fourteen inches wide and twenty inches long, it could easily fit into my own portfolio. Signed by an artist named A. Fabrizi, whom I believed I'd heard of, perhaps, but I was blanking out on exactly what I'd heard. This was the Madonna and Child, all right, just like the one in the photo stolen from Aunt Penelope's album.

Except for one stupendous difference—the way it made me feel when I looked at it. That stunned thing that happens to you when you turn a corner in a museum, and a particular painting seems to leap right at you, grab you by the throat. I felt mesmerized, as if I were suddenly rooted to the spot, my feet nailed down, and wild horses couldn't drag me away. I simply couldn't take my gaze away from the picture for a second, not even to blink.

The painting's background was done in those rich ochre tones that I had become so familiar with in my research on Italian art at the turn of the fifteenth century to the sixteenth. There was even, I think, real gold painted on it, amid dark autumnal colors of burnished brown and blood-red, smoky blue and golden yellow, burnt orange and olive green and dusty plum.

But the faces of the Madonna and her infant had a radiant lightness about them, in soft creams and pinks, opaline whites, even a shimmering violet, which gave them an eternal quality, a vernal sweetness in contrast to the darker background and clothing. The infant, unlike so many paintings of cupids or babies, did not have that usual awful face of a wizened old man attached to a baby body. This one really looked like a baby, gazing up in calm wonderment and adoration at his mother as if she were the sun, the sky and the clouds. What made the Madonna so remarkable, though, was the almost ordinary quality of the sweetness of her face. She looked young, human, girlish except for her mature serenity; and the effect was that you felt as if you had just walked down a street, entered a house, and opened a door on a real young woman who just happened to be living in another century but was archetypal of all young, sweet mothers from Italy. It was as if she'd looked up and caught you with her soft brown eyes and delicate rose mouth, emanating a pure but natural and touching innocence as she gazed benevolently not just at her baby but at you as well.

I felt that time had stopped and I'd found a portal to eternity, a captured moment of the past. I had to make a supreme effort to shake myself out of my reverie and tear my gaze away. For once, I thought I understood Rollo and anyone else who was obsessed with a work of art.

"Oh, God," I whispered, "this is the real thing." My heart, which had just begun to resume its normal beating, now started rat-tat-tatting again. Strangely enough, the thought that occurred to me then was, "I'm in bigger trouble than I thought." I suddenly knew that I had to wrap this all up and get out, fast. I had just finished tying the string when my phone rang. It was Jeremy.

"Got it," I breathed. "Proceed with Phase . . ." I paused forgetfully, still dazed.

"Six, you idiot," Jeremy said. "Get your ass out of there. Now. Rollo's boy is cashing in his chips, and Rollo's stopped winning, and he's looking restless."

"Okay, I'm out of here," I promised.

And damn it, I would have made it out of there, if it hadn't been for the maid.

She stuck her key in the door right after one short, useless knock of warning. All I could do was dive under the bed. This is not a place you want to be, even in the best hotels. I won't discuss dust balls and such, here and now. Suffice it to say, it was a suffocating spot to be in.

I at least had my wits about me enough to shut off my phone so it wouldn't ring and expose me. Now my heart seemed to be pounding against the floor. The maid took her time, turning down the bed, plumping up the pillows, adjusting the temperature, whatever it is they do when the room is already clean but they are giving it that final dumb thing, which I always find a nuisance but which, I suppose, some people like, I suspect because it is so psychologically maternal, offering a parental, loving good-night tuck-in.

So of course Rollo came in. Very sharply he said to her, "What the devil are you doing? Get out of here, you wretch!" He must have scared her, because she rushed out before he had time to holler about the package being pulled out from its hiding place. When he saw it, he sucked in his breath and said, "That stupid, stupid bitch! Leaves it right out on the table in the damned sunlight!" She had apparently taken the parcel off the bed where I'd been forced to leave it, and when she turned down the covers, she must have put it on the table near the glass sliding doors. I watched Rollo's white-leather-shod feet pacing around the room. While he was seething, his telephone rang. He picked it up on the first ring.

"Hello," he said in the sharpest tone I'd ever heard him use. "Yes. Yes. Of course I have it. Those morons botched the whole thing in Antibes, but you just do your job, and then nobody can prove a thing. Is the copy ready? And you have it? All right. I'm leaving now."

And he hung up. He sounded more aggressive without his mother around. With another gusty sigh, he went into the bathroom and peed. Then, I'm sorry to say, that without washing his hands, he picked up the package and went out.

I didn't move right away, because I didn't know for sure if he'd taken the painting, and I was afraid he'd come back for something, even though there was nothing else in the room. Finally I popped out, saw that the package was missing, and frantically called Jeremy.

"Christ!" he hissed. "Where the hell have you been? I've been wild—"

"The maid screwed me up," I said. "Then Rollo came in. I hid under the bed."

"God Almighty," Jeremy groaned.

"Did you get the valet to bring the car around?" I asked.

"Of course. He's parked it in the turnaround. I'm in the lobby, waiting for you."

"Jeremy," I said, "I saw the painting. He's taken it with him. You can't let him out of your sight. If you have to follow him without me, go."

It was almost intolerable, waiting for the elevator. A German family with two little girls came straggling out with a lot of shopping bags. It was a different elevator this time, run by a plump, slow-moving woman. Every time we stopped for someone I could feel my throat clutch, but I somehow managed to make it down to the lobby without fainting dead away.

Jeremy met me at the elevator and yanked me behind a marble pillar. "He's waiting for his car to come round," he said in a low voice. "He hasn't seen me. We'll let him get in his car, then we'll jump into ours and follow him. He's alone, because his buddy took off in another car as soon as he cashed in the chips. I got the license number of the other guy's car. Severine can give it to the police. I left a message on her machine."

Chapter Thirty

FORTUNATELY FOR US, IT TURNED OUT THAT ROLLO WAS A CAUTIOUS driver. I suppose he was being especially careful so that no gendarmes would pull him over and get a look at what he was transporting. Still, it was torture trying to keep him in our sights in the dark of night, once we pulled away from the well-lit main streets and hotels. He was driving a silver Mercedes, and just following him out of Monte Carlo itself was dicey.

"He isn't heading for the airport," I observed. This didn't surprise Jeremy.

"He can't," he said. "He's got stolen art. He'd have to show it at customs. What did it look like? Is it the one in the photo?"

"Yes. It's beautiful. A Madonna with Child, by Fabrizi. Reminds me of Dossi, Albertinelli . . . where the hell is he going?" I said as we followed him onto the highway. I looked at the letters and arrows painted on the ground to let you know what direction you're about to go in. "Ventimiglia," I read aloud.

"He's heading for the Italian border," Jeremy said. "There's no border patrol there anymore. If you manage to smuggle a stolen work of art into certain countries, then sometimes it can be resold to someone who, for instance, innocently believes it's only a copy—and that sale might still be legal. The point is, the real owner often can't do a damned thing about it, especially if he doesn't figure out where it went until years later."

"You think he's going to sell the real painting?" I asked. "I thought he'd keep it. I think the plan was to steal the original and replace it with a copy in the garage, and nobody could prove that the copy wasn't the one that Aunt Penelope owned and Denby saw."

"Sooner or later he'll sell it," Jeremy said. "If it's worth a lot, he won't be able to resist. He obviously has contacts over there who are ready, willing and able."

"Sure. That guy who phoned him. The one I heard while I was under the bed."

"Let's get this straight: there will be no more hiding under the bed for you," Jeremy said.

"Gee, what a shame," I said sarcastically. "I do so love doing that."

"Hoo, hoo," Jeremy said. "What else did Rollo say on the phone?"

"Just what I told you. That his pals in Antibes screwed up, that we can't prove a thing, so long as this guy he talked to 'does his job,' which is to give him that fake, the copy. I'll bet he's going to pick it up right now," I added. "Yessir. I could tell there was definitely a deal going down."

"You're talking like a gendarme again," Jeremy said.

"I believe you mean 'carabiniere' now," I replied.

It was eerie, going past the border. The old customs booths and lanes were still there, like a ghost town. You just floated through them, feeling slightly guilty. At least, I felt like I was sneaking in. I'm incurable. I feel guilty even when I'm not the one with a stolen painting in my clutches.

The immediate effect of crossing into the first town in Italy was a huge traffic jam because of an outdoor music festival drawing in

the tourists and locals alike. The cars barely crawled along, and mo-
torcycles swarmed around us like big noisy bees. I could see Rollo, at
one point, throwing up his hands in frustration. It was hot and dusty,
and the smell of car exhaust filled the air. Finally, mercifully, we made
it out of the clogged little town and up onto the main highway. I expected things to pick up speed and become difficult at this point, but
Rollo had other problems. He had to pull into a gas station and fill
his tank. We pulled over to a section where the campers and families
stopped to park and stretch their legs.

It was a self-service station, and Rollo grimaced, apparently finding this distasteful and difficult. Right in front of our eyes he yanked
on some gloves.

"Ho-lee cow," I breathed. "It *was* him who busted into the apartment." We watched, spellbound, as he stuck the nozzle in the fuel
tank. When he was done, he yanked off his gloves, climbed back in his
car, started it up . . . and pulled off into a parking space near the men's
rooms, where all the weary camper dads were bringing their tired
little boys . . . just a scant few yards away from us. We froze.

"I can't believe he has to pee again," I said in a low voice.

"You didn't see all the gin he knocked back," Jeremy muttered. We
watched covertly as Rollo, who never saw us, got out and headed for
the loo, slamming his car door behind him.

And his seat belt got caught in the door-frame.

So, although the door itself was technically closed, it failed to completely connect with the car and didn't shut tight into its slot, because
the belt was wedged between the door and the car. It looked as if it
had shut properly—but it hadn't. Rollo didn't notice. But I did.

"That door isn't shut tight!" I squeaked. "This is it! Our last
chance."

"Not you," Jeremy said. "I'll do it."

"You'll look too suspicious," I argued.

"You'll get all the men looking at you in that dress," he said.

We almost blew it then and there, bickering as we were. But it was Jeremy who did the deed. And I must say, he was ever so cool. Really, I admired his nerves. He went over to Rollo's car as if it were his own, casually yanked open the driver's door, and reached for the package tied with string, which was sitting right there on the passenger seat, covered with a blanket. Then he sauntered back to me and chucked it in my lap. Just as debonair as when we played Secret Agents.

Then he got behind the wheel of his mighty Dragonetta, and floored it.

I was too scared to look back. But whatever Rollo was doing in there, it took longer than I'd dared hope. Because Jeremy, who wasn't afraid to look back in the rearview at all, said Rollo hadn't emerged from the men's, yet. Jeremy headed rapidly for the highway.

"North or south?" he said when we reached the highway divide.

"East," I said. I already had an idea, because I'd been thinking about all the things that Erik had jokingly told me about becoming an art forger if my career with him went bust.

"That is, follow the signs for Genoa," I explained. "I know of a man there. He can authenticate the painting for us."

"I feel it is my duty to point out, for your personal edification, that technically, we should be notifying somebody in France," Jeremy warned me. "And taking the painting back where it came from. France."

"Phooey," I said. "We're not the ones who brought it across the border. And you know perfectly well that if we take it back, we'll be at the mercy of a French court and it could get tied up for a long time. I want to know what this is before they take it away from me again."

Chapter Thirty-one

WE DROVE INTO THE WEE HOURS. BUT BY SUNRISE WE COULDN'T push on any farther and had to pull over at a rest stop to get some coffee and bread. We found a good parking spot behind some shrubbery where we could stay incognito.

In Italy they know that you are human. They know that you need sustenance. Therefore whenever you stop for gas, you usually can buy not only coffee and bread, milk or juice, but also something substantial, something hot to eat, or, if you prefer, a salami, a hunk of cheese, even uncooked pasta and canned tomatoes to take home to the wife. But the thing is, it's all normal food, really good food, too, not just fast food or faux food for the road.

I devoured my bread, drank my good hot coffee, and promptly fell asleep with my head on Jeremy's shoulder, where I dozed until his snoring woke me up. His cheek was on the top of my head. The morning sun streamed through the windshield, mellow, golden, warming. As soon as I stirred, Jeremy woke, saying, "What? What?" as if ready to take off at high speed.

Jeremy's phone rang and we both nearly jumped out of our seats. "Hello?" he said guardedly. Then he relaxed. "Yes, how's Denby?" he asked, and he mouthed to me that it was Denby's wife on the phone.

"Good, good," Jeremy said. Then all of a sudden he shut up. "Where is it?" he asked rather sharply. Then he was silent again. Then he said, "I see. Tell him thanks. Hope he's feeling better tomorrow. Good-bye."

He turned to me. "Denby made his wife call us right away, because he remembered something he meant to tell us. While he was working on the car, a girl from the village stopped by. She did chores for Aunt Penelope when she was in town, and she was there the day Aunt Penelope died. Aunt Pen had given her money to buy food—and a letter to send by registered mail to my law firm that day. But when Aunt Pen fell ill, the girl went to fetch the doctor, and she forgot to take the letter to the post office. She left it in that little porch beside the kitchen. Denby said there's a bench with a lift-up seat for storage underneath, where the girl kept her grocery bags and lists. Denby saw the address on it, and told her he'd be seeing us soon, and he says he locked the letter in the glove compartment of my car just before his accident. You'd better have a look, Penny. He said it was addressed to both of us."

"Us?" I echoed. He handed me the key to unlock it. And there it was, an envelope from her linen stationery, written in Aunt Penelope's familiar handwriting, to two names, *Penelope Nichols and Jeremy Laidley*, addressed in care of his London firm. I thought of the photos of Jeremy and me, in the writing box on her bed, and I got goose-bumps. I opened the envelope.

My dearest Penelope and Jeremy,

I tried to reach you by telephone, Jeremy darling, but you were unavailable today. I have managed, all this time, to look after you without interfering in your life; and I've always respected your parents' wishes, but I do believe that, in the end, a person has the right to know who he truly is, how beloved he was by both his families, and what his own legacy is really all about. I do so hope, Jeremy, that you will love the

villa as much as I and your great-grandfather did. Accept it as a token
of my love for him, and for you. His name was Giulio Principe, and I
cherished him more than any other creature on earth. You, Jeremy, are
the real gift he left me, and watching you grow into the fine man of our
family has been the sweetest joy of my life. I hope you will forgive me
for being cowardly and not telling you all this directly. So many times,
gazing at your face, I longed to. As for all the rest about your father,
you must ask your mother all about it.

Now Penny dear, no one knows better than I that a girl ought to
have a start in life—and a car of her own to drive to the ball. Otherwise she may find herself at the mercy of men, fate and history, as I
did for a time. I have been thinking a great deal about life, how dear
it is, how fragile we all are, and how history can shake up your entire
little world and throw you some unexpected turns. Penny, with your
bright, inquisitive mind and your caring heart, I feel that you will
know how to tend to something else that I hold dear. Inside the door
on the passenger side of your little car is a hiding place with a painting
that Jeremy's great-grandfather gave me. He made over a bill of sale to
me (which I enclose) so that if the situation arose, I could legally prove
ownership. I kept the painting in my library for a time, but recently
decided that it was safer back in its original hiding place. It may be
very valuable, and I'm afraid that it's caught the eye of Rollo Jr., who
would surely mishandle it. I always meant to sell it to a museum one
day, but I thought it brought me luck and I was reluctant to part with
it. However, when you own something too valuable, and you have to
hide it, then you may never get a chance to look at it anymore. You
always think that you'll have more time to enjoy what you've got.

But darlings, I believe I'm running out of time. What's the point of
surviving history, if one can't pass on some hard-learned wisdom along
with one's earthly possessions? All I can tell you both is that you must
live every day as if it counts, which means to love all of it. Never let a

single one go by without noting the color of the sky, the song of the bird,
the face of the one you love best. And don't let yourself get talked out
of the things you really care about, don't put off what you want to be.
Don't be bitter, Jeremy. People are fallible, but if you aren't too quick
to judge them, they can surprise you. Penny, there's no storybook on
earth more exciting than being alive yourself. So go forward without
fear, and do be kind to each other, no matter where life leads you. I
know that I can trust the two of you to do the right thing with that
which I leave in your hands.

Love to you both,
Aunt Penelope

I read it aloud, haltingly, trying to make out Aunt Penelope's hand-writing. It had her usual hurried, dashing quality, except that the letters were larger, and at the end, a little jagged, as if she were rushed, tired. The village girl had witnessed it by signing at the bottom. By the time I got to the end, I had tears in my eyes.

Jeremy looked touched but bewildered. "Did she go barmy or something? What is all this?" he asked.

Of course none of it made sense to him. But I said excitedly, "She was superstitious about it. She didn't want to think about revealing the painting, until finally she had to," I said. "Then she needed to move fast, and was frantic to tell you all about it, without Rollo finding out. Remember, you said she tried to telephone you the day she died. Now you know why."

I looked at the smaller page enclosed with the letter, a delicate tissue-thin kind of parchment. "It *is* a bill of sale. June 30th, 1940, signed by one Giulio Principe to Penelope Laidley! I bet it was Giulio who put it in the car door in the first place. He told her what to do, so she could get it—and his son—out of Italy if he or his parents died.

See, he wanted the painting out so that the Nazi army couldn't steal it."

Jeremy was staring at me as if trying to decide if I'd taken complete leave of my senses. He said, "What are you *on* about? What the hell did she mean about 'my great-grandfather' and 'ask your mother'? Is she talking about Mum's father? Or Grandfather Nigel?"

He picked up the letter and the bill of sale and looked at them. "Who the bloody hell is Giulio Principe, and 'little Domenico'?" he asked.

I took a deep breath. "I've been meaning to tell you about this all along, but I wanted to check with your mother first to see if what I heard was absolutely true."

His blue eyes darkened as if he didn't know exactly what I was talking about, but some instinct was telling him the general direction already. Yet his voice was cool when he said, "Does this have something to do with me personally?"

"Yes," I said, deciding that the only way to do it was to blurt it out. "I looked up a man who was Aunt Penelope's singing partner in those cabaret duos they performed back in the twenties and thirties. He told me all about Aunt Penelope, and a man she loved very much . . ."

Once I started, the words just came pouring out. I told it to him as directly as it had been told to me. The whole time, from beginning to end, Jeremy never said a word. Which was completely unlike him. Never interrupted once, never fired off a question. Sat there in silence, looking straight ahead, his profile never changing. So I just kept talking, telling it to him as gently as I could, but leaving nothing out.

"You see, I wanted to tell you, but I also wanted to make sure it wasn't just some geezer gossiping," I concluded. I had reached the end and I had run out of breath.

Then Jeremy got out of the car. I know I was supposed to stay put, to give him a chance to think and all that, but I got out with him anyway. The soft golden sun had been sneaking up higher in the sky for some time, but it wasn't until now that, yawning and stretching, it was really raising its face above the morning fog, which was slowly dissolving, so that the effect was like a curtain rising to reveal the stunning view of the Mediterranean. And, like a fairy-tale city emerging from the mists, there was the beautiful old city of Genoa, with its ancient cluster of forts and castles and turrets and hidden secrets.

I don't suppose Jeremy was really seeing it, of course. But he gazed broodingly out at the spectacular world spread there before us, and after a rather long silence, he spoke.

"So—now I'm to believe that Aunt Pen convinced my father—sorry, stepfather, to marry my mother so that she could keep me—all in the family, so to speak?" he said, shocked. "That I am actually the great-grandson of her *driver?*" He paused, then said, "Her servant?"

This irritated me back into my old voluble self. "Oh, don't be such a jerk," I said. "He wasn't really a servant. I told you, that was just cover, socially. He was the only man she ever really loved—"

"And that makes it all better," he said with sudden sarcastic vehemence. "You women are all alike. You think if you say, 'I loved him' that makes it okay. Well, it doesn't. Do you have the first idea what it's like to have people keep pulling the chair out from under your ass? Can you imagine thinking you're one sort of person and finding out that, no, you're not anymore, you're another sort, and you came from a bunch of foreigners you've never met in your life and never will?"

"If you'd listened to me, you wouldn't feel like they were a bunch of foreigners, as you so snobbily put it," I retorted. I suppose I could have been a bit more sympathetic to the pure shock value of what I was telling him, but I was tired of being growled at no matter how carefully I approached him.

"As for your lineage, well, relax, because Giulio, your great-grandfather, was from a good aristocratic family in Italy," I said. "And his son, Domenico—your grandfather—was a brave little boy who got shunted around during the war and ended up in America, but was smart and successful and married the girl he loved and had your father, Tony, a kid who loved music as intensely as you do. And *he* came to England and fell passionately in love with your mother, who loved him so much that even now she runs that soldiers' home in his memory, just to keep him alive for her. You're the only one in this crowd who's a snotty sourpuss. Maybe love doesn't count in the social register, or whatever it is you Brits call it—"

"Debrett's," he said automatically, absently.

"But you had all this love in your lineage, you idiot," I continued, undaunted, "and love is more rare than rubies. It's in your soul, whether you want to admit it or not. It's probably, when you think of it, the best news you've ever had."

"No it's not," he said, suddenly and unexpectedly.

He faced me with what I can only describe as a bucked-up courageous look, as if what he was about to tell me required more guts than anything else he'd ever had to say to me. There we were, all dusty, rumpled and bedraggled, since we'd been driving all night and morning, fueled simply by the adrenaline of the chase. In short, we'd reached that odd, fearless euphoric stage when you just don't have the need to keep up your usual defenses against your feelings and the ridicule of others.

"The best news I've ever had," he said slowly, "you pain-in-the-ass, impossible, stubborn, thickheaded woman—"

"Stubborn and thickheaded are the same thing," I pointed out automatically, not able to stop myself. Because if he needed courage to say something to me, I just might be too terrified to hear it.

"There, you see?" he said triumphantly. "That's exactly what I'm talking about."

"What's the best news you've ever had?" I said, half in dread, half fascinated now.

"The best news I've ever had is that you are no longer my cousin," he said. "I no longer have to look out for you. I no longer have to put up with you. I no longer have to worry that somebody is about to kidnap you, or swindle you, or seduce you for your money . . ."

It was his tone that got to me. I could hardly believe I was hearing it right, but I knew that I was, because of the way it felt. That roller-coaster surge again; only now, having already made that plunge down a steep drop, we were right back on the upswing before I could even catch my breath, climbing higher and higher into the blue sky.

"And most of all," he concluded, "I no longer have to protect you from *me*. You wretched girl, you made me care about you from the first time I saw you being chased by that bee at the beach, but then you just vanished for years and years and never looked back, so I told myself I was glad to be rid of you. But then, in your usual irresponsible way, you waltzed right back into my life, heedless of the consequences and leaving it all up to me to behave properly. Well, now I don't need to feel guilty for all the heretofore primal feelings I've been having about you ever since you showed up in London at the hotel look-ing so beautiful, and you made me wonder if you were doing it on purpose just to torture me or if you simply couldn't control your own heretofore primal feelings— Are you listening to me? Have you grasped precisely what it is that I'm trying to tell you?"

"Yes," I said in a small voice. "Heretofore, as you put it, you have had, for quite some time now—the hots for me."

"And?" he prompted. "Go on."

I couldn't help it. I widened my eyes and said, "What?"

" 'What' indeed!" he said ferociously, and grabbed me and pulled me close and started kissing me hungrily, again and again, and say-ing in between, "Well? Are you going to say it, or are you going to make me make you say it?" And then he'd kiss me again and demand, "Well?" and honestly for a minute there I couldn't catch my breath to speak.

"Yes," I said finally.

"Yes, what?" he said, and kissed me again.

"Yes, I feel the same way, you big bully," I said. I kissed him back as ferociously as he kissed me, and then you couldn't tell anymore who was kissing who, and we kept that up until we simply had to come up for air. The sun was streaming across the whole earth, warming every creature on it now, pushing hard against the sky.

"Well, then, that's settled," he said, and he grinned. "Now perhaps we ought to be seeing about your legacy? Before Rollo figures out that we didn't go back to the villa."

"*Our* legacy. She wants us to share it, Jeremy," I reminded him.

He stared at me and shook his head. "You will never learn to look out for yourself," he said reproachfully. "Technically it's all yours. And I mean to see that Rollo doesn't ever take it away from you again. Then, at our leisure, I'm going to find out, once and for all, how I got all mixed up with this Laidley clan." He sounded energized, like his old confident self, and I knew why. Shocking as the whole thing was, Aunt Penelope had practically anointed him as a bona fide, and very much beloved, member of this family.

He gazed up at the view as if seeing it for the first time. And I thought that, perhaps, he was seeing the city of Genoa the way a warrior prince might, after he'd been away fighting battles and slaying dragons, glad to come home triumphant.

"Fifty-fifty," I said recklessly. This is why I don't go around kissing just anybody. I can never do it without throwing myself totally into it.

"Come on, then, Penny Nichols," he said. "Let's at least find out just what it is that Aunt Penelope wanted us to have."

Part Eleven

Chapter Thirty-two

GENOA WAS A FAIRY-TALE CITY, GUARDED BY MOUNTAINS AT ITS back, with its face gazing out at the salty, sensuous sea. Ships slid regally to and from its harbors, and at each labyrinthine turn of its ancient streets you could find yourself in the time period and locale of your choice—a Roman house from the first of the "A.D." centuries, medieval walled forts from the Dark Ages, Renaissance churches and palaces, vestigial buildings bombed in World War II. Go round a corner to a nearby museum and you'd stumble across streets made of marble, galleries glinting with gold, halls of mirrors. You'd find artifacts said to be a dinner bowl from the Last Supper, letters written by Christopher Columbus, Paganini's violin rumored to be the gift of the devil, a blue plate that supposedly served Saint John the Baptist's head to the queen; and various stunning mosaics, frescoes, sculptures, and tapestries in buildings surrounded by fragrant gardens of roses, lemons, oranges and olives.

Under normal circumstances, a person like me could have gone delirious with delight, dashing around trying to see every historical tidbit. But Jeremy and I were on a mission, to locate an expert I could trust who might identify, in this city of countless treasures and priceless art, one little painting of the Madonna and Child. His office was in the medieval part of Genoa, not far from the museum of fine art.

"Dr. Mateo will see you now," the secretary said, and she showed us into his office anteroom in an old stone building. It was a narrow, modest workroom with no windows, dominated by a high, big wooden table with one lone high stool; three windowed bookshelves filled with musty old tomes; and, in a corner alcove, a very large light table.

Dr. Mateo was seated in a tiny office just beyond the anteroom. His door was open and he was on the telephone when we first arrived, but now he rose from behind a desk heaped with stacks of portfolios and file folders. He was a neat little man with a headful of black and silver hair and a matching trim little beard, and black-rimmed eyeglasses, and one of those tweed suits that professors wear which smell vaguely of pipe smoke.

I had telephoned ahead, so he was expecting us. He gave me the smile of pleasure with which older academics sometimes greet young women; he nodded very politely at Jeremy. Dr. Mateo waited patiently through our murmured preliminaries, but as soon as I opened my portfolio and unwrapped the painting, removing the cardboard and tissue, he leaned forward eagerly, bringing his nearsighted eyes close to it. Even before he reached for his magnifying glass, he had begun murmuring to himself, "Hmm, mhmmm, hmmm, ah-hem . . ."

He turned to a book written in Italian and perused it. Jeremy had raised his eyebrows at the humming sounds, looking at me inquiringly, as if to say, "Is this guy for real?"

But I knew what the humming meant. Dr. Mateo was excited, intrigued, trying to keep his emotions at bay while using two methods—scientific inspection of the canvas, and historical documentation. These may seem like compatible techniques, but many authenticators actually choose either one or the other, as if choosing soccer teams;

some rely on intricate machinery, DNA and lab samples if they lean toward the scientific-inspection approach; or, if they favor historic research, they rely more on cumulative documentation from historical archives.

And then there are men like Mateo, who see their job as picking up the pieces of a shattered whole, as if the truth to each mystery were a rare, delicate and precious vase whose shards needed to be painstakingly and intelligently pieced together, not further dissected. He once wrote a paper describing the world that any artist lived in as a complete cosmos, requiring a unifying eye . . . and an understanding heart.

So you can't rush a guy like Mateo. Most of all, you can't act like a lawyer interrogating a witness. But Jeremy didn't know this, so when he asked, "Have you ever heard of Fabrizi?" he wasn't prepared for Mateo to smile at him with supreme but impenetrable tolerance.

"*Certo,*" Mateo murmured, without feeling any compunction to volunteer further information. Jeremy turned to me pleadingly, with barely concealed exasperation. I tried to signal him to shut up, but Mateo glanced up, caught our signals, and looked amused.

"You are perhaps a professor in America?" Mateo asked me politely as he continued to inspect the painting with the magnifying glass. His tone indicated that one must be patient with people from a younger civilization whose experts were eager and smart, but limited in experience.

"No," I said. "I am an art history researcher. I work with professors, and also for the movies." It was the first time I'd ever mentioned my modest income ahead of my more supportive one. He nodded gravely, very carefully lifting the painting up to the light.

Dr. Mateo is known for his fine instincts and his precise theories. So when, after more "h'mm"-ing, he asked if he might X-ray the painting, I was prepared to give my assent. When he left the room Jeremy could barely contain himself.

"Will that hurt the painting?" he demanded. I shook my head. "For Christ's sake, he's maddening," Jeremy hissed. "He won't even let on if he thinks the thing is valuable or not."

"He doesn't want to rush to judgment," I said. "It would alter the way he conducted his investigation if he did. He knows who Fabrizi is, but he doesn't want to draw preliminary conclusions until he's sure it isn't something other than Fabrizi."

"You mean it could be another artist's?" Jeremy demanded.

"Or a copy, or an outright fake," I said. "I don't know what he's on to, but trust me, he's like a bloodhound on some scent. He may not look excited, but he is."

We didn't have to wait long. Dr. Mateo returned with the painting and set it back on the table with the same polite reverence he would give any painting. Then he disappeared again.

"Now where's he going?" Jeremy groused. "To eat his lunch?"

It did seem like forever before Dr. Mateo returned with an X-ray, which he put on the light table, much as a doctor would in order to deliver a prognosis. He glanced at Jeremy and me, saw the look of suspense on our faces, and smiled.

"Doctor?" I said softly. "Do you have an idea what this might be?"

For the first time Mateo looked excited, like a boy who wants to show you something he found. "See for yourself," he said, and motioned for us to approach the X-ray. "These figures in the background. They are a clear indication of underdrawing. You see here?"

Without ever touching the X-ray he used his little finger to trace the ghostly figures he saw in the background so that we could make them out. What at first appeared to be background scribbles, or even long curls of human hair caught on film, or random scratches on a negative . . . soon emerged as deliberately drawn figures, smeared and smudged at some points as if erased and redrawn on the canvas, before the artist changed his mind and decided to paint the study from a very different angle of the Madonna and Child.

"This underdrawing, I believe, is a preliminary, abandoned sketch of the Madonna and her infant. See the different way the Madonna's head is turned? The way she is seated? The arms, too, and the position of the Child? Even the background is altered, with the window much wider. Can you see this?"

I had already begun to make out the heads and arms of the ghostly figures beneath. As I gazed harder they emerged with more clarity, and all during Mateo's narration, I actually felt a chill through my body that made me shudder with delight, as if the painter himself were alive and had just sketched the images for us right here and now, and we were watching him do it.

"I see it. Yes. Yes. What does it mean?" Jeremy asked respectfully.

Dr. Mateo's voice was like a rich deep humming, calm and steady. "If it were a copy, I do not think that there would be an underdrawing of a different angle of the same study. And see also, that even in the underdrawing there are changes, alterations? A man who paints a copy simply copies what he sees. He does not create in this way, searching for his subject."

"Then—this is an original?" Jeremy asked in a deadly quiet tone.

Dr. Mateo looked up slowly, as if awakening from a dream of his own thoughts. "Oh, dear boy," he said. "Yes, this is clearly an original work of art. That much I do not think will find argument. The question is, whose original?"

"I don't know about Fabrizi," I admitted. "Was he important enough to have imitators or students? I simply assumed—you know, a Renaissance artist, with the work dating from the late 1400s, perhaps early 1500s. I've been studying this period rather closely because of research I'm doing on the Borgias."

"Ah, yes, the Spanish pope," Mateo said. "Your dates are correct.

Then of course you would know with whom this artist was likely to study, in those days." His eyes twinkled as he gave me a hint. "Fabrizi found some favor with Ludovico Sforza in Milan . . ."

"Who was the uncle of Lucrezia Borgia's first husband," I told Jeremy, unspooling some of Lucrezia's Spunky Woman chronology that my head was stuffed with. "But they say her family wanted to bump off her husband. Politics. She probably warned him, though, because he escaped. Her second husband wasn't so lucky. Stabbed in a dark alley, survived, but was finally murdered in his own bedroom while he was still recuperating!"

I turned to Mateo and said, "Was Fabrizi from Milan?"

Mateo looked pleased and amused. "Born and died in Milan, but there was a lot of travelling in between. After the plague, for instance, Fabrizi went to Florence for a time, and did some portraits for the king of France. Fabrizi also studied in Modena, Ferrara . . ."

"Oh," I said, gazing at the beautiful brushstrokes of the painting. "Well, judging by the tones of this canvas, and the places where you say the artist worked, Fabrizi probably was a student of . . ."

Suddenly it hit me. Not in an intellectual way, strangely enough, but with a physical sensation of light-headedness, as a sensual illumination like light breaking across the sky.

"Oh my God," I said.

"What? What?" Jeremy demanded. Dr. Mateo smiled at me, knowing what I was thinking and, above all, what I was feeling. He was pleased, as only a teacher can be, that he had guided me to think of it myself.

"Was—did Fabrizi study with Leonardo?" I whispered.

"Yes, I believe so," he said.

"Oh, God," I repeated. There was a long pause. Nobody moved.

"You don't mean . . . da Vinci, do you?" Jeremy asked tentatively, struggling with his own feelings of, for once, being out of his depth and therefore, like a true Englishman, not wanting to make a fool of himself by voicing something that he might have gotten completely wrong.

But in trying to play it cool, he sounded even funnier, to me, than he dreaded. I guess it was the unusually tentative voice, so unlike him—it just made me giggle. And once I started giggling I couldn't seem to stop. And this of course made Dr. Mateo smile rather broadly. Then he allowed himself a deep, throaty chuckle.

"What? What is it? Am I wrong?" Jeremy asked a trifle defensively.

But Dr. Mateo was not a man who enjoyed another's discomfort. Quickly and reassuringly he said, "No, no, my boy. You are quite right. Come closer and I'll show you. I thought so the moment I saw it, of course, because I have made an especial study of Fabrizi, who is a particular favorite of mine. You see, there was a triptych attributed to Fabrizi, known as the 'Three Virgins.' The first painting was the engagement of Mary to Joseph; the second was Mary with her mother, Saint Anne, and then there was the third—this one—which has been missing for years. I am very familiar with the first two panels of the series, for they are owned by private collectors who kept the paintings in their families; and I spent twenty years waiting for the owners to trust me enough to allow me to examine each Fabrizi closely.

"And then of course there were the rumors that all of the Three Virgins were only copies," he continued, "and that the originals had long been stolen or destroyed. But I do not believe that there were ever any copies made of these paintings. Then, there were other rumors that the third Virgin never existed, except in studio sketches that were never painted because Fabrizi didn't live long enough to paint the final study. But I'd heard that this last painting did, in fact, exist, and the owner simply did not wish to bring it to light. Now here I find the proof I need."

He turned to me with the first real sign of earthly curiosity when he said a bit too casually, "May I ask how you came into possession of this painting?"

Jeremy was ready for that. "She inherited it," he said. "Her family has documentation of its sale from the original Italian family who possessed it for generations."

Dr. Mateo bowed his head politely to me. "Well, your family evidently understands its value so well that they were wise enough to keep—how is it you say, 'a low profile,' " he said. "I have always thought that in Fabrizi's work—at least, in the Three Virgins—I could see not merely the student of Leonardo, but the hand of the master himself."

Jeremy and I were stunned into momentary silence. "Do you mean to say," Jeremy said finally, as if he had to say it aloud, bluntly, to believe it, "that you think this painting is an original Leonardo da Vinci? That Fabrizi didn't draw it at all?" Dr. Mateo held out his hands with the palms up toward Jeremy, as if to slow him down, steady him.

"No, no. I think, as is often the case with student and teacher, you have a bit of both. Here is where I see the hand of the master," he said, pointing to the outstretched fingers of the Madonna, reaching to the baby who was holding out his chubby hand to her. "In the fingers, the folds of the clothes. I am not so certain of the surrounding work—the window, the background . . ."

"But the baby," I said. "Babies usually have the faces of little old men, or wise old cupids, with too many thoughts in their heads. But this one looks like a real infant."

Dr. Mateo gave me a smile that was like a reward. "That is perhaps because," he said, "Fabrizi was a woman. Annamaria Fabrizi. She was quite a remarkable woman. She died at the age of twenty-eight."

I gulped. I hate it when people die younger than I am. And a woman, no less. It makes me hear that clock ticking again in my own life. It makes me think about how foolish it is to imagine you've got

all the time in the world to do what you want. I'd imagined him—
her—older, because of her obvious skill. What else might Fabrizi have
painted if she'd managed to live long enough?

Jeremy, however, was having no such struggles with the meaning
of the brevity of existence. He was in that knight-errant mode, and he
wasn't going home until he'd gotten the information he came for.

"Do you think other people will be inclined to agree with you?"
he asked.

Dr. Mateo shrugged patiently. "It's possible, it's possible. I expect
that many others will want to test my theory, see the painting and decide." He sighed, as if anticipating the sharp wrangling, the posturing,
the egos that would be involved. "You must be prepared for a reaction.
People always want to fight about these things, because there are often
opposing interests involved."

"Can you tell me," Jeremy asked delicately, "even in a general way,
of course—if people agree with you and say that the painting very
likely had some work done by Leonardo—what might the painting
then be worth?"

It's never easy to raise the issue of money with guys like Mateo,
even though money is what's been lurking under the discussion the
whole time. I half expected Mateo to hedge, hem and haw, and indicate that it was crass to even bring it up.

But Dr. Mateo looked Jeremy straight in the eye. "Here are the
possibilities. If it is thought to have nothing to do with the school of
Leonardo, then its value at auction would not be, in my estimation,
worth the sale of it. If it is a copy of a lost original by Leonardo—a
copy that was, say, painted by one of his assistants—even then it could
be valued at say, four million pounds," he said calmly.

And before Jeremy could say a word, Dr. Mateo added solemnly,
"And if it were thought that Leonardo had painted some of it but not
all of it, that would still increase the price to perhaps ten or fifteen

million. But of course if it is determined that it is the great man's original, then it could go to forty million pounds, or, if the auction was handled by those who know how to do this sort of thing, and the buyers wanted it badly enough, they say such a work might even fetch one hundred and forty million pounds."

At that point, I did feel dizzy. I had to sit down, and I plonked myself right onto his high wooden stool, which was the only seat available. Jeremy looked a little pale, but steady on his feet. He was accustomed to dealing with rich clients, and when he heard that such astronomical sums were at stake, some electric current of energy seemed to perk him up like a racehorse snorting for the gate to spring open. When Dr. Mateo's secretary buzzed him to say that his wife was on the telephone, and he excused himself, Jeremy took me aside.

"Okay," he said briskly. "This little package has to go under lock and key right now. My firm has offices in Rome. They can hold it in a vault for you."

"All right," I said, feeling dazed.

"And while we're there," he said, "there's a little lady I think we'd better pay a call on."

Chapter Thirty-three

"MUM'S GOT PLENTY OF ROOM IN THE VILLA SHE'S RENTING, SO WE won't have to stay in a hotel," Jeremy insisted as we drove south to Rome to deposit the painting in the vaults of his firm's Italian offices. "And she's got plenty of explaining to do," he added darkly. He telephoned to alert her that we were on our way. I made him promise that no matter what happened, he wouldn't get sarcastic or holler at his mother.

But by the time we'd dropped off the painting and reached her villa late that night, she'd already gone to bed. The servants had left us a cold supper, and we ate like sleepwalkers, then drifted upstairs into our bedrooms and tumbled gratefully into bed. I just lay there with my muscles twitching and my nerves vibrating, and then I fell into a deep sleep, disturbed only briefly the next morning by a shy maid who delivered a tray of coffee and boiled eggs, and a note from Aunt Sheila saying she had a morning engagement but would meet us for lunch. I ate, bathed, sat on the bed trying to work up the energy to dress, and fell asleep all over again. Then I woke in time for lunch.

The house had been spooky-dark when we arrived at night, but now in the daylight I saw that it was a fine old villa on a hilltop of Rome, with tall doors and high vaulted ceilings, and when you flung

the shutters open you could see beyond the bustling streets and buildings to the surrounding hills with their tall, imposing poplars standing
like cool green sentinels.

Jeremy had slept late, too. I met him on the wide, curving staircase.
"Don't act like a lawyer," I warned him. He shot me a weary look as
we went inside the cool terracotta-colored sitting room with a marble
floor that made the sunlight undulate as if it were reflected on water.

Aunt Sheila looked wary as we entered. She was seated on a dark
blue sofa, and she wore a trim, green and white A-line sleeveless dress
that ended above the knee, with white stockings and white flat shoes
with a bow on them. And with those frosty blonde bangs and dark
eyeliner, she seemed like an elegantly coiffed model from the early
1960s.

"Jeremy darling," she murmured, offering him her cheek to kiss as
he dutifully bent toward her. She appeared to wish that she could get
this over with as fast as possible. But she gave me an especially bright
smile.

"Hallo, Penny," she said. "Would you two care for a drink?"

"What are you having?" Jeremy asked.

"Gin and T, dear," she said.

"Same," he said. "Penny?"

"Sure," I said, on the verge of adding *what the hell*. I had no idea
what, exactly, was going on here, but they both seemed suspiciously
chummy and civilized all of a sudden, which made me dread that a
whacking big storm was brewing underneath.

"Harold's been keeping me up on what you two have been doing,"
she said quickly. "He seems to think it's all going to turn out okay for
you both?" Her sentence turned into a question at the very end.

"Hope so," Jeremy said.

"Fingers crossed, then," she said.

Key-hrist, I thought to myself. Right now there was immense screaming and yelling and threatening going on back in France, because Jeremy had phoned Harold, who got Severine to alert the police, and the police had traced the license number and caught one of Rollo's thugs—the one who'd gone to Monte Carlo with him, who was wanted for other crimes and therefore was spilling the beans on what Rollo had hired him to do—namely, steal the painting and hire a guy to make a fake replica of it that would turn up on the estate again so we'd all assume that Aunt Penelope had owned only the copy in the first place. My parents had been alerted, and were going to let me know when they could get a flight to London. Yet here we were, Jeremy and I, having drinks with Aunt Sheila, because Jeremy refused to leave Rome until he got some answers to some rather more personal questions.

Jeremy cleared his throat, and his mother flinched slightly in apprehension. He saw this, and his gaze softened.

"Mum," he said with amazing gentleness, "Penny came across a fellow who used to perform with Aunt Pen, and he told us a few things about her that we want to check with you."

"Oh?" Aunt Sheila said with a falsely casual lilt to her voice as she reached toward the tray a maid had brought in and set on a low table. The maid vanished quietly, and Aunt Sheila handed each of us our drinks. She took a few sips of her own as she sat back on the sofa.

"Yes . . ." Jeremy began, then hesitated. "A man, name of Simon Thorne." Nobody could miss the flicker of recognition in her eyes, but she was silent. "Mum, was it true that Aunt Pen asked you to marry Da—I mean—" He suddenly looked agonized.

"Uncle Peter," I supplied quickly.

Aunt Sheila set her drink carefully on a cocktail napkin. "Well," she said slowly and controlledly, "I suppose it's true, though at the time I didn't quite understand it that way."

She paused, as if hoping this would be enough and she would not be forced to elaborate. Jeremy was motionless, however, with his eyes trained on her like a hunting dog who's spotted a duck and won't move until you deal with it. She gulped.

"You see, I met Penelope when I was working in a little theatrical agency as a secretary," she went on. "It was a nice mix of the old troupers like Simon, and the up-and-coming kids. I got to see all the new acts, and a lot of them were musical groups. Anyway, Penelope used to have parties and invite all the people from the agency that she knew from her cabaret days, and that's how I got to know her. And she seemed to take quite an interest in me, I thought because she sympathized with women who were defying convention, not marrying."

"Did Aunt Pen introduce you to Peter Laidley?" Jeremy pushed. She looked from him to me, as if imploring me, as a woman, to understand.

"Yes. She was sort of matchmaking, I thought," Aunt Sheila said, "at a time when I was feeling all alone in the world. Tony had died, and I was miserable, and I was still on the outs with my family—"

"Why?" Jeremy interrupted ruthlessly. Aunt Sheila leaned forward.

"Well, darling, because of you," she said, with a glint in her eye.

"Because your mother wouldn't get rid of you, you dope," I said. I turned to her. "Right?" I added. She nodded. "Did Uncle Peter know that Aunt Penelope was trying to throw you two together?" I asked.

"Not at first," she said, keeping her eyes on me but obviously very conscious of Jeremy's attentiveness. "Penelope encouraged him to notice me, and she said nice things about me; so did your grandmother Beryl. Peter saw that his auntie and his mum approved of me. I don't think he knew that I had a baby. So when I saw that he was serious, I told him. And introduced him to you, Jeremy. Peter liked you straight away. Said you were bright as a button."

Jeremy's face had that look I'd come to know well enough by now, indicating that he was trying not to be emotional, or susceptible to his mother's charm. But it was still briefly, touchingly obvious that it meant a great deal to him to hear that Uncle Peter had wanted him. I pictured Jeremy as a baby, after his real father had died, being presented to Mom's brother. In those days an unwed mother with a child was a much bigger deal, and the fact that Uncle Peter accepted Jeremy made Mom's brother seem like a more open-minded, big-hearted guy.

"Peter proposed to me that next Christmas," Aunt Sheila said, looking at me for understanding again. "I told him I didn't know if I could do it. Be a wife, I mean, in the conventional sense. I wanted to, because he was so good and kind and we were cozy together. But there were moments of panic when I thought of Tony and I—I—didn't want this to be the beginning of forgetting about him." She looked at Jeremy now. "When people die," she said softly, "it doesn't necessarily mean you're ready to give them up."

"Then—what made you decide to marry Peter?" Jeremy asked.

"Penelope invited me to tea and she talked very woman-to-woman and made me cry and confess why I wasn't sure about marrying," Aunt Sheila said. "She said she understood, about mourning for a soldier, because she'd been in love with a man who was killed in World War II. She said I mustn't let my grief for Tony overshadow the care of his son. She told me how hard it was for a mother and child alone, especially in show business, and that I'd need to give my son some stability in a world that was so uncertain."

She turned to me and explained, "I rather thought that in her own way, Penelope was offering me a chance to do good. Nobody ever quite put it to me that way before. It is really quite irresistible to young people. That's why they go marching off to war. I wanted to do something right and good with my life, something that Tony would want me to do, so that I would survive, and his son would survive."

"So you married Peter for me—is that what you're saying?"

Jeremy said sternly, in that reproving way that men revert to so easily. She looked back at him, steadily and evenly.

"Not entirely," she said. "I did tell you that I was fond of Peter, happy with him, not as I was with Tony—your father—but in a way no less valuable. I wasn't so afraid of the world when Peter was by my side." She returned to her drink.

I looked at Jeremy. "Well?" I said. "Are you satisfied, you big ape? There are lots worse ways to grow up than being loved and cared for by everybody in sight."

Jeremy looked startled. "Why do you always turn on me where Mum is concerned?" he said. "I go along thinking you're 'for' me, and then bang! there you go." Aunt Sheila studied him, then broke into a giggle.

"Jeremy, stop it. She doesn't know that you're teasing her," she said.

"Oh, I'm used to taking his abuse," I said theatrically.

"Mum," Jeremy asked cautiously, "how much do you know about my real dad's family?"

Aunt Sheila said, "Quite a bit, actually. Tony's mother's name was Rose, and his father's name was Domenico. They met in America; both left Italy because of World War II. Domenico's father, Giulio, was killed in that war, actually."

I could barely contain myself. "And did Aunt Penelope ever tell you the name of the man that *she* loved, who died in World War II?" I asked. Aunt Sheila shook her head.

"No, I don't believe so," she said. "Why?"

"It just so happens that Aunt Penelope's lover was also named Giulio," I said, fairly bouncing on my chair cushion with excitement as I hauled out my diagram of the family tree and slapped it down on the table. Aunt Sheila looked mystified.

"What's this chart?" Jeremy said, glancing first at it, then at me.

"Crib notes? On our family? Good God. Detective Penny Nichols strikes again."

"Yeah, right," I said defiantly. "And don't think it was easy, either. Just when I thought I had you people all figured out, new secrets came popping up." They both peered at it.

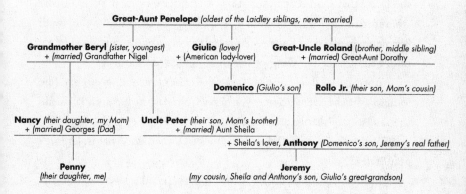

I pointed to the trail down the middle, leading from Aunt Penelope's lover, Giulio, to Aunt Sheila's lover, Anthony, and in the end, to Jeremy. At the center of it all was Domenico, whom I saw as the key to all this.

"Aunt Penelope's lover, Giulio, had a son, Domenico, who got stranded in Italy when Giulio died in the war," I said. "Aunt Penelope managed to get Domenico to London. But his American mother took him back to the States. That's why Domenico grew up there, and *he* had a son named Anthony. That's your Tony, Aunt Sheila," I said.

"Tony," Aunt Sheila repeated, turning so pale that for a moment I thought she was going to faint. "Oh, God," she said. "Oh, my God." She caught her breath and glanced away.

I turned to Jeremy. "And Jeremy, that little boy Domenico who went to America is actually *your* grandfather." Jeremy had a stony look on his face, and at first I wasn't sure he'd heard me, but then he

frowned and I knew he had. I realized that, while all this was a fascinating jigsaw puzzle to me, for Jeremy it was his whole identity, up
in the air.

I turned to Aunt Sheila and said encouragingly, "Aunt Penelope
was keeping tabs on Domenico because he was Giulio's son. And when
she heard that Domenico's son, Tony, died after serving in Vietnam, she
wanted to help you, Aunt Sheila—so, by putting you together with
her nephew—Uncle Peter—she found a way to take you and Jeremy
under the protective wing of her own family. My family."

Aunt Sheila, still stunned, had fallen silent, listening closely. She
looked as if she were going over her whole past in her mind. "Well,"
she said softly, "that explains quite a lot."

Cautiously I asked, "What became of Domenico? That is, Jeremy's
grandfather?"

Aunt Sheila, still trying to absorb it all, glanced up as if in a dream,
and said, "Domenico? Why, he lives in Italy now."

"See that, Jeremy?" I said triumphantly. "Your grandfather is still
alive! Where does he live?" I asked in excitement.

Aunt Sheila answered, "In a little town not far from here, actually.
Tony and I used to look in on him occasionally. I still do, whenever I
come here."

We both stared at her in amazement. "You do what?" Jeremy asked
in a choked voice.

Before he could roar at her I said hurriedly, "Do you have an address for him?"

"Of course, darling," Aunt Sheila said. "I can call ahead and let him
know you're coming. If you want to, of course."

Chapter Thirty-four

"JESUS," JEREMY SAID. "DID YOU HAVE TO OPEN YOUR MOUTH AND ask for the address? I have no memory of this Tony bloke, even if he is my real father. So why on earth would I want to meet *his* father? I don't know these people. I have absolutely no desire to do this, damn it."

" 'Cause like it or not, the old guy is your gramps," I said. We were sitting in his car outside Aunt Sheila's rented villa, and Jeremy looked as if he'd suddenly forgotten how to drive.

"What is it about women that they always want to control a man's life?" he fumed. "First Aunt Pen, thinking she could play God, match-making and all. Then Mum, keeping her little secrets and then hey-presto, she arranges for me to meet my so-called grandfather, just like that. And you, going right along with it."

"And isn't it funny," I said, "that out of all those women, I'm the only one you're hollering at? You certainly never would have hollered at Aunt Penelope, and you were very well-behaved with your mother, but with me you just explode like Vesuvius."

"I suppose that's a slur on my Italian ancestry now," he said darkly. "And I'm not hollering. I do not holler. I merely raised my voice to impress upon you—"

"Come on," I said coaxingly. "I'll go with you."

"That's just what I'm afraid of," he said. "With you by my side, I know I'm guaranteed to get into more tight spots. Car chases. Casinos and international art theft. What's next?"

"Your mother told me more stuff while you were bringing the car around," I said eagerly as he started the car and descended the drive. Within minutes we were bumping along the narrow side streets of Rome. "And you'd better listen," I continued, "because it's about Domenico's American mother. You know, the lady who snatched him back from Aunt Penelope—well, she was from an old Boston Brahmin family, and her name was Lucy. She died of tuberculosis not long after she brought Domenico to Boston. Once she was gone, the Boston relatives were rotten to Domenico and treated him like a servant, which is why he ran away to New York. Where he married an Italian-American girl, Rose—your grandmother—and together they ran a little grocery store. And they raised Tony—your father—as an American kid, and he went to university in New York. After Tony graduated, his parents moved back to Italy, but Tony came to London, to be part of the rock-and-roll scene. He had a band, Jeremy, just like you. And Tony—your father, kept in touch with his parents right up until . . ."

"He died," Jeremy supplied.

"Right. Rose—your grandmother—died here in Italy in the early eighties," I said. "Your grandfather Domenico still lives with her relatives. He's probably in his mid-seventies now." I paused. "He's known that you existed, but he and Rose didn't want to interfere while Uncle Peter was alive. He'd like to see you. You don't have to go and see him, but personally I think you'll be sorry about it your whole life if you don't."

"For Christ's sake, Penny," Jeremy said with a sudden burst of desperation. "Will you just shut up for two minutes so I can hear myself think? Just when I imagine I've heard it all, you come up with more. You haven't stopped chattering since we crossed the border!"

Now that was unfair, even if it was true, which it wasn't, not really. At least, I didn't think so. Even though Aunt Sheila had given us beds to sleep in and bathrooms to wash in and some food, I still felt punchy, sleep-deprived, and high on adrenaline from chasing Rollo across the freaking border and finding out that we'd got hold of a possible Leonardo worth gazillions. I mean, Jeremy could have cut me some slack. But no, there he was, using THAT TONE with me again, a scant day or so after kissing me. I don't see how a man can kiss a woman like that, then turn around and use tones of pure sarcasm bordering on contempt.

We'd just come to a lurching halt at a traffic light. So I did what any self-respecting, slightly punchy woman would have done under the circumstances to salvage her wounded dignity. I said, "Fine!" and opened the car door, stepped out, slammed the door behind me, went plunging off into the city, walking as rapidly away from him as possible—and I promptly got lost.

Look, it's easy to do in Italy. Go down one cobbled street, turn a corner, cross a piazza, and there you are. Lost. Suddenly you can't remember which end is up and which way is south and where the hell you were when you started. That's what I did, and I really didn't mean to, but he annoyed me so much that I wasn't looking at street signs. The city was waking up from its post-lunch slumber, so the shops were flinging open their doors, the cars were suddenly zooming around and honking their horns, and I was thoroughly exhausted and utterly disoriented, not knowing where to turn first.

Naturally what I did was turn down a blind alley, which was scary. It was, actually, like a bad dream, where you're running down one street that looks like another, but the closer you think you are to where you want to be, the farther away you keep getting, and then you hear someone calling your name and you call back but you can't tell where they are, and they can't tell where you are, and you keep fruitlessly calling out to each other . . .

"Penny!" Jeremy shouted. I could hear his footsteps and the panting of his breath as he came running closer when he saw me. "Why the hell did you *do* that?" he demanded angrily.

"To get away from you, you beast," I said wearily.

"You are *impossible!*" he exclaimed in exasperation, taking me by the shoulders and giving me a shake. "I thought you were kidnapped! I pity the man who marries you—because you will be nothing but trouble for him for the rest of his life!"

I really, truly hate it when men say things like that. "Well, I pity the woman who marries *you,*" I shot back, "because you think you can just *holler* any old time you want to, and say the most sneery, snide things in a tone you wouldn't use for a *dog,* much less someone you love."

I broke off and we stood there looking at each other, breathing hard. Then something dawned on each of us at exactly the same time, because the anger on our faces turned to surprise. I was also aware that he was still holding me by the shoulders and hadn't let go.

"Is that so?" he said lightly, under his breath. His tone dropped deeper, and some of the old note of teasing crept back into his voice, but there was something more to it this time, something a little more serious. "Now just who said anything about . . . love?" I didn't answer.

He took my hand and said softly, "I am sorrier than words can say for the miserable, wretched way I treated you just now, even though you *are* a bit of a chatterbox. But I would rather listen to you than any other person on the face of this earth. Except that thanks to you and my mum, I have to go and see about a grandfather right now. So will you please come with me? Because I'm absolutely terrified."

Chapter Thirty-five

JEREMY'S GRANDFATHER LIVED IN A SMALL TOWN OF TERRACED HILLS and stone farmhouses ringed by fields with rows and rows of beautiful olive trees that had their dusty-green-leafy arms outspread as if they utterly worshiped the sun. The street that we pulled into was dotted with umbrella pine trees that looked exactly like their name—like the generous shady evergreen parasols of the gods. We stopped at a pretty white and pale peach house.

"That's it," I said, squinting at Aunt Sheila's scribbled address. When we reached the front door, it was opened by a little girl who had to stretch her arms straight up to reach the doorknob. She had long, luxurious wavy dark hair, and wore a pink-and-white-checked dress, and she stared at us with enormous round brown eyes. Jeremy bent down and said, "May we come in?" She broke into a wide smile that made her cheeks even rounder, and she nodded shyly and led us down a dark corridor.

The house was a cool stone affair that echoed our footsteps slightly as we walked past an open, large parlor furnished with heavy old furniture and white lace, and then a few other closed doors, and then we ended up in the kitchen at the back of the house, where Domenico's sister-in-law, a stout elderly woman, was busy at the stove but smiled at us encouragingly.

Jeremy spoke to her, surprising me when he managed to come up with enough correct Italian words to make a few comprehensible sentences. He and the older woman in the kitchen exchanged understanding looks as they spoke. She turned to the little girl, and must have told her to take us into the garden, because the girl called out to us, *"Venite qui,"* with sudden authority. She led the way out the back door and across a lawn to a pebbled sitting area under a pear tree where an old man was seated on an iron lawn chair and cushions.

As we went outside I said to Jeremy, "I didn't know that you speak Italian."

"I understand some of it, especially the—melody of it," he said. "When I was very young I got bronchitis for three winters in a row, and I had an Italian governess who took care of me and taught me my sums and kept me up on my homework. She slipped in a little Italian vocabulary when I got restless. I thought she was teaching me a secret language."

Jeremy drew himself up a bit taller as we approached the old man sitting in the garden. Domenico was reading his newspaper, but he looked up and put it aside as we drew nearer. He was a tall, trim, wiry old man with a whole beautiful headful of silver hair. He was exquisitely combed, shaved, groomed—and he wore a three-piece suit of the softest lightweight wool, and good well-shined leather shoes that were not brand-new but were finely made and elegant. He looked like a man dressed to go to church on Sunday—but a Sunday from another era. He sat erect, proud, self-possessed and alert, with a dignified demeanor that was perhaps a little stern. As we drew nearer I caught a whiff of a lemon verbena aftershave, and something about the scent was rather touching. For it occurred to me that despite his slightly reticent demeanor, he'd dressed and prepared himself very carefully for this meeting.

"*Buongiorno,*" I said as we drew nearer, since Jeremy suddenly went mute as a post.

The old man smiled. "*Buongiorno,*" he said politely. He gestured toward two other iron garden chairs with cushions on them, for us to sit down. We did, and I looked at Jeremy, who was gazing at the old man. I had not expected to see a family resemblance because I didn't have the time to give it much thought, but now I saw the high foreheads, the elegant wave of the lustrous hair, the intelligent curve of the eyebrows.

They studied each other quietly. Finally they both turned to me. So it was up to me, I realized, to get these two lions to talk to each other. My Italian vocabulary was of the teach-yourself-at-home variety, to figure out art terminology. "*Lei parla inglese?*" I asked hesitatingly.

The old man said, "*Scusi,* not so good anymore." Aw, nuts, I thought. I nudged Jeremy, and he remembered the gift I'd made him buy. It was a small bottle of a good, smooth brandy, a label that I'd seen on my father's shelf. Jeremy had slipped it into his jacket pocket, as if it were a good-luck talisman that he was hanging on to for dear life. It was wrapped in a gold and red shiny-paper gift sleeve, with a tasseled red drawstring. Jeremy handed it to the old man, who slowly pulled the drawstring and extracted the bottle, held it up in the light and nodded approvingly, then set it on the iron table near him and said, lightly and genuinely, "*Grazie.*"

Then he folded his hands in his lap and waited, intently scrutinizing Jeremy rather expectantly, pleasantly but a bit wary. Jeremy shot me a pleading look that quite nakedly said, *Help me!* Something had to be done, or these two sphinxes were going to sit here staring at each other till the end of time.

I tried to imagine this elderly gentleman as a wide-eyed little boy, riding alongside Aunt Penelope in her Dragonetta auto, escaping out of wartime Italy. Then I remembered something I'd stuck in my handbag back at Aunt Pen's villa. The little toy soldier I'd found in the car. In all the excitement I'd forgotten about it. I pulled it out now and gently handed it to Domenico, and said, *"Si ricorda?"* Then I held my breath, wondering if he'd really remember it.

I knew that I was taking a chance, dredging it all up. Possibly Jeremy would want to throttle me if I screwed this up for him, judging by the way he raised his eyebrows and shot me a slightly panicked look, as Domenico leaned forward and bent his head over the toy to examine it.

"Ah!" Domenico said, immediately lifting the hat on the soldier's head and making the arms and legs jump. That gesture, and the fond smile of memory that broke across his face, making an old man look suddenly like a wistful little kid, well . . . it told me everything I wanted to know.

Domenico's eyes misted over as he looked at me and said wonderingly, *"Ha mai conosciuto Penelope, quella bella signora?"*

"Sure we knew her!" I exclaimed. I hesitated, then plunged on. *"Penelope era mia grande zia—la sorella di mia nonna,"* I said. This was a sentence I'd been rehearsing in my mind all the way over here: Penelope was my great-aunt, the sister of my grandmother. Aunt Sheila must have prepared him for this little news flash, because he nodded as if he understood perfectly. The fond smile of memory had softened his expression now.

"Era una signora molto generosa, Penelope," he said, infusing the words with a great deal of heart as he recalled Aunt Penelope as a woman of supreme generosity.

I felt victorious about communicating well enough, but now I looked at Jeremy, and my glance said, *Okay, buddy, you're on. Talk to your grandfather.*

Jeremy cleared his throat and looked uncharacteristically nervous as he reached into his pocket and extracted the photo that I'd given him from Aunt Sheila, the one with his father as a grown man in the kitchen with him. This took me by surprise. He had kept it all along, but this was the first I'd seen of it since I gave it to him at his apartment. Now he handed it to the old man.

"*E questo uomo è tuo figlio?*" he asked tentatively.

"*Ah, si, si!*" Domenico exclaimed after he peered at the photo of his son Tony. He pulled something gold out of his pocket, which at first I thought was a pocket-watch, because it was round and connected to a chain. But then he detached it carefully from the chain, and opened it, and handed it to Jeremy, who reached for it and held it out so I could see it, too. It was a locket with two photographs. One was a pale-skinned, dark-eyed woman with a cloud of soft black hair piled up on her head—his wife, Rose, no doubt. The other photo was of a boy about six years old, wearing a Yankees baseball shirt and cap, and a broad grin on his face.

"Tony," Domenico said proudly. His eyes misted a little as he gazed at Jeremy's picture of Tony as a grown man in bell-bottom jeans. "Tony was a good boy, a good boy," Domenico muttered. He peered closer at the baby in the picture, then stared at Jeremy.

"*Il bambino?*" he said inquiringly before the two of them handed each other their pictures back. Jeremy nodded vigorously, then looked directly at Domenico.

"*Io sono il figlio di tuo figlio,*" Jeremy came out with unexpectedly. My jaw dropped. It was the way he said it, so firmly, as if he'd accepted it for the first time. I am the son of your son.

I held my breath. How was the old man going to take it? Was he going to suspect that a foreigner would have no reason to come all this way after all these years to claim kinship unless he wanted money or something? Was he going to tell Jeremy to go fly a kite, and give him a complex for the rest of his life?

Domenico leaned forward intently. Jeremy gulped and sat very still. Domenico looked at Jeremy and then reached out and patted his cheek affectionately. *"Si, si, è vero,"* he said. "Your mama says you are a good-a boy, too."

Jeremy sat perfectly still, like a dog who can't believe his good luck at being wanted, loved and petted after having been lost and miserable, and who doesn't dare move a muscle for fear of dispelling the perfect moment. His eyes were huge, as if he were fighting back emotion.

Domenico saw this and chuckled, and then he took something else from his pocket. It was a knife, like a camper's jackknife, only this was a more beautiful and a very serious one, with a gold and ivory handle. The old man reached out to the tree, which was heavy with ripe fruit, and which was attracting a few wasps that I had been keeping an eye on. He plucked a pear with total concentration, as if it were being served to him on a tray and he was selecting the best one. Then he took a lovely linen handkerchief that had been neatly folded in his breast pocket, and wiped the pear to clean it. Then he proceeded to peel the pear, letting the peelings collect in an empty ashtray on the wrought-iron table beside him. Then he expertly sliced a nice chunk of the pear, and, still holding the slice on the knife, extended it and offered Jeremy the first slice.

"Per il figlio di figlio mio," the old man said with a slight twinkle of amusement. I recognized the gesture because my father used to do these things for me when I was a little girl. He would cut slices of apples, pears or peaches and hand them to me, slice by slice. I knew the affection such a gesture carried, and, apparently, so did Jeremy, because his eyes were very bright as he accepted the slice and popped it into his mouth. The old man calmly cut another piece and offered it to me. But when he spoke, he addressed Jeremy.

"Per la donna di questo figlio-di-figlio-mio," the grandfather said, finding it a good joke to tease a younger man by referring to me as "the woman of this son-of-my-son." Jeremy glanced at me to see if I got

it, and I grinned. Domenico saw this and chuckled, and continued to
carve that pear, giving a slice to Jeremy, then to me, then to himself,
until it was finished. It was the softest, sweetest pear I'd ever tasted in
my life.

Silence descended again, and Domenico still had that expectant
gaze. Jeremy looked choked up, even though he'd chewed and swallowed his last slice of pear. So I, brightly and boldly, decided to revert
to being the social director of this cruise. Haltingly but determinedly,
I worked up enough schoolgirl vocabulary to string like beads into a
sentence, in which I thought that I was asking "What was Tony really
like?"

Only I must have put the words in the wrong order; I think it
came out "What did Tony like?" instead, because after a slightly puzzled look, Domenico said, *"La musica."*

The little girl was coming toward us, carrying a silver tray with
three china espresso cups and saucers on it, and a small bowl of tiny
sugar cubes. Domenico spoke to her and she nodded, set the tray on
the table, turned and ran back to the house. He reached for the bottle
of brandy from Jeremy, opened it, and put a modest drop in his coffee,
then held the bottle over our cups and glanced at us inquiringly to
ask if we each wanted it. And none of us said no. We sipped our spiked
coffee in a silence that had become natural and companionable.

Moments later the little girl came marching solemnly and impor-
tantly across the lawn, carrying something as if it were a baby. She
handed it to the old man, and he, in turn, handed it to Jeremy. It was
a mandolin.

"From your fadder," the old man said distinctly. Jeremy looked
startled as the mandolin was placed in his hands. The old man held up
his palm and made a gentle pushing gesture, suggesting that Jeremy
play it. Jeremy hesitated.

"Aw, g'wan," I said.

Haltingly at first, and then with more confidence, Jeremy plinked out a little melody. The mandolin had a beautiful sweet tone, rather high, like a young boy in a choir. Halfway through I thought I recognized the tune, dimly, and then it came to me, and somehow I managed to smile and not giggle ferociously as I wanted to when I identified the dulcet melody of "Norwegian Wood" by the Beatles.

Chapter Thirty-six

"IT WAS ALL I COULD THINK OF TO PLAY," JEREMY TOLD ME LATER, when we were back in the car on the road. "I drew a complete blank at first."

"Well, he loved it," I said. The mandolin was sitting on the backseat. Domenico insisted we take it, because it belonged to Jeremy's father. Jeremy had choked out a thank-you in Italian, and when we'd said good-bye and crossed the lawn, he turned back once more to look at the old man in the garden, who looked up and waved to him, raising his hand in that genuine benediction that Italians so naturally offer to travellers.

As we drove off, Jeremy blinked more than once and then glanced at me fearfully as if to see if I was watching him in this extremely emotional moment. I pretended to be rooting around in my purse for the highway map, and I didn't dare look at him until he began talking normally again.

"Thanks for coming with me," he said in a tone that indicated the impact of comprehending, finally, who his father was. He seemed truly calm for the first time in all these weeks of fury, uncertainty and tension.

"I liked him a lot," I said.

"So did I," he said. I fell silent.

"Mum's gone back to London," he said finally. "She said we could stay at the villa overnight. I think we should, because Harold wants us to come straight back to London, which means we should start out early tomorrow."

"Okay," I said, feeling strangely compliant about everything.

When we returned to the villa the chef was still there, cooking busily, and a maid was laying the table for dinner for two, with candles and flowers in delicate cut-glass holders. She had flung open the doors, which led to a stone balcony. Everything seemed so ancient, eternal, as if it had been here forever.

And suddenly, as we stood there admiring the view, it hit me. Here I was, not just acting out, but living out, my favorite time-travel fantasy—the villa, the balcony, the cocktails, a nice fella to talk to, and I even had decent new clothes to wear for a change, though they were a bit crushed, having been stuffed in shopping bags in the trunk of Jeremy's car all this time.

We gazed down at a beautiful, shimmering blue pool at the back of the house, which we'd been too nervous to notice when we first got here. It had a tiled floor, and a stone sculpture of a dolphin in the center, spurting water out of his mouth, as a fountain. I'd bought a bathing suit on my shopping spree, and Jeremy said he always traveled with one because he liked to swim in hotel pools to work out the kinks of traveling. So we decided to go for a swim. And, I'm happy to report, the hives from my wax job at the spa were all gone, and I was now as sleek as a professional swimmer all spruced to win a race. We hurried down and plunged right in, grateful for the shock of cool water after all the dust and heat of the afternoon.

I felt straight as an arrow as I sliced through the water. We swam side by side, back and forth, while the dappled sunlight leapt and flickered across the water. I watched our shadows crawling along at the bottom of the pool, keeping pace with us. We finally paused to rest, tilting our faces up to the fountain-spray of water coming from the dolphin sculpture in big benevolent arcs. Jeremy demanded to know why I, a mere slip of a girl, swam faster than he, a hulking male. It was the kind of demand he'd have made when we were kids.

"You weigh more," I said, and I stuck my tongue out at him. He stared at me in disbelief at my audacity. Then he chased me out of the pool and into the house, and didn't catch up with me until we reached the upstairs bedrooms.

There he pulled me closer to him, slowly but inexorably, with a determination that told me, *This time I won't let you get away.* The tug of his will gave me that thrill of inevitability, and when he put his head down to kiss me, I could finally let myself dare to really, completely feel that fierce hungry ache that I'd had all this time, ever since I first "clapped eyes" on Jeremy at the hotel, which I'd tried so hard to ignore during this whole trip to London, all through the reading of the will, and all the while we'd been chasing around the villa and up and down the whole ding-danged Riviera. Every step of the way I'd been pushing back the pleasure of being with him, and now suddenly, at last, I didn't have to hide the simple fact that the sight of him, the scent of him, the warmth of him just filled me with utter joy. I could greet it all with open arms.

And along with this ferocious hunger, I felt a new and sweetly secure sensation of coming home, where I belonged. We kept pushing closer and closer as if we couldn't ever get close enough, and it seemed as if, after years of endlessly swimming around each other in the cool and salty sea, we'd at last emerged from the turbulent waves, stumbling onto a warm and sandy shore, collapsing into each other's arms, where we lay happily gasping and giddy with the sun and the sky reeling overhead, exultant in our mingled delight.

Chapter Thirty-seven

WHEN WE ARRIVED AT AUNT PENELOPE'S APARTMENT IN LONDON we didn't talk much at all. We seemed to be moving in tandem, as if each of us knew what the other was thinking, feeling, wanting, in that blissful state of harmony. Such a natural thing, harmony is, that when it happens you wonder why on earth you've lived so stupidly that you actually forgot about how great it is to be in sync with another human being. As if once long ago, you knew. When you were pure and innocent and weren't trying so hard to be something other than human.

I put the key in the door and we were smiling at each other as we went in, until we heard a strange noise coming from the kitchen. Amid tremendous clattering of pots and pans, I could make out the deep hum of a man's voice and the high sound of a woman's laughter. They seemed to be calling out and shouting to each other over the clatter. I couldn't hear the actual words, but I could comprehend the uproarious tone.

Jeremy said, "Who the hell is that? It sounds like somebody's crashed the apartment to throw a party!"

"It's my parents," I said meekly. Jeremy paused.

"What are they doing?" he asked in a hushed, fascinated tone.

"They're cooking," I said.

My parents didn't even hear us come in, at first, so busy were they having a good time peeling, chopping, sautéing, teasing and joking with each other, already hilariously revisiting every funny or idiotic thing that had happened at the airports and on the trip over.

My mother glanced up first, and well, you know how it is when you see from the expression on another person's face that your own face has just given you away, and you realize that you've been walking around wearing your happiness all over you for all the world to see.

When my mother observed me wearing this loud cloak of lucky twinkledust, she looked a bit startled, but then she quickly, in her inimitable English way, gave me a wry smile of comprehension that said to me, *Well darling, it's nice to see you happy for once.*

My father's reaction was actually more like several looks passing over his face in rapid succession. He went from surprise, to amused comprehension, to a brief look of paternal sorrow. He recovered and smiled fondly, but then he gave Jeremy a look of mingled understanding and yet tiger-watchfulness, the way men do when they communicate, *I know this is inevitable but if you don't watch yourself you'll have me to answer to.*

And Jeremy was looking back at him, respectfully but tigerish himself, the way a younger man communicates, *You can't keep her all to yourself any longer, Dad.* I must say this primitive exchange was a bit shocking, and yet I felt as if nothing could surprise me today because everything was so wholesale astonishing.

My mother took control of the situation and, with typical composure, broke the silence with words of assurance and civility, and said things like, "How was your trip? You must be hungry." They were both wearing aprons on top of their shirts and slacks. My mother had a little flour on the tip of her nose, and my father's hair was slightly askew in that way it gets when he's been cooking in earnest.

They explained that Rupert had let them in. He didn't know what else to do with them when they phoned, and the poor kid didn't stand a chance against their playful logic and the way they coordinate their persuasiveness by speaking back and forth more to each other than to anyone else, and sometimes both talking at the same time. My father told Rupert that he simply must get near a stove so that he could cook some food, which my jet-lagged mother had been craving since they left New York. Rupert surrendered and gave them the spare key.

My mother took me by the arm and led me into the dining room, suggesting that we set the table together, which gave my father the cover he needed to have a few moments alone with Jeremy. I'm sure that nothing so gauche as direct questioning occurred, but when Jeremy returned to us, looking visibly relieved and a touch pleased with himself for surviving it, I couldn't resist whispering to him as my mother discreetly went into the kitchen for more cutlery, "Well? Did he threaten you with a meat cleaver?"

"Not exactly," Jeremy said, "but I watched him mince an onion in seconds flat, dismember a chicken without a sound, and pound the hell out of a puff paste. I got the message. Now he wants to see you." He paused. "He let me slice the bread. Is that a good sign?" he asked hopefully.

"Very good," I said.

My mother returned and said, "Penny, dear, see if your father needs any help." Then she took over Jeremy at that point, talking to him, smoothing the way for him, and the two of them with their nice English shorthand managed to make each other feel assured that neither would say or do anything to embarrass the other. Whereas I suddenly felt as if someone, possibly me, was going to shout from the rooftops with irrepressible joy. I tried to control this as I went into the kitchen to help my dad.

"Everything all right?" he inquired in that low, easy French tone that I find so soothing.

"Yes, of course, why?" I said, momentarily lapsing into my old schoolgirl-trying-to-pretend that I didn't just sneak into the house at dawn after a school dance.

"No reason," he said in a rich Burgundian chuckle. "We only get our news these days in *leetle* bits and pieces. We hear you've been running around all of France in fancy cars, going to gambling casinos, chasing after a mysterious painting, and making everyone in three countries delirious with worry."

He said all this casually while placing chicken sections into individual-sized servings of pastry wreaths, then brushing them with sauce and popping them into the oven on a tray. Without pausing for breath he reached out and did some fast flipping of sizzling vegetables in a sauté pan on the stove, without a spatula, just with a few quick, astonishing jerks of the wrist that made the vegetables fly up in the air and dance before landing perfectly right back in the pan. Then he peered into a bubbling pot.

"The soup is ready," he announced. "Why don't you pour it into the tureen?"

"Gladly," I said. "Does Aunt Penelope have a tureen?"

He looked at me reproachfully. "After all the time you've been here, you didn't acquaint yourself right away with the kitchen?" he asked. "You must be a foundling. No daughter of mine could possibly do such a thing."

"Wait, I remember," I said. "Here it is."

"That's better," he said. "Let the soup wait. Come here and help me with the appetizers." We worked side by side as we have before, and he asked me about everything that had happened in France, without once permitting me to forget the importance of the platter we were arranging to feed the people we loved. I told him about how dicey it had gotten with Rollo, and what happened with Jeremy and his mother and his Italian grandfather.

"And yet," Dad drawled, "in spite of it all, here you are, safe and sound." He reached out and gave my cheek a gentle pinch.

"Hallo in there!" my mother called out. "We're famished!" My father handed me a tray.

"Here, carry this out and feed the boy," he said.

Part Twelve

Chapter Thirty-eight

WHILE WE WAITED FOR THE FRENCH COURT TO SCHEDULE THE DE-cision on Aunt Penelope's will, I was being advised about what to do with the painting if the judge decided that I possessed sole ownership.

Personally I thought this was tempting fate, to start counting chickens and crossing bridges. But I really had no choice. Word got out that the painting existed, starting with whispers and murmurs, then small newspaper items, which people actually do read. So the world came knocking at my door, in some cases banging at it, and making the telephone shrill at all hours of the night with urgent messages from collectors, museum and auction house executives, all heedless of the time difference and eager to beat each other out, thinking that greed would make me amenable even when they'd just yanked me out of bed. I had to have all my phone calls forwarded to Jeremy's law office, just to get some sleep at night.

I had a long talk with my parents and Jeremy about it. We decided that, after the experience I'd had of someone breaking into the house in the dead of night to steal the painting, we didn't want to keep it in an apartment, where it would have to be insured by people who might prefer to devalue it so that if it were stolen they wouldn't have to fork over a lot of money. We didn't like the idea of keeping it buried in a vault, where, as Aunt Penelope had pointed out, you'd never get to see what you had. So we agreed that I should sell it to a museum or gallery.

First off, I wanted to split the money four ways—for me, for Jeremy, for my parents, and the final fourth divided between Aunt Sheila and Jeremy's grandfather. My parents emphatically said they wouldn't take a cent from me, and they couldn't be budged.

"Don't be silly, darling," my mother said. "We know you'll look after us in our old age. What do we want with more bank accounts and investments to manage? And when we die—which I suppose we will, you know, someday, eventually—it would be a tax mess for you. No, dear, you keep it."

To which my father added, "Just make sure you keep me in good coffee and good wine and good fruit. The fruit will be the hardest for you to find. I don't know what they're doing to it these days," and he was off and running, fuming about the poor state of produce.

Aunt Sheila also said she was "fine as I am," and Jeremy's grandfather refused to take anything from me or relatives he'd never seen, but Jeremy said he thought the man would accept gifts from him, over time, whenever Jeremy visited him.

"Then it's you and me, kiddo," I said.

"Get hold of the money first, and then let us know what you want to do with it, you fool," Jeremy said.

So the painting had to be evaluated by the potential buyers' experts, a process, we realized, that could go on forever. After more X-rays, and the scrutiny of specialists, most of the experts agreed on one thing, which was that the Madonna and Child came from a student of Leonardo. Many believed that the Master had not painted the whole thing himself, though there were a few stalwarts who thought it was entirely his work. But even "fractional participation" by Leonardo could make the numbers soar to dizzying heights.

Dr. Mateo had written up his assessment for us—that the Master had made a stroke here and there on Fabrizi's original painting. Most people believed that it was either a copy of a lost Leonardo sketch (which would still be quite valuable) or else the original work of Fabrizi, a "minor female artist" who had studied "briefly" under the Master and possibly been helped by him.

I had Erik and Tim take a look at it when they stopped by in Italy; then they showed up in London on their way home. They arrived looking sated and suntanned from their travels. We had a swell time because I threw them a real English tea party and showed them all around the apartment, including Aunt Penelope's vintage dresses, which made them moan with joy.

"Will you marry me?" Timothy asked me. "Then I can be around this fabulous stuff for the rest of my life."

"Good. You marry her, and I'll marry Jeremy," Erik shot back. For to my chagrin, they spent more time discussing a photo I'd shown them of Jeremy than they did the painting. Jeremy was in Brussels when they visited, but I promised they'd meet him next time.

When Erik and Tim finally settled down to tell me their opinion of the Madonna and Child, they grew very serious and professional, and they assessed it soberly and respectfully. They believed, as I did, that Fabrizi had sketched the underdrawings and was the creator of the piece.

"Maybe Leonardo put a stroke here and there, that's entirely possible, but this is *so* original," Timothy declared excitedly. "I've never seen anything like it."

"But leave it to the experts, honey," Erik advised me, "and the experts are the ones who can get you the most cash. If they see a total Leonardo, then baby, *let* them."

But certain compulsive collectors with money to burn and time on their hands wanted only to beat each other to the punch, buy it and figure out who did it later. These people were the hardest to deal with, the kind who would think nothing of hopping on a jet to London and then stalking me. They were not accustomed to hearing "No" and didn't handle it very well when I, a snip of a girl, said I'd have to think it over. They got ugly very fast, resorting to one basic tactic of negotiation—force—being positive that relentless bullying would make me bow to their wishes. I had to call the cops on more than one of them. This didn't scare them as much as the fear that their competitors might get their mitts on a masterpiece that one day might be decreed an authentic, new Leonardo.

The museums by and large used the "dangling carrot" approach, calculating that fear would motivate me if they feigned only mild interest at first, then casually made an offer of a comparatively more modest sum than the private collectors proposed. Still, even from them I got some pretty strange phone calls in the night, offering me, *sotto voce*, tens of thousands of pounds if I'd sell it to them right now, tonight, before it went to auction.

Big money is tempting, but oddly enough, when it gets that big it becomes unreal and a little frightening. You get the feeling that bad luck will come with it, because nobody forks over that much without expecting to extract some of your flesh and blood if it turns out that they miscalculated and the painting was later, somehow, proved to be what they would consider a fake. I had nightmares that such a buyer would tell himself that I'd somehow swindled him on purpose, and he'd come looking to get his money back or dump me in the Thames, or both. Of course, with all that money I supposed I could hire thugs of my own, and become like Rollo or worse; but even people with thugs and bodyguards, I've noticed, are not immune from fear and paranoia, and they still do a lot of looking over their shoulders. No, thanks. I'd seen enough of this shadowy underworld, and I didn't want to cut any deals like Persephone.

Besides, I was concerned about how and where the painting would be kept. In the end, the offer that I liked best was from one little museum on the Italian Riviera suggesting that they would put it in a special glassed-in gallery where visitors could view it from either inside the gallery or from an adjacent tearoom, where they could rest and revive and feed their kids while gazing at art through the glass walls. If they wanted to view it up close inside the gallery, they were restricted from bringing things like phones and food and noise with them. Being Italian, the curators said *certo*, they understood my concerns about a proper and protective environment for the painting, but, they reminded me with an amused tone, one couldn't always control the behavior of tourists. Best of all, though, it would stay in a place that I would be glad to come and visit and say hello to the Madonna and Child whenever I wanted.

Jeremy liked this gallery, too, once he heard the offer that this surprising little museum came up with. "Twenty million pounds," he said in a tone of satisfaction, as if he'd finally gotten me what he'd wanted to all along. "Now all we have to do is convince the judge that Aunt Pen was sane and not unduly influenced by me when she wrote her will."

Chapter Thirty-nine

AUNT PENELOPE'S WILL WAS JUDGED IN NICE. ALL OF US WERE there—my parents, Harold, Rupert, Severine, Louis, Jeremy and me . . . and Rollo and his lawyers. Only Great-Aunt Dorothy was AWOL; she had a headache or heart palpitations or something, they said, while the fact was, she just couldn't stand to see all that lovely money go to somebody else.

Because a deal had finally been struck. All family members agreed to it, and it was this: Rollo wouldn't contest the will, and we wouldn't press charges for theft and send him to a French prison, thanks to his thuggy friend who "sang," as Jeremy told me.

"Now who's talking like a cop?" I asked him as we took our seats in the courtroom.

"Behave," he hissed. "The French don't like cutups in the court."

I saw my parents glance inquiringly in our direction, and I sobered up, feeling as if I were a kid again who didn't want the grown-ups to know how much I liked Jeremy.

The judge, a serious-looking but dapper man in his mid-sixties, eyed us all with the bright, alert eyes of a bird of prey while hearing the case presented to him. It was all spoken in French and then repeated in English, even when he rendered his decision with great formality.

The gist of it was that Aunt Penelope's will would stand as written. It helped to have her handwritten note, dated, signed, and witnessed, indicating that she knew who Jeremy was, regarded him as a special member of the family, and had reasons to bequeath what she did to him—and me. So Jeremy got the villa; Rollo got the furnishings, which must be removed under supervision by such-and-such date, no going back later, etc.; and I got the Dragonetta, the garage, and its contents. Which included the painting. When it was over and the judge retired, even cool old Harold let out a sigh of relief and mopped his brow with his handkerchief.

Rollo, too, could not prevent himself from uttering a gusty regretful sigh when the painting was announced as mine. As he rose to go, he shrugged his shoulders as if rearranging himself, like a dog shaking himself off after a fight. He and his lawyers walked out of the courthouse without a single backward glance, and climbed into a long black limousine.

"You know, of course, that we'll have to look after him," I told Jeremy as we watched Rollo's car pull away. "He is family, after all."

Jeremy understood and he didn't argue, but he rolled his eyes. "Oh, Lord," he groaned. "Just don't let *him* know your plans."

My parents and our triumphant lawyers behaved as if they had just passed their last final exam and would never have to return to school ever again. Not that anybody whooped; we were all too sober and dignified for that. But suddenly everyone was hugging and slapping each other on the back.

My parents had decided to stay on in Nice for a week. So as we lingered on the sidewalk outside the courthouse in the beautiful sunlight, savoring the fine weather and our good luck, my father and mother were trying to decide which restaurant they'd like to take us to. I glanced over at Jeremy, who was conversing with Rupert and Louis. They were beaming, as if Jeremy was praising them. Severine joined them, and they all looked triumphant.

Harold came over to me, shook hands formally, and said with a twinkle, "Well, Miss Nichols, what on earth will such a young lady do with such a windfall?"

I grinned. "Oh, share it with the one man in the world I can trust most," I said happily and automatically. But when Harold harumphed and said, "Ah, well, excellent," and excused himself, I thought perhaps I'd been a bit too honest.

He went to speak to Rupert and Louis. Severine, I noticed, gave Jeremy a single kiss on the cheek, which I thought was far more intimate than the customary one-on-each-cheek kiss. Jeremy glanced somewhat guiltily at me, I thought, and didn't kiss her back.

Severine's gaze followed his, and she studied me from afar, then looked back at Jeremy again, as if she suddenly comprehended something for the first time, and it didn't sit well. A sharp, territorial expression crossed her face as she looked back at me again, and all I could think was, "Uh-oh."

Sure enough, she came walking toward me rather purposefully. "Congratulations, Miss Nichols," she said. Jeremy had followed her, looking slightly alarmed at the two of us together.

"We really have Severine to thank for a lot of the way this was settled," he told me softly as if trying to make peace, not war.

"Yes, thanks-very-much," I said, and my own voice sounded very English to me for the first time. I looked at her and she looked at me, but then she glanced away as if she couldn't bear the sight of me anymore. We managed polite nods and a handshake. Her fingers were cold, and I was glad when she went back to talk to Louis, Rupert, and Harold.

"Okay, I thanked her," I said when she'd left us. Jeremy laughed and rumpled my hair. Severine, alert as a cobra, sensed something and flicked a backward glance at us, then resumed talking serenely to Louis and Rupert, while Harold stepped away to answer his mobile phone.

"Penny," Jeremy said, "you know you can change your mind about sharing the money."

"No," I said, "I talked it over with my parents. They understand, and agree."

"You *will* go on making me feel like I have to protect you, even from myself," he said.

"A deal's a deal," I said. "We'll split everything from France fifty-fifty, including what I get for the painting. Which also means I get to use the villa, and you can drive my car."

"You're impossible," he said, and he looked as if he might kiss me, but my parents were watching us and waving. He took my arm and we joined them.

"Jeremy!" my mother said, taking his arm in a friendly way. "Are you hungry? We're starved!" I was going to dine out with my folks, then leave them in Nice, to have their little second honeymoon. I'd thought Jeremy, too, would come with us and celebrate, but he told us that Harold had assigned him a new client from Texas who insisted on seeing him tonight in London. And he would probably have to fly out of London with him tomorrow afternoon.

But he assured me that he and my father's lawyers had already gone over some routine papers that I was supposed to sign, so Jeremy wanted me to know that he'd be in his office in the morning, and if I came down there early to sign them, he'd be able to answer any last-minute questions. "Okay, I'll see you tomorrow," I said.

My mother gave him a kiss, which pleased him, and he shook hands with my father, and kissed me, rather formally because my parents were watching; then Rupert stopped by to tell me, in his nervous, responsible way, that he'd booked me a flight to London for later tonight.

Chapter Forty

THE NEXT MORNING, I KNEW SOMETHING WAS WRONG THE MINUTE I set foot in the law offices in London. A silver-haired secretary led me back to Jeremy's office, which had a big modern desk, a high-backed leather chair, a beautiful view of the Thames . . . but no Jeremy. She told me that Rupert was on his way to "explain all." I knew she meant explain about Jeremy's absence; my father's American lawyer had already sent me an e-mail assuring me that these papers were okay to sign, for they just made me a legal heir.

Rupert came in looking especially nervous, even for him, and proceeded to tell me that Jeremy had not only left the building earlier than he'd expected but also would be out of the country longer than he'd thought. The client wanted him to stay abroad for at least two weeks, because after a stop in Canada, he'd be needed in Texas.

"I can't understand it," I said to Rupert as he laid out the papers for me to sign on Jeremy's desk. "Jeremy usually calls me to tell me these things himself, and he didn't."

"No?" said Rupert with mild surprise. "Well, it all happened this morning, very rush-rush. Client's private plane was leaving early for Canada. Fellow wants Jeremy to go fishing with him at his special private retreat. Out on some island that they have to be choppered in to. No phones or modern conveniences there."

The secretary poked her head in the door and said there was a phone call that Rupert must take. Rupert left me alone to sign "whenever you feel comfortable."

So there I was, sitting quietly in Jeremy's office, in Jeremy's chair, looking out of Jeremy's window ... but no Jeremy. I had my pen poised when I felt someone watching me. It was Severine, standing right outside the door, talking to the secretary. As I signed the papers, I could feel Severine's eyes watching my every loop.

"I'm getting paranoid," I thought, when she walked away. The secretary returned and collected all the papers, and she said, "Oh, by the way, your fiancé is here, come to pick you up. He was here earlier but went down to the restaurant for breakfast. He said to call him when you were done, so I did and he's out in the reception now. Shall I send him in?"

"My *what*?" I said, astounded.

But Paul was never a man to be kept hanging around a reception area. He'd been right behind the secretary, following her in. He was coming at me right now, with that familiar arrogant tilt of his head, the ruthless, determined look in his eye, the status-symbol clothes, and that aggressive, bullying stride. The only thing I didn't recognize about him was the warm, bighearted grin on his face. I'd never seen that before. But now it positively stretched ear-to-ear.

"Penny Nichols, *hello!*" he said in a low voice as he put his arm around my waist and pulled me in for a possessive kiss. "Pentathlon Productions just isn't the same without you."

"Paul!" I gulped. "What—what—are you doing here—in London?" It was a nightmare come true. Paul in London. Here in Jeremy's office. Two separate and distinct compartments of my life, New York and London, now horribly overlapping. I felt a jolt of absolute panic, knowing what Paul's like when he's got quarry trained in his sights.

"I'm here on business—and pleasure," he said meaningfully. He had a most peculiar gleam in his eye. "I've come to rescue the only woman I've ever loved, and bring you home."

Paul never talked like that. Declarations of love were, to a warrior like him, tantamount to surrender and defeat. So, not having sincere words of love in his arsenal, he'd merely borrowed them from any one of Pentathlon Productions' scripts. I felt embarrassed for both of us.

Rupert's head peered round the corner. He looked stricken, even somewhat guilty. And behind him were a couple of other curious office onlookers. I stepped away from Paul.

"Uh—that's nice, Paul—er—have a seat, I'll be right back," I choked out, and darted out of the room and chased Rupert down at his little desk.

"Okay, Rupert," I said. "Out with it. What's going on here? How did Paul know I'd be here? Who let that monster in?"

"He was here earlier," Rupert whispered. "Apparently he tried to reach you, but all your calls are still being forwarded to us. Somebody told him you were expected here this morning, and let him in."

"Did Paul talk to Jeremy?" I asked, horrified.

"Yes. Your fiancé told Jeremy he'd come to take you back home to America—"

"Stop calling him my fiancé," I said. "Do you think for one minute that I would actually *marry* that guy? Good God," I said. "I'd rather eat nails."

Rupert looked surprised and relieved. "I say, that's good news," he said cheerfully.

"How come you all believed him?" I pressed, even though I know how convincing Paul can be. The trick of being a good liar is to actually start believing your own lies.

"Well," said Rupert, looking a bit fusty, "Harold said *you* told him that you were going to share your inheritance with 'the one man in the world I can trust most'— your exact words."

I groaned. "Drat that Harold," I said. "The soul of discretion, until now."

Rupert said, "So, naturally, when this bloke showed up he rather gave the impression that you'd summoned him as soon as the estate was settled and you'd got your money."

Bingo. The money. That explained it. Erik had warned me that Paul knew why I'd gone to London. And the story of the painting had been in all the Euro press. Oh, Christ, I thought. This must be what it's like to hit the lottery or something, and have all your friends and relatives come out of the woodwork, suddenly impressed with you.

"Did Jeremy say anything to you about me when he left?" I asked. Rupert looked up as if he'd finally made a decision to spill the beans, but he still couldn't quite look me in the eye.

"Oh, you know," he said. "He went about muttering about the treachery of women. Men do that among men. It doesn't mean any-thing," Rupert assured me. "It's just that Jeremy truly fancies you, and it kind of looked as if once you got what you needed from him, you called up your real boyfriend. He said this was the fellow who'd bro-ken your heart and for whom you still carry a torch. So—you didn't tell this man to meet you here, then?" he inquired.

"Of course not!" I said hotly. "Invite that creep back into my life? Share money with that bum? Never! He came here all on his own."

"Ah," said Rupert, looking as if he wished we would stop talking about it. "That explains the whole kerfuffle."

"No, it doesn't," I said. "Who told Paul that I was going to be here in the first place? And let him in this morning?"

Something made me look up then. At the far end of the corridor was Severine, watching us closely. When she saw the look on my face, she darted toward the ladies' room.

"Pardon me, Rupert," I said. "And don't disappear on me. I'll be right back. Keep Paul as busy as you can."

I chased that snake-woman right into the ladies' room and cornered her at the mirror, where she was very cool and casual, smoothing her hair and applying blood-red lipstick. All the while we spoke, her eyes were on my reflection in the mirror.

"Well?" I demanded.

When I didn't say anything more, she said, "Congratulations on your engagement."

"There is no engagement," I said hotly. "And suddenly Jeremy's gone, too. Would you like to explain why you took it upon yourself to arrange this little fiasco?"

From the look on her face I knew that she was the one who did it, all right.

"Don't worry about Zheremy," she said, patting her shiny hair in that perfect twist. "He always gets what he wants from women." Her eyes looked hard, but bright. I knew she meant that he'd lost interest in her. I might have even felt sorry for her—except for what she said next. "Especially now zat he has his villa . . . and a generous allowance from *you*." She shook her head scoldingly, as if I'd played the war of the sexes all wrong. "You make it too easy for him. Now he can stay independent, even from you," she said on her way out.

I stood there alone for a moment. Well. Someone had just told me that a man had seduced me only for my money. Now that was truly a new experience.

When I came out of the ladies' room Paul was in the hallway, waiting to pounce.

"Okay, Penny, let's find somewhere beautiful and expensive to have lunch," he offered, as if he'd made up his mind for both of us. I was amazed that he still thought he could impose his strong will on my uncertain one. "You and I have a lot of catching up to do," he murmured softly. "For the rest of our lives."

I stared at him. I could remember a time, not that long ago, when such attentiveness, fidelity and affection from him would have filled me with joy. Now, well ... I could see from the hard little sparkle around those loving eyes, that I was simply, in his mind, the rich woman he'd been searching for all his life—and, as an added bonus, I was also sweet Penny Nichols, who he always thought would make a nice, loyal, compliant little wife.

"Sorry, Paul," I said calmly. "I've got to track down a certain lawyer. And by the way," I added, "do stop going around introducing yourself as my fiancé. You and I both know that our little moment in the sun together ended a long, long time ago."

On my way out, I caught up with Rupert, who was going out to lunch. "It was Severine who did the deed and put Jeremy and Paul in the same cage together," I announced.

Rupert looked nonplused and said, "Really? I'm quite surprised at Severine. She's usually so professional. I don't know why she would do such a thing."

"Because she's in love with him, for starters," I said. "I think they were an item once."

Rupert mumbled that well, if it were true that Jeremy and Severine had been an item once, it must have been before he, Rupert, had "come on board."

"Look, Rupert," I said. "Now I *have* to talk to Jeremy, that moron. You must have a number where you can reach him."

"Actually, I don't," Rupert said, sounding surprised himself. "The guy from Texas is a secretive sort of fellow. He does his deals at some lodge where there are no phones. Jeremy told me he'd try to find a landline somewhere, but I haven't heard from him yet. Don't worry. He'll phone in eventually. He always does."

"I certainly hope so," I said. "Meanwhile, I have to go to Italy, to the museum that's bought the painting. To approve where they're putting it."

"I understand, and I'll tell Jeremy as soon as he calls," Rupert promised.

Chapter Forty-one

S O THERE I WAS, SITTING ON A BENCH IN THE MUSEUM, STARING AT the Madonna and Child, wondering what on earth I was going to do with the rest of my life. The day was sunny and benevolent, and the walled-in museum gardens were fragrant with lemon and orange trees whose perfume wafted into the corridors through its open windows. I'd been ushered in via a private door, and led to the special wing where my painting had its own glassed-in alcove waiting for it, with a quaint, tiny thermometer that would make sure it always had just the right atmosphere and temperature to protect it.

The curator had been wonderfully kind, and sensed that I was feeling a bit subdued, so after the workman finished the job of hanging the painting, he left me there alone with my thoughts. I could hear his footsteps retreating across the cool marble floors.

I sat there gazing at the Madonna. She gave me a maternal, comforting sort of look. She may have even said, *Pull yourself together, ducky . . . you're still young . . . more or less . . .*

But just as I'd begun to calm down and feel philosophical, a man plunked himself down on the bench next to me and cleared his throat and rattled his newspaper. Irritably I realized that the museum had just opened for the day, and people were already streaming in to get a look

at the painting. It was obvious that I needed to be left alone. But this
man couldn't sit still, he harumphed and blew his nose noisily—and
still I didn't catch on. Till finally he spoke.

"For a detective, Penny Nichols, you can be a bit obtuse at crucial
moments," I heard Jeremy's voice say in amusement. I looked up into
his grinning, dopey face.

"I don't believe it," I said. "You're supposed to be on a boat or
something. In Texas."

"And you're supposed to be winging your way back to America
with that uncouth beast," he said. "According to Severine. You didn't
tell me Paul was still your boss, you know."

"Nobody's going to be my boss ever again," I said.

"Nevertheless," Jeremy said, "when he showed up at my door,
grinning like a monkey, talking about marrying you, I guess I went
a bit doolally. God, I just wanted to wring his neck. And yours. I remembered how tortured you looked when you told me about him."

"That is not, you know, love," I muttered.

"Yes, well, it almost made a murderer out of me," he said wryly.
"Fortunately I was summoned away, to the sodding wilderness in
Canada. On a boat that's really a car, or else it's a car that's really a boat,
for Chrissake. All I could see was that smug grin of your wretched
'fiancé.' But the farther out to sea I got, the more it occurred to me
that I'd been royally duped."

"Correct," I said. "He lied to you. But Severine set the whole
thing up."

"Ah," he said. "Then I see it's Severine I should strangle. Or maybe
you can do it for me, there's a girl." He exhaled deeply. "When I finally
got through to the office, I heard conflicting reports. Severine said, as
far as she knew, you'd signed your papers and gone back to America
with that hound. Rupert said you chased the hound out of the office

and told Rupert he'd bloody well better get hold of me and tell me you were here. So, here I am."

"What happened to your client?" I asked curiously.

"Far as I know, he's still on his boat, but I told him it couldn't be helped," he said.

"You came back—just for me?" I said in a small voice. Nobody had ever done anything remotely like that. Crossed an ocean and all . . .

Jeremy gave me a look that went straight to my heart. "Yes, well, I started to imagine what it would be like to live in a world without Penny Nichols in my life. It seemed unbearable. I couldn't give you up without a fight. So you see, you've made a whole new man of me. An utter lunatic. I never act this way. Thanks a lot," he said ruefully.

"Yeah, it was pretty lousy without you, too," I said frankly. "Let's promise never to let anything come between us like that again."

"I promise," he said, and he kissed me. For a long, long, *long* languorous time, as if he had all the time in the world, and yet as if we both thought we'd never have enough time, even in a lifetime, to tell each other how much we loved each other.

Bless Italy, nobody disturbed us as we sat there in each other's arms. Nobody thought it was strange, or bad, or a violation of the rules for two people to be so happy. People just moved quietly around us, the curators and the patrons alike. Until, of course, it was lunchtime. Then one of the guards gently told us that the museum would be closing for a couple of hours. We rose from our little bench, and I nodded good-bye-for-now to our painting on the wall. As we walked through the museum to get to the front door, Jeremy said regretfully, "I have to go back to London. Pick up the pieces at the office."

"Are you in deep trouble, mild trouble, or—?" I asked.

"It'll be okay, mostly," he said. Then he looked at me and said seriously, "But I've been thinking a lot, about what Aunt Pen said in that letter to us. About not letting anyone talk you out of living the life you want. I mean, I could go on being a lawyer in this firm, hoping to make partner, just another rat in the rat race. But I wouldn't be doing a lot of the things I'd like to do, might never have had a chance to do if it weren't for Aunt Penelope."

"I know what you mean," I said instantly. "I love working with Erik and Tim, but I don't want to be in thrall to Pentathlon Productions for the rest of my life, and frankly, Paul may just have already decided that I'm history over there. Erik has other clients, I guess, but . . ."

"Penny, dear," Jeremy said in amusement, "I don't think you've quite grasped the situation. You are now a woman of some means. You could start your own production company if you wanted to."

"Hmm," I said, "you're right. It hasn't really sunk in yet."

"The point is, if we just continued as we are, we'd hardly ever see each other," Jeremy concluded, "flying around on business-as-usual and feeling lucky if we managed to pass each other in airports. I think we can do better than that."

I tilted my head at him. "Whadja have in mind, pal?" I inquired.

He grinned. "Why, we could start some enterprise of our own. After all, I'm a well-known, fairly respected, high-powered international lawyer—"

"Modest to a fault, too," I commented. He went on, undeterred.

"You are a rather good historical expert, and, moreover, a natural-born snoop," he said. "So there must be some way that we can put those two things together. But the point is, we should give ourselves time to figure out what we really love to do, and why, and what it all means to us."

We were walking through room after room of antiquities, moving past ancient statues of the Roman gods, past spooky medieval displays of armor and golden chalices, through the Renaissance Room, where portraits gazed back at us pensively, watchfully. I drew a deep breath, and somehow in that instant, I knew that the world was opening up for me in ways I'd never dreamed possible, and that my life had just made some fundamental shift. It was as if a veil had been lifted and I was seeing everything for the very first time. I didn't know exactly what it all meant and where it would all lead, but I knew that my feet were already on the path.

And then my stomach growled. Loud. Jeremy said, "Was that you?"

"Look. I can't figure out my whole future on an empty stomach," I said. "All of Italy has stopped its business to eat lunch. Can't we grab something before the flight back?" Because I had a return ticket for today, too.

"Of course," Jeremy said. "And tonight, let's meet at my apartment after I handle things at the office. The doorman will let you in if you get there ahead of me. We could cook dinner together like your parents do. I'll pick up champagne, to celebrate our good luck properly."

"Great!" I said. "I'll shop for some stuff at the market when we get back to London."

Chapter Forty-two

I HAVE TO ADMIT, I LOOKED RIDICULOUSLY HAPPY WHEN I SHOWED up at Jeremy's apartment with my arms full of bundles of groceries. A short, middle-aged doorman with big ears sticking out of his uniform cap smiled at me when I entered, so I didn't expect any trouble when I told him I was going up to Jeremy's apartment to wait for him. A strange look crossed the guy's face, and his smile disappeared.

"*You?*" he repeated falteringly. "Then ... who's the girl sitting upstairs in his flat?"

I felt as if I'd just been dropped to earth without a parachute. I said, "There must be a mistake. I'm the one Jeremy told you to let in." He came out from behind his doorman's station and irritably pressed the button to call the elevator. The door opened.

"We'll 'ave to go up and see about this," he said. "You come with me, young lady."

On the ride up he muttered to nobody in particular, "People comin', people goin', all the time." I could hardly stand it. Finally we stopped at Jeremy's floor.

I sailed down the corridor like the *Queen Mary,* with the muttering doorman in my wake. Impatiently I waited as he knocked first, then put his key in the lock. As the door swung open, a woman called out.

"Hello, darling," she said in the most delighted of tones. When we didn't answer, she floated into view. She was a slim blonde, wearing a very low-cut dress of black and red chiffon. When she saw us she stopped dead in her tracks and looked at us sharply.

"You have the wrong flat," she said in annoyance to the doorman.

"This young lady says *she's* the one Mr. Jeremy Laidley wants—and *you're* a mistake," the doorman said with stupendous tact. "Name o' . . ." he paused. "What's your name, dearie?"

"Penny Nichols," I said, then asked the woman, "Who are you?"

"I am *Mrs.* Jeremy Laidley," she said with supreme confidence.

When she turned to look at the doorman again, I realized, with a sinking heart, that I recognized that pretty profile. From the photos in Aunt Sheila's Christmas cards.

And then I began to understand what Jeremy and I might now be up against. The money again. Already this inheritance was wreaking havoc, with all our nearest and dearest showing up from here and yon, all ready to stake their claims. Whatever had made me think that this future life was going to be easy?

She was staring at me rather coolly when she said, "I'm afraid you'll just have to go."

Well, I figured it was time to start acting like an heiress. I had no idea where to begin. So I stepped into the apartment, tossed my coat and bag on the sofa, and said, "I believe you mean you're the *ex*–Mrs. Jeremy Laidley. True enough?"

My mother had this ancient board game from the 1960s that she found in the attic of our house, which she occasionally hauled down for me to play with when I was a little girl and home sick in bed, or when my friends came over and it was raining and we were bored. It was positively quaint, and called Barbie, Queen of the Prom. To win, you had to do three things—become president of a school club, have a formal gown to wear, and have a steady boyfriend to escort you. You didn't have to be smart, pretty, rich, or well-connected. Just lucky. You rolled the dice and moved around and around the squares on the board, drawing cards until you managed to get all three.

So okay, I never really wanted to be president of anything. And Jeremy, I can see, is going to be nothing but trouble. I do, however, have a beautiful vintage wardrobe, a great London flat, a fantastic antique car that's being restored, and even a bank account.

I mean, hell, it's a start. Isn't it?

Acknowledgments

Special thanks to my husband Ray, for his spirited wit, unfailing support and insightful advice. To Margaret Atwood for her generous, continued encouragement. To the intrepid Jennifer Unter, whose confidence and good cheer steered us through in fine style; and thanks to everyone at RLR Literary. I wish to express my gratitude to the terrific publishing team at Penguin, particularly Rachel Kahan, Kara Welsh, and especially to my thoughtful, perceptive editor, Kara Cesare. I would also like to thank Elizabeth Corradino of Moses & Singer, for her advice and amiable humor. Thanks to family and friends; and finally, to all those who love to read novels, in a quiet celebration of the time we have together here on this beautiful earth.

A Rather Lovely
Inheritance

C.A. Belmond

A CONVERSATION WITH C.A. BELMOND

Q. *This novel has a first-person narrator with characters who seem very quirky and real. Is the story based on your own life?*

A. No, although I have some similarities in my background; my husband's family is English on his father's side, and we both have personal and professional connections to Europe. But this story and the characters are entirely fictional. The French author Colette described the writing of a novel as following one fundamental command, *"Regarde!"* or "Look!" She was talking about a kind of looking that involves all of the senses, where you collect powerful impressions of how people, and animals, and the earth itself react to events. These impressions go into a free and unfettered part of your being, and when you've stored up so many of them, you're like a cup that's overflowing. It's this overflow that compels you to create a story, a poem, a picture or a song. It's almost as if you've stopped time, and captured a slice of life, so that others can also respond to it and explore it at their own pace. That's why I disagree when people say, "Fiction is a lie." Not so! Fiction is a made-up story compared to, say, the daily report of journalism. But a novel can distill the dailiness of life into a private, meditative, sensory realm where we might experience the deeper, eternal truths that run underneath us like a hidden stream.

Q. *But what about the heroine's voice and the plot of the story? How do you find and shape these things? Where do you get your ideas?*

A. In the bathtub, or swimming. For some reason water does it for me. Maybe I'm part fish, and maybe that's why the Mediterranean has such a hold on me. I just find that a good splash gives me clarity and insight. With this novel, I knew that I wanted to write about an American abroad, since I've studied and worked in the places where Penny bounces around. Geography is definitely a factor—there's just something about the Riviera that implies the possibility of a high-spirited caper, a stylish romp, replete with surprise twists and red herrings. And throughout Europe I find that the existence of modern life cheek by jowl with ancient buildings, narrow streets, sculptures, landmarks and other mementos of a bittersweet legacy, makes you appreciate how quickly life can go from madly hilarious to truly awful to heartbreakingly beautiful. I could imagine an idealistic heroine there, thrust into funny, exciting, sometimes alarming circumstances. Penny's wry voice came naturally out of all this—slightly aggrieved yet ever hopeful. There are many ways to tell a tale, but it evolves from the character, who usually leads you along; she'll let you know if your choice doesn't suit her, like a dress that doesn't fit. I envisioned her as a redhead because she has such a peppery personality, and because I saw Severine as a brunette and Jeremy's ex-wife as a blonde. I mused about what kind of redhead my heroine would be—not a carrot-top red, she'd be something copper-colored, copper like a penny. Yes! Penny and Great-Aunt Penelope. When it fits, you know it. Then you follow the trail of cookie crumbs, wherever they lead.

Q. *What about all that history, those details of long-gone time periods? What makes you pick one time period over another?*

A. History, I think, is one big inheritance story . . . with lots of pages torn, smudged or missing. Again, you're gathering the bits and pieces, like a detective, an archaeologist, or a rag-bag lady collecting ribbons here and scraps of leather there. Travelling makes you want to know more about who's been here before you. You're standing on a beach and then you find out, quite casually, that Napoleon landed there when he was trying to make a comeback. You discover, beyond the cave murals, the footprints of a prehistoric man who was running like mad from some animal who's now extinct. You eat in a local restaurant where, years ago, starving artists couldn't afford to pay for lunch, so the owner accepted a painting as payment instead—and now those paintings are worth a small fortune. You can't help asking, where did they all come from, and where have they disappeared to? Yet they never really vanish completely, and that's what makes it so intriguing. Boats that sank in the Mediterranean Sea in the days of the ancient Greeks still turn up today when divers stumble over them. They were there all along, just waiting to be found.

In this novel, it was necessary to invent the history of an entire family. I devised a family tree for my characters that was far more complicated than the one that Penny eventually makes. I worked out birth dates, deaths, and the years of the important events in their lives, and how old they were at each turn. Well, once you have those dates, you know that, for instance, Great-Aunt Penelope and her friends were barely recovering from one world war when they were plunged into another. They saw their pals die young, so they weren't pretending that death doesn't happen, or that it can be outfoxed, as we tend to do today. People are very much shaped by the politics and social restrictions of their time, although some ideas and feelings, of course, transcend time completely. History bequeaths to us the treasures and the debris of those who came before us. The trick is to be able to distinguish which is which.

Q. *The relationship between the hero and heroine is what really drives the story. How did that come about?*

A. I have a real fondness for the clever yet wistful songs, movies and theatre of the 1920s and 1930s. I love the rapid-fire, sassy bantering; it was the era of the wisecrack, because people were disillusioned, wary of being lied to in the wake of the First World War and the Great Depression. The tension is relieved with the snappy comeback, the underlying *Oh, yeah, says who?* Then you add the sexual and romantic element, and it's great fun. This is not to be confused with today's concept of the so-called "battle of the sexes," where, I fear, we've come to expect a nastier edge to arguments, and a doomed incompatibility. But Penny and Jeremy genuinely like each other and are willing to communicate it all the time, even when they're bickering. There isn't any real hostility in their banter, they're just prodding and teasing and trying to break through.

And yes, Penny and Jeremy's back-and-forth certainly "drives" the story, which may be why they spend so much time in a car together. When you're jaunting around for long hours at a stretch, pretty soon you're confiding, reflecting, ruminating in ways that are more free, perhaps because you're defying gravity and time and all the things that pin you down. For Penny and Jeremy, their "chase" is more than just a treasure hunt, because while they are sifting through the family's past, they are actually being released from their own pasts. The chase lifts them into a special zone of eternal present-time, where they can really find each other before coming back down to earth to deal with the demands of everyday life and the future.

Q. *What about the other characters? What's to become of everybody?*

A. I love all these characters. I don't see anybody as "good" or "bad." They are people in certain circumstances, reacting well or badly or wearily or foolishly or generously or greedily. And as in life, a friend can sometimes screw you up, and someone you thought of as a foe can unexpectedly, perhaps accidentally, point you in the right direction. So I see a rich and fascinating future for Penny and Jeremy, Aunt Sheila and their family and friends and even good old Rollo. These characters are so alive to me that even when I'm not consciously watching over them, when I come back to them I find that they've been up to all sorts of mischief and have plenty of new stories to tell.

QUESTIONS
FOR DISCUSSION

1. The theme of the innocent American abroad is a recurring one in Western literature. The heroine often finds herself in uncharted waters that she must navigate with her intelligence, wit, and instinct. Yet when it comes to social conventions, she's bound to make some missteps. Often the heroine arrives hoping that a fresh start might be possible. What are some other expectations of such a character? Are they realistic? Are they in some sense self-fulfilling, or do they rely on unpredictable events, other characters, circumstances and setting?

2. The heroine is seemingly full of contradictions; Penny loves her work, but doesn't care for office politics. She appreciates beautiful clothes and fine things, but doesn't particularly like shopping. She's slightly world-weary, yet she deliberately refuses to become jaded and cynical. Penny her-

self says that she's "incurably" hopeful, a not-quite-thwarted idealist. She persists in believing that she might find a soul mate in life. In short, she's gambling that she can succeed on her own terms. Does the path she's chosen in life make her journey simpler? More difficult? What will it require of her? Is there a point of no return, where she has no choice but to go full-speed ahead?

3. The hero is also a man of complexity. Jeremy is self-assured, worldly-wise, yet as Penny noted, there has always been an undercurrent of rebellion in his nature. Then he is thrown into an unexpected crisis that leads him to question not only his comfortable assumptions about life, but his actual identity. How does he handle it initially? Does he change tactics at any point? How do the other characters influence his responses?

4. It's Penny's job to be able to tell what's authentic and what's fake, as well as to find out how time and history influence people. Is she able to do this in her daily life? What are the turning points in the story that shed light on the circumstances, and what leads her to these moments? Are they random, or do they occur as a result of her own endeavors? She also believes that history can serve as a "map" or guide

to finding out what's important in life. What do you think of that? The heroine also concludes that, historically speaking, "life is awfully short." How would such a revelation alter the way a person conducts her life? Does it influence the choices that Penny makes?

5. Both Penny's and Jeremy's parents keep secrets from them. How do these secrets emerge? Why were they kept quiet in the first place? Why are so many family histories so fragmented? What was Great-Aunt Penelope's real legacy to them all?

About the Author

C.A. Belmond has published short fiction, poetry and humorous essays. She was awarded the Edward Albee Foundation Fellowship and was twice a Pushcart Press Editors' Book Award finalist. She has written, directed and produced television drama and documentary, and her screenplays were shortlisted at Robert Redford's Sundance Institute and the Eugene O'Neill Playwrights Conference. She has taught writing at New York University, and was a writer-in-residence at the Karolyi Foundation in the South of France.

Visit her Web site at www.aratherlovelyinheritance.com.